HOW DID THAT HAPPEN?

Holding People Accountable

—— *for Results* ——

the Positive, Principled Way

ROGER CONNORS

AND **TOM SMITH**

PORTFOLIO/PENGUIN

PORTFOLIO/PENGUIN

Published by the Penguin Group

Penguin Group (USA) Inc., 375 Hudson Street, New York, New York 10014, U.S.A. ·
Penguin Group (Canada), 90 Eglinton Avenue East, Suite 700, Toronto, Ontario, Canada M4P 2Y3
(a division of Pearson Penguin Canada Inc.) · Penguin Books Ltd, 80 Strand, London WC2R 0RL,
England · Penguin Ireland, 25 St Stephen's Green, Dublin 2, Ireland (a division of Penguin Books Ltd) ·
Penguin Books Australia Ltd, 250 Camberwell Road, Camberwell, Victoria 3124, Australia (a division
of Pearson Australia Group Pty Ltd) · Penguin Books India Pvt Ltd, 11 Community Centre, Panchsheel
Park, New Delhi – 110 017, India · Penguin Group (NZ), 67 Apollo Drive, Rosedale, Auckland 0632,
New Zealand (a division of Pearson New Zealand Ltd) · Penguin Books (South Africa) (Pty) Ltd, 24
Sturdee Avenue, Rosebank, Johannesburg 2196, South Africa

Penguin Books Ltd, Registered Offices : 80 Strand, London WC2R 0RL, England

First published in the United States of America by Portfolio, a member of
Penguin Group (USA) Inc. 2009
This paperback edition published 2011

5   7   9   10   8   6   4

360° Accountability™; Above The Line®; Accountability Attitudes™; Accountability Connection™;
Accountability Conversation™; Accountability Reality Check™; Accountability Sequence™;
Accountability Styles™; Accountability Training®; Alignment Dialogue™; Alignment Meeting™;
Below The Line®; Building An Accountable Culture Track™; By When™; Creating A Culture Of
Accountability®; Cultural Beliefs®; Culture of Accountability™; Do It®; Expectations Chain™;
FORM Checklist™; Holding Others Accountable Track™; How Did That Happen?®; Inner Ring®;
Inspect What You Expect™; LOOK Model®; Outer Ring™; Own It®; Partners In Leadership®;
Phantom Reality™; Reality Window®; See It®; Solve It®; Steps To Accountability®; Taking Personal
Accountability Track™; The 5-D Fast Training Model®; The Oz Principle®; The Results Pyramid®;
Three Tracks To Creating Greater Accountability™; Why-What-When® are trademarks of Partners In
Leadership, used with permission. The trademarks referenced herein as registered are registered in the
U.S. and/or other countries.

The various self-assessments, models, charts, and lists used in this book are owned by Partners In
Leadership, used with permission.

ISBN 978-1-59184-258-3 (hc.)
ISBN 978-1-59184-414-3 (pbk.)
CIP data available
Printed in the United States of America
Set in Minion
Designed by Mia Risberg

We dedicate this book to all of our clients who,
over the past two decades, have partnered with us
and have proven unequivocally that
greater accountability produces results.

Acknowledgments

A book of this scope becomes a reality only when a team of people in complete alignment personally invest themselves in the "cause." We have been blessed to work with just such a team.

We express gratitude to Adrian Zackheim, our publisher and partner, who immediately and personally envisioned the impact greater accountability always makes on business results. From the outset he has remained committed to our goal of developing a comprehensive set of literature, which includes this, our third book, that accurately describes how to create greater accountability for results in business.

We deeply appreciate our own senior management team, each of whom is, in his or her own right, experts and field practitioners on this subject. Each has made invaluable contributions to this book by way of client stories and developmental feedback. Specifically, we thank Tracy Skousen, Marcus Nicolls, Jared Jones, Tony Bridwell, Tanner Corbridge, Mike Evans, Maury Hiers, Kirk Matson, Brad Starr, Adrienne Sigman, and Ran Jones. For their faithful research and ever-attentive support, we are grateful to John Jacobsen, John Grover, Michelle Murray, and Jennifer Zarback.

Heartfelt thanks also go to Mike Snell, our agent and friend, whose thoughtful input, feedback, and editorial contributions helped us shape the nature of the book and the manner of presentation. His attention to detail and his contributions throughout have made this book much more useful and relevant than it would have been otherwise.

We also appreciate Brooke Carey, our editor, who forthrightly told us what she thought and candidly encouraged us to make adjustments where needed. We'd also like to thank Courtney Nobile, our publicist, for her tireless efforts in promoting the book. The entire Portfolio team was wonderfully supportive and encouraging throughout the writing of this book.

Many clients and colleagues read advance copies and chapter selections, providing feedback about what did and did not work in early drafts of the manuscript. Their input helped refine this book into an even better tool. We thank each of them for their thoughtful contributions.

Finally, we must acknowledge the ongoing support of our families. Without their encouragement, patience, and understanding we could not possibly have written this book while running our successful and growing business. They make our every endeavor more meaningful.

Contents

HOW DID
THAT HAPPEN?

Introduction

HOW DID THAT HAPPEN?

During the closing days of the historic 2008 presidential campaign in the United States, nothing preoccupied the American public more than the deteriorating economy. Seemingly overnight, a global financial crisis blindsided the country and changed the entire landscape of the financial markets. The stock market crashed, with the Dow Jones Industrials losing almost half of their value. Markets all over the world followed suit. In October of that year, a number of the world's stock exchanges suffered drops of up to 10 percent, some of the worst declines in history. The ramifications of the sudden and overwhelming crash of the American financial markets extended well beyond the United States. The banks in Iceland failed, bankrupting the entire nation. Bank failures in Europe signaled that most developed countries in the world were sharing the pain. The head of the International Monetary Fund cautioned that the global financial system was on the "brink of systemic meltdown," and the deputy governor of the Bank of England declared that this was "possibly the largest financial crisis of its kind in human history."

With the meltdown of the world's financial markets, individuals began losing their wealth at astonishing rates. Taken together, the devastating decline in the value of individual investors' 401(k)'s, the record-high foreclosure rate on home mortgages, the soaring unemployment rate associated with the cutback of corporate budgets, and the lack of credit to both consumers and businesses, brought the calamity to a very personal level. These sudden and consequential changes left both Main Street and Wall Street asking the question: "How did that happen?"

No one seemed to see it coming. Financial experts, market gurus, business leaders, government officials, and the average Joes and Janes on Main Street were caught completely off guard. Nevertheless, a close observer might have discerned telltale signs of impending doom. Housing prices were rising faster than incomes. Personal savings had dropped to the lowest rate since 1933 and the Great Depression. Mortgage lenders were issuing so-called subprime loans without validating a buyer's income or requiring a down payment. Financial institutions, including many of the largest and most respected in the world, bought billions of dollars' worth of these shaky mortgages in the form of mortgage-backed securities. In hindsight, these high-risk investments and other financial decisions, such as artificially lowering interest rates, disregarded proven economic principles. Still, in spite of all this, this great and troubling catastrophe that reached global proportions seemed entirely unanticipated. In fact, the collapse of the global financial markets in 2008 will, in our estimation, go down in history as the most significant "How did that happen?" business story in the last fifty years.

This question—"How did that happen?"—usually leads to its corollary, "Who should be held accountable?" You could point the finger at a number of culprits: the politicians and government agencies that had failed to regulate the mortgage industry; ratings institutions that gave mortgage-backed securities the highest credit ratings, thus implying that they were safe investments; the home buyers—many of whom assumed they would be able to flip their homes sometime before their adjustable interest rates rose to a point they couldn't afford; the banks that lent them the money and gorged themselves on the short-term profits of the subprime market; greedy investors and market speculators betting on how bad things would get; and let's not forget the wizards at many Wall Street financial institutions who invented the complicated financial instruments that no one really understood, and that finally brought down such venerable companies as Lehman Brothers, Bear Stearns, Morgan Stanley, and AIG.

Who would have envisioned the chief executive officers of the big three American automakers making a pilgrimage in their private jets to Washington, D.C., to beg the U.S. Congress for billions of dollars to bail their companies out of the crisis that had been building for decades? And who, wondered exasperated Americans, can we hold accountable, not just for the mess, but also for turning things around? Even as the federal government began working to help solve the problem, people were left wondering, "How did that happen?" As the Troubled Assets Relief Program (TARP) Reform and Accountability Act was implemented, no one seemed able to account for where the money was going. Apparently, the leaders of these banks felt no need to account for what they were doing with billions of dollars of taxpayer money. Astoundingly, many of the former heads of institutions that received significant assistance from public monies, such as Freddie and Fannie Mae, received large bonuses and payouts while their organizations were fighting to stave off insolvency. Whether they realized it or not, the government, Wall Street, and businesses around the world were mired in a serious accountability problem.

Accountability? Everyone talks about it, shareholders demand it, taxpayers want it, and stakeholders insist on it. But exactly what is accountability, and how do you get people to take it? Our firm, Partners In Leadership Inc., widely considered the worldwide leader in Accountability Training, has spent more than twenty years studying and teaching accountability because we believe that no other attribute of individual or organizational life contributes more to the success of individuals, teams, and organizations. As the founders of the company, we have developed approaches to accountability that have helped major companies produce billions of dollars in shareholder wealth, provided fulfilling and positive work environments for hundreds of thousands of employees, and delivered exceptional products and services to customers.

Throughout our work with thousands of top-producing industry leaders, however, we keep hearing the same questions: "Exactly how do we prevent the surprises that so often blindside us, despite all our best efforts to make things happen the way we expect them to happen? How can we improve our follow-up so that we get the results we want? And how do we do it without making people feel resentful, resistant, manipulated, and controlled?" To answer these questions we have crafted the essential and sequential steps that enable anyone to establish the right expectations and to manage any unmet expectations in the positive, principled way that inspires people, makes them feel good about their work, and gets results. When an organization provides the clarity that comes with this approach, they also build accountability into every level of its culture, and results naturally follow. Unfortunately, too few leaders do it the right way. When people hear the question, "Who's accountable for that?" they often duck for cover, fearing that someone is about to get punished. Those who use this approach invariably find that the harder they try to hold others accountable, the worse the situation gets. Disappointment mounts, results dwindle, and most everyone gets frustrated or ends up feeling betrayed.

The workplace has become too complex for the old methods used to create accountability. The new generation of workers differs markedly from the Greatest Generation Ever that fought World War II, that generation's baby boomer children, and even the more recent Generation X. If you don't respect these differences with an appropriate new management style, you can hardly expect these workers to respond to you with the enthusiasm and hard work you expect.

A recent Zogby International nationwide poll (the largest representative study of its kind in the United States) recently documented the extent to which corporate management uses accountability the wrong way. The poll revealed that 25 percent of employed Americans describe their workplace as a "dictatorship," and only 52 percent said their boss "treats subordinates well." Barely half (51 percent) said their co-workers "often feel motivated or are mostly motivated at work." So, what's the problem? Are people lazy? Do they put too little effort into their work? Do they care too little about their own and their company's success? Or do they just not know how to go about holding each other accountable in a way that motivates everyone to get the results expected of them? If asked to generalize, we would almost guarantee that it's a matter of know-how and not a lack of motivation or a lack of willingness to take accountability.

True accountability is not about punishment. It is not about taking revenge against someone who has failed to meet your expectations. So, exactly what is it? For some, accountability is a way to "act," a behavior you display only when threatened with punishment for poor performance. To others, accountability is an "attitude," a way of looking at your circumstances, good or bad, and taking the view that only you are responsible for what you do next and that blaming anyone else for what happens will simply waste time and energy. To us, accountability, in its truest and most authentic form, is a personal "attribute" that exemplifies who you are. It is "a way of being" that empowers you, each individual on your team and every single person in your organization, to meet and even surpass your highest expectations.

THE TWO SIDES TO ACCOUNTABILITY

Over the past two decades we have worked with clients intent on meeting the high expectations of their marketplace, shareholders, customers, and all the other stakeholders. As we have helped companies of all types and sizes cash in on the organizational currency of accountability, we have become convinced that there are two very distinct sides to the accountability coin: one side of the coin is *taking* accountability yourself, and the flipside is *holding* other people accountable.

In our first book, *The Oz Principle*, we focused on the importance of people *taking* accountability for results. Recognized as a groundbreaking work, *The Oz Principle*, with its proven Steps to Accountability and its Above the Line philosophy, begins to establish the necessary foundation on which an organization can build an accountable workforce, from top to bottom.

In organizations without this foundation, it is easy to spot people lacking the personal engagement necessary for achieving results. Instead, they externalize the need to change, expecting someone else to supply solutions to problems and challenges. While they readily see the need for change in others, they fail to see it in themselves. People who *take* accountability for results internalize the need for change and embark upon the Steps to Accountability. They become self-motivated and resourceful, focusing entirely on what else they can personally do to achieve the desired results. They make it a habit to See It, Own It, Solve It, and Do It. They know that they can overcome whatever obstacles they face and create the results they desire.

Our second book, *Journey to the Emerald City*, also broke new ground as it explored the path an organization must take to create an organization-wide Culture of Accountability. A Culture of Accountability, by definition, is a team, department, division, or companywide culture in which people take accountability to think and act in the manner necessary to achieve desired organizational results. When an organization clearly defines the results it expects, it can more effectively pinpoint the shifts in culture required to achieve those results. Alignment around these shifts and clear accountability for moving in the defined direction, coupled with the integration of key culture management tools and the implementation of needed changes in organizational systems, accelerates the transition to a Culture of Accountability.

We have worked with over seven hundred companies and hundreds of thousands of individuals to implement the models and methods described in our books and our Accountability Training. As we work with executive leaders, middle managers, and frontline workers in organizations around the world, we rarely meet anyone who does not, in the end, want to take accountability, get results, and help their organization achieve its objectives. We are convinced that people are motivated by meaningful work and want to participate in a cause larger than the duties outlined in their own particular job description. They take satisfaction in solving problems and overcoming obstacles. They are happiest when they demonstrate a can-do attitude and refuse to participate in the damaging cycles of blame, fear, apathy, confusion, and frustration that so often arise when results fall short of expectations.

Now, in this book, we examine the other side of the accountability coin: *holding* people accountable for results in a way that conquers all the damaging behaviors that permeate so many organizations today.

This book shows you how to hold others accountable for delivering on expectations in the positive, principled way that produces results. Never again will your attempts to hold people accountable backfire in a way that actually *hurts* your objective. Never again will you feel at a loss, wondering what else you can do to get others to deliver on expectations. Never again will you be surprised at the outcome, wondering, "How did that happen?" in spite of all your very best efforts. By following the steps in what we call the Accountability Sequence, you will learn how to avoid the unpleasant "surprises" that plague almost every project and discover the key to getting things done through others. This was brought home to us while we were overseeing a backyard project, the construction of a pool and pavilion. It required the efforts of a number of tradespeople: a backhoe operator, a plumber, an electrician, a roofer, and a landscaper. All the usual "surprises" plagued the project. The backhoe severed a buried cable, the electrical conduit was initially laid out in the wrong place, and the construction crew couldn't match the shingles on the house. Despite all those setbacks, it all came together one day, and we all stood around admiring the result. One of the concrete finishers who had been with the project from the beginning was leaning on a shovel nearby. "Hey," he exclaimed, "this looks really good!" It did. We stood there looking at the finished product recalling all the challenges we had overcome and wondered aloud, "How did *that* happen?" While we asked this question about a success in a lighthearted way, we imagine that you have often asked it in dead seriousness about a surprising failure, one you might have avoided had you more effectively held others accountable for results.

Over the last twenty years, we have accumulated a library full of stories and case studies that illustrate how accountability, correctly understood and applied, produces results for companies all over the world. The stories you will read in this book have drawn heavily upon our own practical and real-life experiences with clients, illustrating both successful and failed attempts to hold people accountable. As you can imagine, many of our client companies have a standing corporate policy that precludes the use of their name in publications, whether the story makes them look good or not. We honor such policies and use such stories anonymously, camouflaging their names, industries, and settings to ensure confidentiality. Rather than repeatedly remind you that we have disguised a company or person, we will place their names in "quotes." Rest assured, however, that the stories accurately describe what really occurred.

Many of these anonymous client stories actually reflect quite well on those involved and provide substantial evidence that the principles we teach really do work. The cases include a nationally branded eyeglass company, whose sales growth shot from 147 percent to 314 percent in one year after utilizing our training throughout their organization; a major exercise equipment manufacturer where, in two short months, revenue and profitability rose by 13 percent and 66 percent, respectively; and a pet care products manufacturer that achieved a 75 percent decrease in accidents, and a dramatic reduction in the time it takes to bring a new product to market. Accountable people get results. Accountable cultures produce results. The positive, principled approach to holding others accountable guarantees results.

THE ACCOUNTABILITY SEQUENCE

It has taken us a lot of time, effort, thought, and experience to capture the positive, principled way to hold others accountable in a simple set of steps we call the Accountability Sequence. The Accountability Sequence is divided into two parts: the Outer Ring and the Inner Ring. In the first half of the book we cover the Outer Ring, where you form, communicate, align, and inspect expectations.

**THE OUTER RING:
ESTABLISHING EXPECTATIONS**

Notice that the Outer Ring deals with establishing expectations, the fundamental activity that both sets up and sustains our accountability relationships with others, and at the same time lays the foundation for effectively holding them accountable.

In the second half of the book, we present the Inner Ring, where you engage in an Accountability Conversation to determine the best way to deal with unmet expectations.

THE INNER RING:
MANAGING UNMET EXPECTATIONS

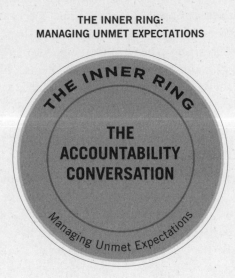

During the Accountability Conversation, you address the four main causes of missed delivery: poor motivation, inadequate training, too little personal accountability, and an ineffective culture. Solving these problems with the right solution (greater motivation, targeted training, a keener sense of personal accountability, and the right culture) can convert any unmet expectation into a success. In these chapters you will find an array of practical tools you can use to help the people on whom you depend solve whatever problems arise and successfully deliver on your expectations.

THE INNER RING:
THE FOUR SOLUTIONS

The complete model presents an overview of the sequential journey we will be taking together in the pages ahead. Moving from the Outer Ring to the Inner Ring, you will learn how to hold people accountable even more effectively than you do now—and probably better than you ever thought possible.

THE ACCOUNTABILITY SEQUENCE

THE OUTER RING

FORM

THE INNER RING

THE ACCOUNTABILITY CONVERSATION

INSPECT

COMMUNICATE

Managing Unmet Expectations

ALIGN

Establishing Expectations

This model suggests a strong connection between expectations and accountability. In fact, we have come to understand that expectations and accountability go hand in hand. Throughout a normal day, we hold many people accountable to fulfill the expectations we have of them: peers, bosses, team members, employees, suppliers, and even customers. When you grasp the inseparable connection between expectations and accountability, you begin to discover the secret to holding others accountable. Consider this: What do you hold people accountable for? We think most of the people reading this book would rightly answer, "Results." We also think that you mean the results you expect others to deliver. At the end of the day, you only hold people accountable for one thing: *the expectations you have of them*. Whether the expectation is for someone to turn in a report on time, make a sale this quarter, build a product according to certain specifications, or ship a part by a certain time of the day, they are all expectations and they are all things you need other people to do for you. The very process of managing those expectations is the act of holding them accountable. Performing this act the positive, principled way not only delivers results, it simultaneously raises both individual and organizational morale.

THE POSITIVE, PRINCIPLED WAY

This book provides a variety of tools that will better enable you to get results through others. These tools show you exactly how you can more effectively get the people you depend on to fulfill your expectations. It shows you how to hold them accountable in a way that motivates, supports, encourages, and helps them to deliver. Each step in the Outer Ring offers a key tool that is easy to put to immediate use in your work.

In the pages ahead, you will find a rich assortment of "how-to" approaches and methods that show you exactly what you can do to implement each step of the Outer and Inner Rings successfully. Every step of the way we encourage you to practice what you are learning with a variety of useful devices: graphic models, self-tests, checklists, tips, and reality checks. Within minutes of finishing each chapter, you can apply a particular principle or practice to your work. It's that practical, essential, and useful. Holding people accountable for results may be an essential philosophy for anyone intent on succeeding in today's complex and fast-changing business climate, but that philosophy won't make much of a difference if you don't have a concrete, step-by-step approach you can use to ensure your success.

How Did That Happen? offers a comprehensive approach to holding people accountable. You will find many models, exercises, tools, tips, and examples that will help you, and the people you depend upon, succeed. We think you will get the most out of the book if you take your time and return to it often to review and practice a particular step in the Outer or Inner Ring. This is a book that you should not plan to read just one time and feel that you have mastered the concepts. Instead, we invite you to take your time and return often to review a step in the Outer or Inner Ring and practice its application by using the tools we have provided. Each chapter contains a suggestion for application in a section called the Accountability Reality Check. We encourage you not to skim over this brief section, but to take some time to experiment with it. Doing so will help you to immediately apply the principles introduced in each chapter and see their positive impact on your daily work.

At the conclusion of each chapter we have included a recap of the major ideas and principles discussed in the preceding pages. This summary's title, "The Positive, Principled Way," reminds you that the tools and practices introduced in the chapter make the process of holding others accountable both "positive" and "principled." The concepts, models, philosophies, methods, and ideas presented in the chapters are, in fact, the principles that cause people to feel that you are implementing accountability in a way that is fair, rational, predictable, and full of integrity. When people experience that kind of accountability, they willingly embrace it themselves.

Applying the skills presented in both the Outer and Inner Ring will help you hold all the people you work with more accountable for what you need them to do, right here and right now. If you make accountability your standard operating procedure, if you do it the right way, they may not know precisely how you did it, but they will know that something has changed: they may enjoy a relationship that runs more smoothly and more efficiently, they may sense a focus that did not exist before, and they may grow ever more willing and able to deliver the results you expect. At the end of the day, you will eliminate the surprises that come with bad news and missed results, and you will no longer find yourself shaking your head in frustration, wondering "How did that happen?"

THE OUTER RING

THE ART OF THE SEQUENCE

Every day we see and hear examples in the business media and from our clients of circumstances that profoundly affect both individuals and entire organizations, largely because someone failed to hold someone else accountable for meeting specific expectations. Almost without fail, we can explain what happened by looking at the situation through the lens of the Outer Ring of the Accountability Sequence.

Case in point: After Hurricane Katrina killed more than twelve hundred people and devastated New Orleans and the Gulf Coast, leaving in its wake a disaster of epic proportion, most observers felt that the U.S. government handled the aftermath poorly. Its failure to provide timely relief to thousands of hurricane victims taking shelter in the Louisiana Superdome in New Orleans made headlines worldwide. The congressional investigation into what went wrong with the government's overall response to the storm reveals a great deal about how a debacle like this can happen. And it highlighted the confusion, resentment, and finger-pointing that typically ensues when people are held accountable for fulfilling expectations that were not clearly established in the first place.

In July 2004, approximately one year prior to Hurricane Katrina, state, local, and federal agencies conducted a Gulf-wide exercise called "Hurricane

Pam" designed to test their collective response to a hypothetical disaster in New Orleans that included evacuating one million people and dealing with damaged levees and the destruction of hundreds of thousands of buildings. As observers later mused, the exercise was "eerily prescient," as it foreshadowed, to an amazing degree, what would happen when Katrina struck. Before the storm ravaged New Orleans, the Department of Homeland Security had been given responsibility for the federal National Response Plan (NRP), designed to set priorities and delegate authority among responding local, state, and federal agencies in major crises in the event of an emergency. When Katrina did strike the coast, Homeland Security Secretary Michael Chertoff named Michael Brown, then FEMA director, as the principle federal officer (PFO) for Hurricane Katrina. Chertoff called Brown his "battlefield commander on the ground."

This delegation decision, and the accompanying unclear expectations that came with it, set off a chain reaction that became the "delegation disaster" of the decade. Chertoff, in his first appearance before a House panel investigating the calamity, commented, "I knew I became more involved in operational matters than I would normally expect to be or want to be. . . . I am not a hurricane expert. I've got to rely on people to execute the details of the plan." How had Katrina overwhelmed his organization? As Chertoff explained it, confusion over roles and decision-making, combined with conflicting information and reports of what was happening on the ground, left him and his team unable to deliver, despite the vast amount of state and federal resources available to his department for solving the problems they faced.

In retrospect, there were a number of clearly recognizable signs, evident from the early hours of the tragedy, that expectations would go unmet. Brown, as the House and Senate report points out, resented his appointment as PFO by his boss, Chertoff, and did not trust the secretary. The secretary did not appoint Brown until some thirty-six hours after Katrina's landfall, despite pre-storm video briefings by the National Weather Service (which, by the way, erred by only slightly in its predictions of where, when, and with what strength Katrina would make landfall) and without regard to the preestablished procedure of appointing the PFO forty-eight hours prior to landfall. In addition, since FEMA was not a first responder organization for large-scale emergencies, the agency had not organized and equipped itself to perform the many duties required by such a monumental disaster— FEMA employs a mere twenty-six hundred people nationwide. Instead of focusing on the immediate challenge, the Secretary attended a conference on the bird flu in Atlanta the day after the hurricane struck land. As a result, the government mounted what the House report called a Category One response to a Category Five event. Secretary Chertoff ultimately came under intense pressure to remove Michael Brown as PFO and assign that role to someone else. In the end, Brown resigned his post as FEMA director, and the House and Senate launched investigations into what went wrong.

Where did Secretary Chertoff go wrong? A thorough review of his actions with respect to the Outer Ring of the Accountability Sequence Model suggests that he did not sufficiently establish expectations for Brown and the other people responsible for the government's reaction to the emergency. Had he formed, communicated, aligned, and inspected the expectation that the right people would be in the right place at the right time with the right resources to deal with such a large-scale incident, Brown, FEMA, and everyone else involved would have done a much better job serving the people of New Orleans. In fact, had Secretary Chertoff properly moved through the steps in the Outer Ring, he might have asked someone other than the reluctant Brown to head up the effort. The resulting failure of those he was counting on to fulfill his own expectations put Chertoff in the predicament that ensnares anyone who has not effectively established expectations: he was left holding the bag, answering questions about missed expectations, failed performance, and dismal results.

THE OUTER RING:
ESTABLISHING EXPECTATIONS

Successfully holding others accountable to deliver on expectations, and doing it in a way that makes others feel good about it, requires real effort and skill, even though the process itself is quite simple. The effort to move deliberately through each step of the Outer Ring develops the skill associated with the positive, principled approach, and it yields predictable and satisfying results, taking away any mystery and confusion about what people are expected to do.

Many people do not take the time to follow such logical and deliberate steps consistently. Instead, they expect people to fill in the blanks and move forward, regardless of their lack of clarity, resolving issues as they go and troubleshooting problems as they arise. When it comes to holding others accountable, they often picture someone with two hands clenched around someone else's neck, asking the question, "How in the world could that have happened?" Their experience has taught them that holding others accountable means issuing threats, shouting rebukes, and doling out punishment.

Unable to account for their own failure to effectively take the steps in the Outer Ring, they resort to holding others accountable by getting people to explain their failures and justify their unproductive actions. When they do that, they immerse themselves in an increasingly destructive process they hope will get themselves off the hook and put others on the spot to explain what went wrong. This process involves four familiar steps: Discover, Hunt, Scramble, and Hide. These four steps occur in most organizations at some time or another. People who follow them first try to *discover* what happened and pinpoint the nature of the "failure"; then they begin the process to *hunt* down the guilty parties, *scramble* to make the best of a bad situation, and, finally, *hide* and hope that no one will figure out the enormity of the mistake and come looking for someone to blame. Unfortunately, Discover, Hunt, Scramble, and Hide too often describes what it looks like to hold others accountable for results in organizations today. Given their experience in corporate life, most people would say that to hold someone accountable means "to follow up when things go wrong to ensure that people answer for their failures."

Our own definition, the one that drives the Outer Ring of the Accountability Sequence, empowers people in a practical and powerful way to influence results *before* things go wrong. To hold someone accountable means "to effectively form, communicate, align, and inspect the fulfillment of an expectation in the positive, principled way that enables people to achieve results now and in the future."

This is not just an abstract, "feel good" dictionary definition, however. We have implemented it in a step-by-step process that works both for us and for our clients around the world. When you use the Accountability Sequence to hold people accountable to deliver on expectations, you win, they win, and each of your organization's stakeholders wins. Had Secretary Chertoff and his team used it, they would have saved themselves, their organizations, and the people their organizations serve a whole world of misery.

Although our approach to holding people accountable springs from a deep and abiding philosophy that accountability really matters in the world, we've taken it to the day-to-day practical level. Yes, you must learn to think about holding people accountable the right way, but you must also treat it as a practical skill you can develop with concentrated effort over time. Deliberately moving through the sequence, step-by-step, produces people who know what needs to be done, view it the same way you do, and deliver what you expect them to deliver, not just once, but every time!

The steps in the Outer Ring, as well as the methodologies within each step, provide a basic pattern you can tailor to each person in a way that works for them. We want to acknowledge that as much as we have worked to turn accountability into a science, there is still a lot of room left in the process for "art." To master the art of the sequence you must learn to work with people using a general framework that you adapt and apply in a way that produces a result unique to the situation and circumstance. Regardless of the variations you may play on the basic theme, a thorough understanding of the principles that provide the foundation for successfully moving through the steps of the Outer Ring will help you hold others accountable the positive, principled way.

THE THREE AXIOMS OF THE OUTER RING

Three axioms form the foundation for holding others accountable the positive, principled way and set the stage for taking the steps in the Outer Ring: the Accountability Fallacy, the Accountability Assumption, and the Accountability Truth.

The Accountability Fallacy

The first of these axioms, the Accountability Fallacy, captures a common mistake people make when they assume that others fail to follow through because there is something wrong with them. This false assumption comes easily to most of us because we so clearly see the evidence that convicts the culprits of not caring enough or not working hard enough to get the job done the way we expect them to get it done. Basically, we assume people to be guilty until proven innocent. When leaders fall prey to the Accountability Fallacy, they not only assume that their people are flawed, but that they themselves can do little or nothing to change those flaws except punish people for having them. Real accountability always requires us to begin by looking at ourselves for anything that might be missing.

The Accountability Assumption

The second axiom, the Accountability Assumption, dictates that you should always begin with the assumption that, in any given circumstance, people are doing their very best to fulfill your expectations. This assumption, consistently applied, will start the whole journey toward holding others accountable on a positive and principled track. Whenever you begin by assuming the worst in others, you will most likely see their worst behavior (not to mention your own) emerge. The Accountability Assumption allows you to begin with the view that people want things to work just as much as you do and that they are doing all they can to make that happen. This approach not only brings out the best in you, but, with some rare exceptions, it accurately reflects the truth about the people with whom you work.

The Accountability Truth

Under all of this lies the third and final axiom, the Accountability Truth, which provides a more effective way of looking at the problem when people fail to follow through and deliver on expectations. By "truth," we simply mean that when things go wrong, there is usually something wrong with what "I" am doing. When you embrace this principle, you take control of future outcomes and internalize the continual need to improve your effectiveness with respect to holding others accountable. Thinking and behaving this way produces better results. You become more proficient at getting things done through others. When you see yourself as part of the problem, you empower yourself to join the team that will do whatever it takes to solve it.

HOW DID I LET THAT HAPPEN?

With the Accountability Truth in mind you can imagine that asking the question, "How did that happen?" does not generally produce an overly productive conversation. Certainly, understanding what went wrong is important, but this question usually places full accountability on those who fail to deliver and sheds little, if any, light on what *you* could have done to keep things on track. That's one reason you should consider asking a better, more effective question when you feel that people have let you down: "How did *I let* that happen?"

Those two additional words can make a big difference. First, adding "I" to the equation shifts the focus from what everyone else didn't do to what you can do to improve the situation. Asking, "How did that happen?" removes you from the picture, as though you played no role at all in whatever went wrong. Once you take accountability for your part in the failure to deliver, you empower yourself to get *more* done through others. Your effectiveness, or ineffectiveness, in applying the steps in the Outer Ring can significantly influence the overall success of anyone in a position to meet your expectations. In fact, in many of the cases we have encountered over the years, we have often found that the person originating the expectation, the one holding others accountable to deliver, actually contributed to the missed delivery. In most cases they could have avoided failure and enjoyed greater success by more effectively working the steps in the Outer Ring. We're not saying that they alone caused the failure, but we are saying that they did not do a good enough job Forming, Communicating, Aligning, and Inspecting their expectations.

"Jim Simmons," the chief executive officer of "Integrated Components" (IC), came face-to-face with the importance of asking that question when he desperately needed to raise capital to fund IC's next stage of growth. Since the task required that he hit the road for several weeks, making presentations to potential backers, he expected his management team to keep the company on track and meet market expectations during his absence.

He had crafted a compelling presentation, highlighting the company's main product, a patented medical device that would revolutionize the treatment of diabetics and ensure IC's bright future. During what appeared to be a well-received presentation to a group of venture capitalists in Boston, he was presented with a set of financial statements generated by a third party that completely contradicted what he had just told the investment group.

Shocked, embarrassed, and dead sure the financials were wrong, he boarded the next jet, flew back to St. Louis, and convened an emergency meeting with his top team. "I can't believe this!" he exclaimed. "This has got to be a mistake!" His people sheepishly admitted that there was no mistake. IC had failed to achieve the results Simmons had expected, results that he had now confidently promoted to the financial community over the past week. Simmons could not imagine a worse situation. As he went around the table, asking his team to explain the fiasco, listening to their explanations, he shook his head in absolute astonishment. "How did this happen?" he wanted to know.

In response, Simmons's management team told him that they did not want to do anything that would take him off the road and interfere with his efforts to raise money. They passionately defended their actions, stating that they knew the immediate future of the company depended entirely upon his fund-raising success. They further justified their actions, explaining to Simmons that they had made every attempt to solve the problems the company faced and deliver the expected results. Simmons couldn't believe his ears: all of this despite continual reports that everything was on track!

Simmons couldn't help reflecting on just where it was that he went wrong. He wondered out loud if it were possible for him to have truly been that distracted to have missed what was really going on inside the company. He admitted to the fact that things can change very quickly in their industry, but he was astounded by just how quickly things had changed at IC. Upon reflection, Simmons began to realize that he was continually sending the message that only one thing was important to him, and that was to secure the financing. In fact, he recounted the numerous times in his mind when he told various members of the management team that he did not want to be in the loop on certain operational issues and that they needed to solve things on their own while he was gone. His reflection helped him take his share of the accountability for how they got into that mess and, more important, helped him realize what he would need to do differently in order not to repeat the mistake.

Including yourself in the accountability equation and accepting your role in getting things done through others provides a number of powerful payoffs:

- Creates more positive relationships where people feel that you deal fairly with them and acknowledge the whole story and not just the part that emphasizes what they did or did not do.

- Helps you learn from your experiences when things go wrong because you no longer attribute the reasons for failure solely to someone else.
- Gets the process of fulfilling expectations back on track because you are willing to look objectively at "what else" you can do to ensure the outcome now and in the future.
- Develops a culture where everyone on the team can follow your example and become part of the solution, not just part of the problem.
- Establishes a positive work environment where people give their best effort because they feel motivated by principles that feel right and fair.

That's a huge return on your personal investment. Adding the two simple words "I let" facilitates a major change in the way you look at problems or mistakes. Those two words lessen the shock that comes when people do not deliver, even when you think you did your very best to ensure the desired outcome. This does not mean that we don't closely examine what others have done when our expectations go unmet. In fact, that is what the Accountability Conversation on the Inner Ring aims to accomplish, as we discuss in the second half of this book. Putting the "I" in the equation allows you to evaluate how well you hold others accountable and to identify where you can improve in your ability to help others fulfill your expectations.

THE ACCOUNTABILITY CONNECTION

You "connect" with the people you work with as you share meaningful experiences and build a working relationship with them. As you have experiences holding people accountable, you form a unique connection with each person that we call your Accountability Connection. These connections are based on both direct and indirect experience with you and are seen as either positive or negative. Every accountability conversation you have with them perpetuates either that positive or negative connection. If someone feels that you have dealt unfairly with them, they will undoubtedly see the connection as negative. If they think you have treated them fairly and in a supportive manner, they will most likely view it as positive. These experiences accumulate with individuals over time and greatly affect people's responses to your efforts to use the steps in the Outer Ring to establish expectations with them. Most people intuitively know whether the accountability connection is positive or negative, but few pay much attention to managing it effectively. A keen awareness of your accountability connections can make a huge difference as you work to form, communicate, align, and inspect your expectations. The more positive your connections, the more successful your efforts to hold them accountable for achieving results. In the interest of space, we have only included five lines on this list, but feel free to make it as long as you like.

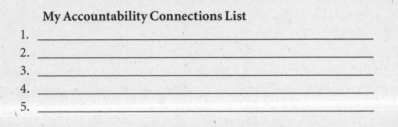

My Accountability Connections List

1. _____
2. _____
3. _____
4. _____
5. _____

Take just a moment now to consider the status of your connections with the people you hold accountable. To do this, we have put together five connection questions that you can ask the people you work with to help you determine the positive or negative quality of your connections with them.

THE FIVE CONNECTION QUESTIONS

After you explain the concept of the Accountability Connection, ask them:

1. Overall, do you feel we have a positive or negative connection?
2. If our connection were negative, how would you rate it on a scale from 1 to 10 (10 being the worse)?
3. What do I do to make you feel that our connection is negative?
4. How often does it seem negative: always, sometimes, or seldom?
5. Can you suggest ways in which I might improve my connection with you?

Opening this sort of a dialogue allows you to explore any current and significant disconnects. There is a tremendous difference between relatively minor disconnects, such as "I think a little more day-to-day courtesy would make people feel better about their work" and the potentially disastrous ones, such as "My fear of retribution prevents me from speaking up when something has gone wrong." As you review your accountability connections with people, consider the clues that often signal a negative connection.

SEVEN CLUES FOR DETECTING A NEGATIVE CONNECTION

1. You visibly detect the other person's frustration during your conversations.
2. You note that they tend to offer excuses even before you get into the subject.
3. You hear virtually no positive feedback about their working relationship with you.
4. You recognize that they talk freely when things are going well and clam up when things are going poorly.
5. You can tell they are avoiding you.
6. You wait in vain for a proactive report on their progress.
7. You find that your conversations with them usually focus on what's not working.

If you detect three or more of these clues, then, no matter how positively someone may claim they feel about their connection with you, it more than likely hinders your ability to hold them accountable.

Interestingly, it is not uncommon for people to have misgivings about holding others accountable. We asked one of our clients, someone fairly representative of those we encounter in a typical organization, to describe the extent to which people in her organization held others accountable. She told us that some people at her company did a great job holding others accountable, some did a fair job, and some were downright lousy at it. When we asked her why some people do it poorly she replied, "35 percent is competency (they're not good at it), 25 percent is a fear of what will happen if they do it, 20 percent is relationships, and 20 percent is due to the lack of clarity around what people should actually be held accountable to do." Informally polling other clients has validated this phenomenon and helped us to tabulate the top five reasons why people don't hold others accountable.

THE TOP FIVE REASONS PEOPLE
DON'T HOLD OTHERS ACCOUNTABLE

1. A fear of offending someone or jeopardizing a personal relationship.
2. A feeling that they lack the time to follow up effectively.
3. A lack of faith that the effort will make enough of a difference.
4. A worry that by holding someone else accountable, they may expose their own failure.
5. A reluctance to spark any potential retaliation.

One recent survey of employees who left their job found that 25 percent said they quit because of "ineffective leadership" and another 22 percent claimed they resigned due to "poor relations" with their manager. Put another way, almost half of all the people leaving their organizations say they are leaving because of a negative accountability connection with superiors. Considering the fact that it costs up to three times the amount of an employee's salary to replace them, we suggest that organizations are paying an enormous price for not addressing and reversing the existing negative accountability connections. You can't calculate the real price organizations pay for negative accountability connections in dollars alone. These negative connections also damage the morale of individuals, teams, and whole organizations, making it hard to get anything done, creating more stress for everyone involved, and throwing people into the resistance mode with all of its accompanying negative consequences.

Turning your negative connections into more positive ones fosters an environment where you can work more effectively with people in the Outer Ring. Doing so will greatly enhance your ability to move through the steps of forming, communicating, aligning, and inspecting expectations the positive, principled way.

If we revisit Jim Simmons, whom we met at the beginning of this chapter, we bet that Jim's assessment of those he works with most closely—his CFO, the national sales manager, and the VP of manufacturing—might reveal that the connections were not as positive as they should have been, which may also help to explain why members of his team were not more forthcoming about missed targets. Remember, evaluating your connections may help you head off potential problems *before* they develop into unmet expectations.

ACCOUNTABILITY STYLES

If you are like most people we know, when it comes to creating your Accountability Connections and holding others accountable, you do so with a particular style. Your own Accountability Style will reflect a natural preference for one of two different sides of a continuum. The continuum describes the extremes of the two styles that we tend to see: Coerce & Compel and Wait & See.

ACCOUNTABILITY STYLES CONTINUUM

The two styles are fairly self-explanatory. Leaders on the extreme left operate with the traditional "Command & Control" style of management, acting like generals directing an army toward victory. To get results, they think they need to use the force of rank to make good things happen. In sharp contrast, those on the extreme right will sometimes bend over backward to do the work themselves and fail to involve others sufficiently to get the job done. While you may think you do not fall into one of these two groups, chances are that you do, at least to some extent. Everyone, to one degree or another, has an Accountability Style and leans toward one of these two categories. Don't worry, though, because neither style is right or wrong and both have strengths and weaknesses. However, it is important to understand that you will not improve your ability to hold others accountable if you do not understand your particular style and how it affects the way you work with the steps in the Outer Ring. Take a moment now to complete the following self-assessment.

Accountability Style Self-Assessment

RESPOND YES OR NO

_____ 1. I often find myself waiting for people to report back.

_____ 2. I frequently find myself reprimanding people for not doing what they say they will do.

_____ 3. I often find myself wondering if people are doing what I asked them to do.

_____ 4. I can be a little intimidating to others when they miss their deadlines.

_____ 5. People can feel I am pretty easygoing when they don't follow through.

_____ 6. I am pretty relentless in my follow-up of others to make sure they deliver on the expectations I have of them.

_____ 7. I freely hand off tasks without a lot of follow-up, trusting that people will get it done.

_____ 8. People often feel that I expect too much of them.

_____ 9. I often assume, without checking to see if it is accurate, that people are doing what I asked.

_____ 10. Frequently, I have to "chase" people down to get a status report.

Here's how you can score the assessment:

Self-Assessment Scoring

SCORING	YOUR ACCOUNTABILITY STYLE
If the majority of "Yes" responses is marked for the even-numbered questions, your style is:	**Coerce & Compel**
If the majority of "Yes" responses is marked for the odd-numbered questions, your style is:	**Wait & See**

Where do you fall on the continuum? If you do not score a clear majority in one or the other style, then you probably spend some time doing
both. However, since we all tend toward one of the styles, you could gain
greater insight into your style by getting some feedback from people who
know you well and will be honest with you. You can also visit our Web site
www.howdidthathappen.com and complete a more extensive self-scoring
survey to determine your Accountability Style even more accurately.

As you can see, your Accountability Style suggests that whenever you
do not effectively hold someone accountable, you probably make a mistake
either by forcing things to happen (Coerce & Compel) or by taking too little
action to follow up (Wait & See). Both styles incorporate certain strengths:

COERCE & COMPEL STYLE ADVANTAGES	WAIT & SEE STYLE ADVANTAGES
Takes action and steps in when things go wrong	Strongly supports people
Exercises persistence in follow-up	Emphasizes giving people freedom to succeed or fail
Doesn't give up easily	Places a lot of trust in others
Ensures frequent, regular reporting	Steps in with great caution
Communicates high expectations	Builds strong loyalty and support in others
Stays focused on the task at hand	Thoroughly thinks through intervention before acting

On the other hand, both styles also display aggravating weaknesses,
weaknesses that will, sooner or later, get you into trouble:

COERCE & COMPEL STYLE DISADVANTAGES	WAIT & SEE STYLE DISADVANTAGES
Intimidates others	Avoids a proactive approach
Overreacts to bad news	Strikes people as disengaged
Tends to "force" things to happen	Makes false assumptions that things are happening
Willingly sacrifices relationships	Does not follow up often enough
Resists a people-oriented approach	Tends to err on the side of not intervening
Lacks sufficient trust in others	Sets low expectations

Your particular style, which reflects your basic personality, greatly influences how you go about holding others accountable. In fact, few other traits make as much of a difference when it comes to getting things done through others.

We see it all the time in our practice. One successful entrepreneur we worked with, "John," demonstrated all the qualities of the Wait & See style as CEO: a strong people orientation, lots of trust, and a preference to allow freedom, plus a hesitancy to step in too quickly. However, people in the organization did not think John was holding his international marketing VP, "Robert," accountable. In fact, people felt John was letting Robert run wild. In his work and in his dealings with people, Robert came off as self-interested, independent, difficult to work with, and secretive. The situation caused one key person in the company to observe that John "totally gave him (Robert) power because there was no accountability." Eventually, Robert moved his international marketing group to Brazil, where he maintained his independent, self-centered approach to getting things done, with John taking no steps to correct the problem, in hopes that things would work themselves out in time. Then things took a disastrous turn. Ultimately, it came to light that Robert was using company resources to do some third-party manufacturing and marketing with his buddies in Brazil for their own personal gain. Of course, John felt personally violated. Loyalty? Robert displayed none. The trust John had placed in Robert? Destroyed.

Contrast John's story with that of another entrepreneurial CEO, "Joan," who launched a start-up in the software development industry. Joan had built her success on the fact that she was always one of the smartest members of the team, engaging in the work wherever it needed to be done. She did not hesitate to skip the chain of command and march into someone's office to make sure projects were on schedule and that people were solving problems as they popped up. She knew the technology intimately. Her entire manner drove her relentlessly to question anyone on any topic in an effort to get results. That approach seemed to work for her until, in the wake of a merger, she inherited a larger organization from a successful but slower-moving company. Joan, always forceful and impatient, acted quickly to move people out of the way and force the organization into a faster operational mode. For the people in the target organization, it felt like "Hurricane Joan had struck." Indeed, it had. Joan left in her wake a trail of dead bodies along with a number of survivors with almost no loyalty and trust. Within a short period of time, Joan managed to dismantle the old culture and install in its place an environment of fear, where people hesitated to try anything new. With all decision-making firmly under Joan's control, loyalty sank to an all-time low. The company did make progress toward its objectives, but at a snail's pace in a market that demanded the speed of light.

Think about it: two CEOs with two different styles reflecting the two extremes on the continuum, and two scenarios where style weaknesses inhibited the leaders' abilities to hold others accountable, to form and follow up properly on an expectation to ensure that people not only fulfilled it, but felt good about it at the end of the day.

Acknowledging and understanding your Accountability Style marks the best beginning for your journey around the Outer Ring. Once you gain that understanding, without feeling that you are "bad" or "wrong" because you act the way you do, you can start adjusting your actions in a way that will put you at a more optimal point on the continuum. We label that point on the continuum the "Positive, Principled Way" and consider it the perfect blend of strengths from both accountability styles.

THE POSITIVE, PRINCIPLED WAY

In the middle of the continuum, you will find a more thoughtful, more deliberate, and more methodical approach to holding others accountable. It is the result of following the sequence of steps in the Outer Ring of the Account-ability Sequence. Whatever your style, however well or poorly you currently hold others accountable, by following the sequence, you will more effectively tap all the strengths of both styles while mitigating their weaknesses.

For each step of the Accountability Sequence, we will point out how the styles affect your ability to implement that particular principle or tool. Since the styles so strongly affect how anyone progresses through both the Inner and Outer Rings, we will offer hints, suggestions, reminders, cau-tions, and recommendations along the way that will help you use your style to its best advantage.

ACCOUNTABILITY REALITY CHECK

In each chapter, we will encourage you to take time to apply what you are learning in your daily work. The Accountability Reality Check provides hands-on exercises that test your learning and, at the same time, provide potentially valuable insights into how you can improve your ability to hold others accountable.

Try this. Revisit your Accountability Connections List completed earlier in this chapter and consider each person you placed on it in terms of the Top Five Reasons People Don't Hold Others Accountable. Do any of them apply? If so, jot that number next to the name of the person. After you have done that for each connection, try to see if a pattern emerges or if the reasons vary from person to person. Have you avoided holding someone accountable? If so, what can you do about that? Having worked with many people just like you, we have become more and more convinced that travel-ing the Outer Ring will largely address the barriers to creating a culture and work environment where people, yourself included, effectively hold one an-other accountable the positive, principled way.

THE OUTER RING

When we introduce the Outer Ring to people, most nod their heads in agreement because it strikes them as basic common sense. To most people

the steps of forming, communicating, aligning, and inspecting expectations seem quite intuitive. In our view, that's what makes the sequence so
powerful. It *is* simple and intuitive. Problems arise, however, because common sense does not always translate into common *practice*. The Outer Ring
captures the essence of what it takes to get things done through others by
effectively establishing expectations. Find someone who does that really
well, and you will have found someone who knows how to follow the steps
smoothly and effectively.

By using a systematic, sequential approach to holding people accountable, you accentuate the strengths of your style, mitigate its weaknesses,
and create positive Accountability Connections. With some thoughtful
preparation and patient practice, anyone can master the art of the sequence.
Mastering it will empower you to help people deliver on all your expectations, and it will help you develop individual talent and organizational
capability, valuable resources needed to succeed in this fiercely competitive
world. To capture all of the advantages of this technology, we recommend
that you integrate the Accountability Sequence, with its positive, principled approach, into your talent management, leadership development,
and performance management efforts. There is no question in our minds
that getting everyone in your organization on the same page with respect
to accountability can make all the difference between average and world-
class performance. Ready? Let's take the first step of our journey around
the Outer Ring by learning how to *form* expectations.

Chapter One

THE POSITIVE, PRINCIPLED WAY

As promised, we will summarize each chapter's main principles and ideas in this brief recap. This summary will capture the practices and approaches that characterize the positive, principled approach to holding people accountable for results with the Accountability Sequence.

The Art of the Sequence
Moving deliberately and effectively through the steps in the Outer Ring will produce success. To hold someone accountable means to effectively form, communicate, align, and inspect the fulfillment of an expectation in the positive, principled way that enables people to achieve results now and in the future.

The Three Axioms of the Outer Ring
Three axioms form the foundation for taking the steps in the Outer Ring: (1) the Accountability Fallacy (when people fail to follow through, there's something wrong with them); (2) the Accountability Assumption (people are doing their very best in any given circumstance to fulfill my expectations); and (3) the Accountability Truth (when something goes wrong, there is usually something wrong with what I am doing).

How Did I Let That Happen?
A more effective question than "How did that happen?" is "How did *I let* that happen?" Adding the words "I let" will enable you to be more effective at getting results through others.

The Accountability Connection
Every time you hold someone accountable, you create an experience for them that leads to either a positive or a negative connection, one that impacts your overall relationship and your effectiveness at taking the steps in the Outer Ring with them.

Accountability Styles

People tend to lean toward one of the two styles, "Coerce & Compel" or "Wait & See." Each style has its strengths and weaknesses. The positive, principled way effectively blends the strengths of these two styles and allows you to implement accountability most effectively.

Chapter Two

FORM EXPECTATIONS

THE BEST EXPECTATIONS

Holding others accountable the positive, principled way begins with Step One in the Outer Ring of the Accountability Sequence: form expectations. It almost goes without saying that you cannot effectively hold someone accountable if you have not first formed clear expectations. Clarifying your thinking about just what you expect from others, guided by the specific principles we will discuss in this chapter, will help you establish expectations and create positive Accountability Connections in a way that ensures people deliver results. Let's face it; you have expectations of all those you work with, from suppliers and vendors to co-workers, team members, and supervisors. You expect them to deliver the results you need, when you need them; and your own ability to produce the results for which you yourself will be held accountable naturally depends on others fulfilling your expectations. Ensuring that those expectations are clearly formed is the essential first step.

When it comes to getting things done, any old expectation just won't do. Years ago Sears & Roebuck gave customers a mail-order catalog of available products that identified each as "good," "better," or "best." Your purchase depended, of course, on what you could afford. "Good" might satisfy you, "better" might please you more, but "best" would give you a "world-class" experience. "Best" would last over time and would be guaranteed to do the job. When it comes to forming expectations, most of us do a pretty "good" job at letting people know what we need. When it's really important, we often do an even "better" job, taking even more care to ensure people know what we need. But when it comes to forming key expectations, we cannot afford to settle for anything but "best." Forming "best" expectations is what the first step in the Outer Ring is all about.

Individuals and companies that fail to think through their expectations clearly often pay an enormous price. Take, for example, Michelin's introduction of the run-flat tire. On the surface, the run-flat tire looked like a great idea to everyone involved: a tire that would allow a driver to continue traveling at up to fifty miles per hour for about a hundred miles, even after a tire had gone flat. Everyone within Michelin projected that this tire would match the breakthrough achieved by the radial tire, which revolutionized tire technology and is still standard equipment on most cars today. Based on this expectation, Michelin made huge investments over many years to bring this new idea to market. However, when Michelin introduced the run-flat tire, the company did not hear the applause it expected; it heard, instead, the "bang" of a blowout. As sales fell woefully short of expectations, everyone at Michelin was left scratching their heads in bewilderment: how had that happened?

The run-flat tire's design required a connection to a dashboard light that would flash when the tire needed replacement. This meant that only cars originally equipped with the appropriate electronics could benefit from the run-flat tire, and very few cars on the market at that time were equipped with the right electronics. In the final analysis, the run-flat tire was doomed from the outset. A decade after the botched introduction, only a few models carried the run-flat tire as standard equipment.

How could a major manufacturer fall so drastically short of its expectations? Why didn't someone somewhere in the product introduction pipeline catch this detail? Certainly, no one expected such a big miss in the marketplace. After all, it *was* a great idea. The product worked just the way the company designed it. Everyone executed the plan effectively and delivered a functional product to the market, just as expected. But looking back, it's not all that hard to explain why all of Michelin's intermediate success with the run-flat tire ended up as a resounding failure.

The explanation for Michelin's failure begins with understanding the fact that a "good" expectation is sometimes not good enough. When it came to introducing its potentially revolutionary tire, Michelin needed a "best" expectation formed up front, the first step in the Outer Ring. Certainly, "best" would have allowed everyone at Michelin, up and down the line, to consider the additional steps required to get the desired result. Someone would have determined that those steps included coordinating with original equipment manufacturers and accounting for the fact that it takes at least four years for a car to go from design to production. Someone would have acknowledged that Michelin would need to incorporate tires with the run-flat technology into the overall design of successful car models, again requiring years of advance planning and successful marketing to the automakers, not to mention the after-market conversion of dealerships, tire resellers, and garages that service the tires, all of whom need to get on board. The Michelin run-flat tire dilemma illustrates the lesson that most people experience at some point in their careers: taking time up front to form expectations effectively leads to success; not doing so paves the road to failure.

Of course, Michelin is not the only company that has failed to form "best" expectations when they needed them and subsequently paid a big price for that oversight. Stories of companies that have committed similar oversights abound, and their artifacts literally dot the business landscape. For a good example, take a look at the large modern office building with a strikingly different design that stands on the outskirts of London just beyond Heathrow Airport. The impressive "Ark" building, fashioned after an architect's idea of Noah's biblical ship, looks just like you might imagine the genuine article—a big boat, only this one constructed of glass and modern materials. It has won numerous architectural awards, and, from the outside at least, it takes your breath away. However, at the time of this writing, no tenants occupy the building. Why? Because the inside of the building fell short of the expectations created by its unique and engaging outer shell. Its exterior captivated the eye, but its interior lacked the user-friendly features tenants demand. For a company looking to rent space and not just win architectural awards, discovering the poor reception of the marketplace to the building's interior utility must have left many investors and designers wondering, "How did that happen?"

Like the run-flat tire at Michelin, a disconnect occurred somewhere in the planning process of the "Ark Project." At the outset, the Ark's owners surely must have expected that this unique design would draw tenants like a magnet. As it turned out, prospective tenants just couldn't imagine themselves working there. Again, when it comes to forming key expectations that must be fulfilled, you simply cannot afford to settle for anything less than "best." The "best" expectation, if properly formed, would have empowered everyone involved, from the design team to the leasing office, to deliver an office building that would attract tenants and turn a profit. Twenty-twenty hindsight? Sure. But the difference between merely having an expectation and deliberately forming one always becomes more obvious after it's too late.

How about applying this to you? Have you suffered a disappointment because you did not form your expectations properly? Take a moment to consider the last time you felt dissatisfied with the outcome of a major project, initiative, or some other endeavor. Could you tell a story about a time when you knew what you wanted, worked hard to have it happen, but, just like the Michelin folks or the builders of the Ark, found out too late that the people you were counting on would never deliver on your expectation?

For some people, forming "best" expectations may sound like the easiest thing in the world to accomplish. For most, however, it's not so easy. But as we have pointed out, it's worth the initial investment. The work of forming "best" expectations begins when you make a very deliberate and conscious effort at the outset to form the expectation in a way that makes the deliverable clearly understood. Managers can form expectations all on their own, but they will always get better results when they form "best" expectations with the input and collaboration of those involved in making it happen. Only mutually understood and agreed-upon expectations can get people 100 percent committed to getting the job done.

Individual and organizational accountability always begins by clearly defining the result, a premise discussed in our book, *The Oz Principle*. However, when it comes to holding *someone else* accountable to deliver the result, you will significantly strengthen your ability to do so as you become proficient in forming expectations. The assessment below will help you evaluate your own ability to do so. As you respond, consider how those you work with might answer these questions if they were evaluating you.

CLUES TO ASSESSING HOW WELL YOU FORM EXPECTATIONS

Answer True or False to each statement.

_____ 1. You wonder why the people you depend on just "don't seem to get it."

_____ 2. You are often disappointed with the results people deliver and routinely ask the question, "How did that happen?"

_____ 3. People feel that they often waste time working on things you ask them to do because your priorities often seem to change.

_____ 4. The people you work closest with are not able to articulate what is most important to you with any degree of certainty.

_____ 5. You tend to understate what you are really asking people to do because you don't want to strain relationships.

_____ 6. You tend to assume people already have the vision of what needs to be done and, as a result, don't take the needed time to form specific expectations.

_____ 7. You often have to re-explain and clarify with people what it is you really want.

If you replied "True" to even a few of these statements, then there is room for improvement. But whether or not you are proficient and effective at the first step of the Outer Ring, you can learn the skills to clearly form your expectations so that everyone you depend upon understands exactly what needs to happen.

THE EXPECTATIONS CHAIN

The first step in the Outer Ring of the Accountability Sequence requires some thoughtful planning and consideration. It all starts with what we call the Expectations Chain, a takeoff on the "Supply Chain" concept. In this case, the chain consists of all the people who are connected to each other in order to fulfill your expectations and deliver the results you want. The decision-makers at Michelin made a big mistake when they did not effectively include the original equipment manufacturers (OEMs) in their chain. Ultimately, the success of the run-flat tire would depend on them. As you form expectations of others (at least if you want to form the kind of expectations that help ensure the result), you must consider everyone up and down the chain.

We never form our expectations in a vacuum. Everyone is part of a chain of expectations in the business world. We all have a boss—someone who has expectations of us, usually high expectations, that we wish to fulfill. That boss can be a supervisor or manager, a parent company, headquarters, the customer, or the shareholders. Whatever the case, someone defines what is expected of us. We, in turn, form links in the chain by defining expectations for others based on what is expected of us. All of these links form a chain of expectations upon which all involved depend for success. Understanding how we are connected and linked together in this chain is critical to forming expectations that help people deliver what we need.

Consider "Rashid" who works as a statistical analyst in the marketing department of "Pullman & Kindle," a major consumer products company. His weekly competitive analysis report depends on information supplied by "Tamara," who sits just two cubicles away from him, and by "Maxwell," a key outside vendor. Both Tamara and the Maxwell contact represent critical links in Rashid's Expectations Chain.

Every week, one or both of his sources fails to get him what he needs on time, forcing him to scramble to complete his report. He's fast, but he makes mistakes when he's under time pressure, and he hates that. When he submits a late or flawed report, his boss gives him a glassy stare and mutters, "No excuses." Like all of us, Rashid is stuck in the middle of the Expectations Chain between those he depends on and those who depend on him. What does he do? He gets mad, he fumes, and he loses his temper. He calls his contact at Maxwell and yells at him. "I expect you to be accountable! If you think you're irreplaceable," he threatens, "stick your finger in a glass of water, pull it out, and see if you leave a hole!" The contact's reaction? "Same to you, buddy!"

He can't threaten Tamara, though. They see each other ten times a day, they eat lunch together in the cafeteria, and he really likes working with her. Except for her frequent tardiness, she does a great job. But then one day, after his boss berates him and suggests he consider transferring to a different job, he can't help himself. Doing what comes naturally to all of us, he falls prey to the Accountability Fallacy—there must be something wrong with *them*! He reads Tamara the riot act. She stops speaking to him, except when absolutely necessary. And what's the result of all of this? Rashid will now find it even harder to get his report done on time.

If Rashid asked our advice, we would begin by helping him look at how he forms his expectations. Exactly what does he expect from the two people most critical to his success? We can only imagine what we might discover. It may turn out that he has a vague expectation that he will receive what he needs when he needs it. Perhaps he feels comfortable with such vagueness and has never bothered to form his expectation in a deliberate, clear, and compelling way. If so, we can confidently tell Rashid that unless he properly forms his expectations, he will not likely communicate them effectively.

Without taking this step in the Accountability Sequence, Rashid will probably never find either Tamara or his contact at Maxwell bending over backward to meet his expectations.

Taking your entire Expectations Chain into consideration when you form your expectations will accelerate everyone's ability to deliver the result. Remember, your Expectations Chain includes everyone upon whom you depend to help you fulfill expectations. Making sure that you have given consideration to all the people both up-line and down-line in the chain will help you craft your expectations so that they apply to everyone involved.

Take a moment to think about a key expectation you need fulfilled. Now, list all the people you will hold accountable, in one way or another, to help make that happen. Your list will include people such as your boss, subordinates, peers, suppliers, and contractors, people both inside and outside of your organization and team.

EXPECTATIONS CHAIN

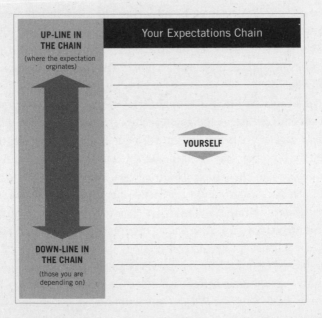

Too often, people think only in terms of defined organizations and teams and fail to take into account the much larger virtual organizations of people on whom we all ultimately depend to get things done. Thinking about the entire Expectations Chain will help you increase your skill at forming expectations in a way that can positively influence everyone.

SUGGESTIONS FOR WORKING WITH
YOUR EXPECTATIONS CHAIN

1. Define the chain in terms of the people you rely on and not just the organizations they belong to. Doing so will create a virtual team of people that more accurately describes everyone who contributes to your final result.

2. Identify the chain by asking others about those on whom they depend as they work to fulfill your expectations. Do this with all of the important people in your chain. Recognizing how far your chain really extends can help you properly form expectations.

3. As you define your Expectations Chain, consider up-line links, not just the more obvious down-line ones. Up-line links include your boss, your boss's boss, and all the stakeholders who contribute to your fulfillment of an expectation, especially your customers.

4. Give due consideration to everyone in the chain, including those outside the range of your organizational authority. Never write off someone in your chain as beyond your influence. Most of the time, people will listen to a persuasive argument.

5. Take extra steps to reach out to people at geographically distant locations. It's only natural to pay less attention to people with whom you do not come into physical contact every day.

Effectively managing your Expectations Chain begins with deliberately forming your expectations in a way that brings clarity and understanding to everyone throughout the chain.

FORMING EXPECTATIONS

We all know what we mean by an "expectation," right? The dictionary defines an expectation as a "strong belief that someone will or should do something." Of course, not all expectations are equal: some matter a great deal more than others. A weathercaster leads you to expect a rainy day? No big deal. You expect third-quarter revenues to meet the predictions you gave to Wall Street? A very big deal! Let's call those "big deal" expectations (where the stakes run high, where you simply must meet them or suffer dire consequences) your "key" expectations. These are the kinds of expectations that require our "best" thinking.

We define a "key expectation" as "an expectation that *must* be achieved and will require the commitment from everyone in the Expectations Chain to do what needs to be done to deliver the result." Key expectations are formed when not delivering is not an option. Everyone in the Expectations Chain must see it, believe in it, and share responsibility for making it happen. This means that when you *form* your expectations, you must carefully weigh the specifics of what you want to have happen, as well as the specific people who will be required to take accountability to make it happen.

We worked with one very effective leader at "Home Grown Foods," who was involved in implementing a districtwide training program designed to engage customers more fully in their stores. In every store in the district, both store directors and their people gave the program high marks, praising the training as the best they had ever received. Those responsible for the training's implementation celebrated the fact that almost 100 percent of the people scheduled for training received it on time and within budget. But that's not all. They were proud of the fact that the training effort brought an increase in sales of about $5 million.

So that's all good, right? Actually, it's not nearly as good as it might have been. Further follow-up studies throughout Home Grown Foods revealed that only about 15 percent of the people who underwent the training were actually using what they learned. This meant that, calculated on the basis of the initial sales increases, if everyone who went through the program had actually applied the training, they could have captured at least another $25 million in sales, for a grand total of $30 million.

The project debrief helped the implementation team realize that they never really formed the right expectation in the first place. A "best" expectation would have gone beyond just making sure everyone got trained to ensuring that everyone who went through the training actually applied it to their daily work. After all, what other target could you possibly set for such training? The target remained the same: to get people to interact with the customer and create the engagement necessary to capture an additional $25 million in sales revenue. But somehow, that key expectation got lost in formation, long before implementation began. As a result, store directors never really understood that the key expectation was not just executing a successful training program, but capturing $30 million in increased sales through effective application of the training.

To their credit, Home Grown Foods used what they learned from this experience to improve implementation of their next district training program. Before doing anything else, they clearly formed their expectation. They discussed exactly what they wanted to have happen and who specifically they needed to get involved in order to make it happen. Once they formed the right expectation, they began the implementation process in the stores with a five-minute prep class conducted by the immediate supervisor of each employee, who explained why they were getting the training. Every person who began the training did so with the belief that their store director expected immediate application and follow-through.

To reinforce the expectation with everyone involved, the instructors began the session by asking participants if they had attended the five-minute prep class with their immediate supervisor. The instructors excused anyone who had not done so, asking them to return for training another day after they had received the proper preparation for the course. After that happened, no one was surprised when reluctant store directors quickly got on board.

Immediately after the training, the instructors conducted another short meeting with the participants, asking what they had learned and reinforcing the need for immediate application. Both the instructor and the store director held the participants accountable for taking the training to the aisles of Home Grown Foods. As a result of better expectations and implementation, the company reaped big dividends on a daily basis. Note that the successful fulfillment of their expectation began with effectively forming one that everyone could embrace. This didn't just provide a happy training experience, but a tangible boost in sales revenue to meet the company's quarterly plan. Based on his success, the leader of this organization won a major promotion and strong encouragement to use his approach systemwide.

APPLYING FORM

The real change at Home Grown Foods began when they understood that a truly effective expectation begins with a statement of what you (individually or as an organization) want to have happen. Stating your expectation this way, making it as accurate as possible, helps you to clarify the outcome you need to achieve. In the case of the grocer and their first shot at implementing the training, they did not emphasize what the company really wanted to have happen: "to achieve $30 million in sales revenue growth districtwide within nine months as a result of implementing the new training in each store." While that's what they really wanted, they had actually formed an expectation that sounded more like just "getting everyone at every level trained in each store in the district on time and on budget." There's a world of difference between these two expectations.

While numerous methods and other popular acronyms have been used over the years to establish and describe processes for setting goals and objectives, we recommend that when you set about establishing best expectations you apply the FORM Checklist, which includes the four characteristics we consider fundamental to forming effective expectations: Framable, Obtainable, Repeatable, and Measurable. Testing your key expectations against these four characteristics will ensure that you properly form the expectation.

FORM CHECKLIST

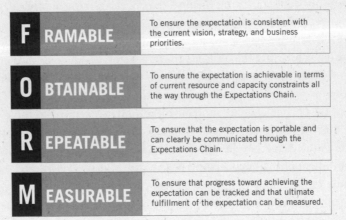

F RAMABLE	To ensure the expectation is consistent with the current vision, strategy, and business priorities.
O BTAINABLE	To ensure the expectation is achievable in terms of current resource and capacity constraints all the way through the Expectations Chain.
R EPEATABLE	To ensure that the expectation is portable and can clearly be communicated through the Expectations Chain.
M EASURABLE	To ensure that progress toward achieving the expectation can be tracked and that ultimate fulfillment of the expectation can be measured.

Once you have accurately identified "what you want to have happen," use the Framable Check to determine whether the expectation is consistent with your current vision, strategy, and business priorities and, more important, the vision, strategy, and business priorities of those who are up-line in your Expectations Chain. If you cannot frame the expectation within this context, then ask yourself, "Do we really need to do this?" The Obtainable Check certifies that, given all the existing resource and capacity constraints, the expectation is achievable by everyone all the way through the Expectations Chain. The Repeatable Check confirms that the expectation has sufficient portability to traverse the entire Expectations Chain with a minimum amount of effort and energy. Finally, the Measurable Check examines whether you have formed the expectation in a way that allows everyone involved to track their progress toward its achievement. Applying FORM to what you want to have happen will increase the likelihood that you take the first step in the Outer Ring smoothly and effectively.

At this point you might want to ask, "Does every expectation I form deserve this level of effort and energy?" Our answer is "No." Remember, not all expectations carry equal weight. When the downside of not delivering on an expectation matters so much that you simply cannot let that happen, then, in our view, it deserves expending the additional energy required to use FORM and give it your "best" effort. Your key expectations may apply to the whole organization or they may apply solely to specific individuals. In either case, you cannot afford not to invest the time and energy needed to do it right because, in the long run, doing it early will save valuable time and resources later.

Continuing the Home Grown Foods example, let's apply FORM to what they wanted to have happen: "to achieve $30 million in sales revenue growth districtwide within nine months as a result of implementing the new training in each store."

"Is it Framable?" Is it consistent with the company's current vision, strategy, business results, and priorities? In HGF's case, its history of emphasizing customer service made the new training feel like a "hand-in-glove" fit with the current business strategy and with what people were already doing to contribute to the company's overall growth and success.

"Is it Obtainable?" HGF needed to look at the Expectations Chain both up-line and down-line to consider everyone's capability to execute the work. That consideration included the availability of organizational talent, the current and future workload of the staff, and all the other factors that affect people's ability to get things done. After careful analysis, HGF concluded that it possessed the needed capacity to implement the training program and attain the desired sales growth. However, this check also prompted the clarification that the $30 million sales increase would need to come from each of the ten stores in the district, with each of them contributing $3 million. The focus on sales increases at each store fits perfectly with the current HGF business model.

Ensuring that people are working on the things that you say are most important to the overall growth and success of the organization may do more than anything else to assure that your key expectations are indeed obtainable. When you make sure that people are working on the right things and that they have the right support (addressing the capacity issues), you will always improve the likelihood of your success.

Company leaders who lack sufficient foresight and fail to plan realistically run the risk of letting a "just get it done" mentality demolish their hopes. For example, "Optical Controls Inc.," with thirty district offices spread throughout the world, expected each office to provide its own customer support. However, with the onslaught of a more competitive market and the need for more consistency across the organization, corporate leaders decided to centralize the operation, charging "Jeff Green," the senior vice president of operations, to get the job done within a lightning-fast, six-month time frame. To make it all happen, Jeff needed to reduce the workforce in the district offices and expand it in the centralized location, getting representatives up to speed on the phone without skipping a beat and without interrupting normal operations. The result? Six months turned into twelve months; twelve months turned into two years. Worse, instead of enhancing customer service, the project took an unexpected toll on everyone involved, including the customer.

Looking back, Jeff acknowledged that the company lacked the capacity to accomplish in twenty-four weeks what would, in reality, take twenty-four months. "Just do it" may work in sports, but it frequently misses the mark in business. OCI couldn't just "flip a switch" and go from a decentralized function to a centralized one in a mere six months, all the while maintaining a high level of customer service. While the strategy made a ton of sense and still does (everyone at OCI still agrees that the centralized model would work best in today's market), unrealistic expectations dashed the company's hopes, putting off customers when OCI most desperately needed not only to satisfy, but to delight them.

Caution! Before we move forward, we must offer some advice about changing priorities. Everything in today's accelerated business environment can change in the blink of an eye. Working recently with one highly respected organizational leader, we were surprised by her resistance to beginning a twelve-month effort to improve the culture of her organization. Her reason? She feared that her leadership team would find itself distracted from focusing on the necessary follow-through. She confided to us that she just never knew when she and her team might be surprised by news that her company had been acquired or merged with another. While she admitted that she was not aware of any imminent plans for such an acquisition, everyone, not least of all herself, expected that an acquisition could happen at almost any time. That, of course, would once again delay implementation of all major initiatives. "Why waste time starting something we won't be able to finish?" she asked. Good question.

Her situation is not unique. Priorities, circumstances, business conditions, and economic cycles all change, often unexpectedly, sometimes slowly and sometimes overnight. Those who wish to succeed in business today must adapt to those changing conditions and, quite possibly, adjust expectations accordingly. Keep in mind, however, that every time you change expectations, you disrupt the entire Expectations Chain. A thoughtful and deliberate formation of your expectations up front will help you avoid the need to change and adjust them later.

"Is it Repeatable?" This check tests whether you've given the expectation "legs," making it simple and clear enough that people can easily transfer the idea to others, both up and down the Expectations Chain. Consider, for instance, the seemingly complicated act of performing cardiopulmonary resuscitation (CPR). As you may recall, for years someone learning to administer CPR had to remember the ratio of chest compressions to mouth-to-mouth breaths. As many times as you may have heard it, can you recall the numbers? To novices, that seemed hard to remember, particularly under pressure! Could it be made simpler and, thus, more transferable? Yes. Not long ago the American Heart Association announced that hands-only CPR—rapid presses on an adult victim's chest until help arrives—gets as good a result in adult patients as standard CPR. Now, if Uncle Joe falls down clutching his chest, you only need to remember two things: (1) call 911 and (2) push hard and fast on the middle of Uncle Joe's chest. The new protocol for giving CPR to adults even addresses the issue of achievability by removing the mouth-to-mouth requirement, something many people hesitate doing, especially with other adults. In this case, making the expectation more easily transferable will save lives.

When forming key expectations, you should consider and follow the communication path through the entire Expectations Chain. Anticipating who will need to know the expectation, as well as weighing their ability to comprehend it, will improve your ability to FORM the proper expectation. This applies to all key expectations no matter how many people are in the chain.

What about Home Grown Foods? How repeatable did the company make its expectation? Looking at the communication path, everyone knew that every store employee, including the baggers and stockers, would need to be involved in the training if they were to hit the target number of $3 million per store.

Ultimately, boiling down the expectation to something that almost sounds like a motto, like "3-in-9" ($3 million sales increase in nine months) makes the expectation easier to talk about and share throughout the organization.

"Is it Measurable?" This check usually means concisely capturing the expectation on paper and describing how you will track progress over time. In the case of HGF, weekly sales numbers would quantify progress. In addition, to further monitor progress HGF would use "mystery shoppers," company employees who would shop in stores just like real customers. These mystery shoppers would rate the quality of their interactions with HGF personnel relative to the training objectives. Together, these reports would indicate the degree to which store employees had applied their training to their customers.

After applying the FORM Checklist, the HGF expectation now reads: "Achieve $30 million in additional sales revenue districtwide within nine months. Do this by increasing sales in each store in the district by $3 million ("3-in-9"), as a result of implementing the new training program at all levels in each store. Measure progress in terms of weekly sales numbers and mystery shopper scores." Having applied FORM, HGF crafted a clear expectation the company can use to tell everyone in the organization exactly what it wants to have happen.

The FORM Checklist is a practical device you can use whenever you are beginning to establish a key expectation. It causes you to become more deliberate and conscious about establishing an expectation, and, with practice, its use can become an ingrained habit. Take a moment to complete the Deliberate Leader Self-Test to discover the extent to which you may have already made forming expectations a habit.

The Deliberate Leader Self-Test

RESPOND TRUE OR FALSE TO THE FOLLOWING STATEMENTS.

PEOPLE WOULD SAY . . .

_____ 1. I carefully consider what I want to have happen before I start communicating what I want people to do.

_____ 2. I have a good feel for how long it takes to get things done and I am fairly realistic in my requests for turnaround.

_____ 3. I give thoughtful consideration to the "key" expectations that I form and always write them down.

_____ 4. I have a good read on organizational capacity and believe I know what is being asked of the organization and how much effort is being required to accomplish it—no one would say I am "out of touch."

_____ 5. I take the time to test my requests against current organizational efforts and priorities to make sure they fit; when they don't, I take those requests off the list.

_____ 6. I consider all the people who will be involved in helping fulfill my expectations, both inside and outside of the organization, before I form my expectations.

_____ 7. I am good at making my expectations simple and clear so that others can easily transfer the idea to everyone up and down the Expectations Chain.

_____ 8. I am confident the people I work with can readily and accurately list what I consider to be the "key" expectations that I have of them.

_____ 9. I always make sure that "key" expectations are measurable.

_____ 10. I am not impulsive and spontaneous when it comes to telling others what I expect of them.

IF YOU RESPONDED TRUE TO . . .	THEN YOU ARE . . .
All 10 statements	an EXPERT at deliberately and consciously forming expectations. People understand what you expect of them.
8–9 statements	a PRO who is very conscious about helping people successfully do what you ask of them. You also recognize that you could improve your skills in this area.
5–7 statements	an AMATEUR or about average in your ability to form expectations methodically. You could benefit from a much more deliberate approach.

3–4 statements	a NOVICE at forming expectations in a way that sets people (including yourself) up to win. Your willingness to see reality will help you succeed in applying the principles in this book.
Fewer than 3 statements	a BASKET CASE (just kidding!). You're still uncertain about how to form key expectations. The good news is that you will see big dividends and greater success working through others as you apply the principles in this book.

What insights did you gain from this exercise? Will your heightened self-knowledge encourage you to form your expectations in a more deliberate and conscious fashion? If so, you are making sure and steady progress on your journey toward holding people accountable the positive, principled way.

FORMING EXPECTATIONS WITH "STYLE"

Remember the Accountability Styles—Coerce & Compel and Wait & See—we introduced in Chapter One? When it comes to holding others accountable, you naturally lean toward one or the other style. As with everything you do, your natural style greatly influences the way you form expectations.

Those who display the Coerce & Compel style may often form unrealistic and, therefore, unachievable expectations. Too often, they discount information that people are operating at full capacity and that the pipeline cannot accommodate any more work. People prone to this style will usually feel they can force "one more thing" into the system if everyone just works a little smarter, and, maybe, a little harder. "Just get it done," they proclaim. Someone with the Coerce & Compel mind-set believes that if you make people stretch, they will rise to the occasion. Do they rise? Not always. They often chafe under a style they can find overly demanding and unrealistic. A person with this style may also feel that people should already know what to do. This assumption causes them to focus on doing their own jobs, thus minimizing the time and energy they fear they might waste on deliberately forming expectations.

When forming expectations, the Coerce & Compel style should recognize these tendencies and ask:

1. If people tell me they think this expectation is unrealistic, would I know why they think so? If not, perhaps I should ask them exactly why they do.
2. When did people in the organization last tell me they felt "stretched to the limit"? If I add another item to the plate, how will that affect morale, and how will I manage that?
3. Have I applied the FORM Checklist and given sufficient thought to this expectation, or am I rushing into it because I feel people should just get the job done and figure it out?

In contrast, someone with a Wait & See style can be overly sympathetic to organizational capacity issues and not ask enough of people. This style often struggles with forming higher expectations that cause people to stretch. A strong people orientation and the desire to maintain rapport can potentially slow down people with this style and inhibit their ability to deliver the result on time. They also may not take the time to apply the steps outlined in this chapter, not because they don't want to invest the time and effort, but because it may not occur to them that people need that much direction in order to get the job done. Because this style tends to adhere to a more unstructured approach, applying FORM may seem cumbersome and potentially a poor trade-off for the planning time required to do it well. As a result, they may stop practicing what they have learned concerning the proper way to form expectations.

When forming expectations, a person with a Wait & See style should ask:

1. In forming this expectation, am I asking enough of the organization? Should I stretch them even more?
2. Do I possess a realistic view of the organization's capacity? How can I determine if any "excess capacity" exists?
3. Have I applied the FORM Checklist and given sufficient thought to this expectation, or am I wrongly assuming that people don't need a lot of direction and will get it done without additional clarification?

Recognizing how your style may affect your ability to form expectations effectively will help you even more successfully implement the principles and methodologies presented in this chapter.

ACCOUNTABILITY REALITY CHECK

As you may recall from the last chapter, we will periodically suggest some simple ways you can apply what you are learning as you progress through the Accountability Sequence. To implement this Accountability Reality Check, ask the people with whom you work most closely to respond to the Deliberate Leader Self-Test on your behalf. You can also go to our Web site at www.howdidthathappen.com and send a link to a complimentary electronic version of the test to any number of people in your organization, asking them to give you a confidential response. Urge their complete honesty, telling them you want to know what they really think. They may respond to the statements on your behalf quite differently than you responded for yourself, either positively or negatively. Gathering their feedback now will prove helpful as you continue navigating the Outer Ring.

THE ACCOUNTABILITY SEQUENCE

The Accountability Sequence provides a series of steps that should be taken in the prescribed order. Each step builds upon the previous one. Skipping one may jeopardize your ability to employ accountability "best practices" in your business. More often than not, any shortcut ends up costing you in terms of lost time, heightened confusion, misspent energy, and, ultimately, failure to get the results you expect and need. By taking the first step in the Outer Ring, and deliberately and consciously forming the key expectations you have of others, you prepare yourself to take the next crucial step: communicate expectations.

Chapter Two

THE POSITIVE, PRINCIPLED WAY

Before you move on to Chapter Three, pause briefly to think about the key concepts we have introduced in this chapter. A brief review will help you summarize the material before moving on to the next chapter.

The Best Expectations
When it comes to expectations, there is "good," "better," and "best." Taking the time to form the "best" expectations is essential to fulfilling critical expectations.

The Expectations Chain
You must take into account all of the people, both up-line and down-line, on whom you depend to fulfill the expectation. Consciously managing this chain will guarantee better results.

Key Expectations
You should take more time to form key expectations; expectations where *not* delivering is *not* an option. You begin by asking, "What do I want to have happen?"

The FORM Checklist
This acronym reminds you to consider four crucial elements when you form a "key" expectation: Framable, Obtainable, Repeatable, and Measurable.

- **Framable:** To ensure the expectation is consistent with the current vision, strategy, and business priorities.
- **Obtainable:** To ensure the expectation is achievable in terms of current resource and capacity constraints all the way through the Expectations Chain.
- **Repeatable:** To ensure that the expectation is portable and can be clearly communicated through the chain.
- **Measurable:** To ensure that you can track progress toward achieving the expectation and measure the ultimate fulfillment of the expectation.

Chapter Three

COMMUNICATE EXPECTATIONS

COMMAND, CONTROL, AND FAIL

The next step in the Outer Ring involves communicating key expectations with such clarity that people understand what is expected and why it is important for them to follow through and deliver. This level of understanding can only come from complete and compelling communication. Incomplete or ineffective communication heightens the risk of failure and leaves you shaking your head, wondering once again, "How did that happen?"

When a major industrial products manufacturer, "Builtwell," promoted "Dennis Jones" from director to area vice president, he took on the job of organizing an entirely new sales region. His boss, "Jerry Snyder," expected him to get the new region up and running and achieving sales targets as soon as possible. Dennis confidently started from scratch, establishing a structure and hiring all the necessary sales reps and district managers needed to fill the new region's seven districts. With the structure in place, he established a system of accountability meant to promote success throughout the organization. But after two years, in spite of initial optimism, Dennis failed to fulfill the original plan, and for the first time in his career he fell woefully short of his boss's expectations. Jerry, disappointed with the poor results coming out of the new region, told Dennis that he needed to boost performance fast.

Quickly, Dennis analyzed the situation. Hoping to spot trends that might help him figure out what was going wrong in his region, he crunched the numbers and analyzed every other region in the division (average calls per day, new accounts per rep, cold call results—you name it). While poring over the data, he finally recognized what was happening. His region was, it turned out, quite different from all of the other regions. Based on his analysis, Dennis determined that the solution to his problem was to put "more boots on the ground." He was convinced that all he needed to do to make sure he hit the numbers and capture the targeted market share was tell Jerry his discovery.

With his analysis in hand, Dennis prepped himself for his meeting with Jerry. He was confident that once Jerry heard his conclusions, he would understand why the region was falling short of plan and would support giving Dennis the resources he needed to turn things around. Dennis confidently made his pitch for more resources and painstakingly justified, explained, and excused his regional results from almost every imaginable angle. At the end of his presentation, Dennis drew a deep breath and asked, "What do you think?"

Jerry smiled, leaned back in his chair, took off his glasses, and said, "I don't care," three words that would forever change how Dennis thought about his work: perhaps this statement should not have surprised Dennis to the extent that it did. After all, Jerry, who had worked for Builtwell for many years, had won everyone's respect as a tough but fair boss. People knew that he always took time to teach and mentor, but they also knew that Jerry never sugarcoated a message he thought someone needed to hear. Jerry continued, "I didn't bring you here to tell me why you can't get it done. I brought you here to get it done. You have the resources you need. Figure it out. You need to know that you're not the only one on the line here. We both are, and we're running out of time."

Ouch! Dennis was now clear on the expectation: he was accountable to deliver the result on time and without any additional increases to his regional headcount. With just a few words, Jerry had reaffirmed his expectation to Dennis in a way that eliminated all of his excuses and cleared Dennis's mind. He knew he had to deliver on the result. He had one more year to get it done, and he had to do it with his existing team. Over the first two years, Dennis had lost focus of the original expectation communicated by Jerry: "Here's what I want you to do. Here's when I want you to do it." Jerry's communication of his expectations had simply followed the classic What-When approach. Not surprisingly, Dennis had just repeated that communication to his leaders and reps throughout the region. Unfortunately, while Jerry's marching orders had motivated Dennis, they had not had the same impact on the region as a whole.

At this point in the story, we want to pause and point out the downside to the What-When approach that Jerry and anyone else communicating expectations need to understand. First of all, the What-When approach reflects the old "Command & Control" attitude toward getting things done, and, as we have discussed earlier, that old model does not do much to motivate today's workforce. Still, people at all levels of the organization tend to favor this approach when tasking someone to get something done because it doesn't take a lot of time to implement and, based upon past experiences, it usually works. It's so simple. All you need to do is communicate to the people you hold accountable exactly what you want and when you want it. Case closed. But, and this is a big "but," anyone who has relied on the What-When approach has most likely come to the realization that this time-honored approach does not work nearly as well as it did in the past, primarily because that approach fails to engage the hearts and minds of people in a way that motivates them to follow through and do what it takes to deliver on key expectations.

We read a funny but poignant example of this problem in an Associated Press release. According to the report, a Chicago man had filed a lawsuit against a tattoo parlor because the tattoo artist misspelled the word *tomorrow* on the customer's forearm. The artist defended the misspelling by saying he spelled the word exactly as the customer had written it on a slip of paper. He claimed, in effect, "I did what he wanted, when he wanted it!" This exemplifies one of the greatest limitations of the What-When approach to communicating expectations: people end up doing exactly what you asked them to do, exactly the way you told them to do it, even if doing so will not achieve the expected result. With "What-When," you only engage hands and feet, allowing both heart and mind to wander aimlessly, unengaged in looking for what else can be done to achieve results.

Over the years, we have observed (and made) all of the most common mistakes people make when they communicate expectations. How many of them have you made over the past week?

THE MOST COMMON MISTAKES PEOPLE MAKE WHEN COMMUNICATING EXPECTATIONS

1. Barking out "marching orders" without making your directions clear enough that people fully understand and accept them.
2. Assuming people need only one explanation in order to understand what you expect them to deliver.
3. Failing to form an expectation clearly yourself before communicating it to others.
4. Excluding any explanation about "why" you want something done within a specific time frame.
5. Asking people to do something, but not clearly explaining when you need it done.
6. Failing to describe the resources available to help people do what you want them to do.
7. Issuing such specific instructions about what to do and how to do it, that people hesitate to "own it" themselves and think out of the box to ensure the result.

If you have committed any of these mistakes, don't beat yourself up. You are not alone. Time pressures, deadlines, and multiple priorities often compel us to trade greater effectiveness for seemingly greater efficiency. Such an exchange requires everyone we work with to become experts at guessing what we want and deciphering what we really mean. Not only does this approach damage our Accountability Connections; it does nothing to ensure that things get done when we want them to get done.

Returning now to Dennis's story, he had used the What-When approach for a couple of years before realizing that it would not motivate his team to get the region humming. While his boss had continued to rely on the old-style communication approach, which had served them both fairly well in the past, Dennis now knew that he needed to find a better way to communicate his expectations to his team if he was going to motivate his region to dig deeper, try harder, think smarter, and deliver the expected results.

Dennis set to work, first bringing together his seven district managers in the same room for two days. Together the team acknowledged that their region was ranked as the lowest-performing one in the division, a fact that embarrassed them all. When Dennis showed his managers his analysis of the region's poor productivity, it inspired a frank and candid conversation about the sad state of affairs. Everyone knew that the success of the region, as well as their future careers with the company, depended on swift action. Time was running out and their jobs were on the line. With a fresh and clear understanding of "why" they needed to change, they began brainstorming ways they could improve the frequency of calling on key accounts without assigning more people to the task. As the discussion unfolded, the mood in the room changed. Instead of glumly going through the motions, the team became more and more excited about turning things around. This newfound energy helped them identify several inadequacies they needed to address quickly in order to supercharge the region's performance. They sorted the problems into three buckets: (1) changing personnel; (2) identifying the correct metrics for the sales process; and (3) improving their effectiveness with key accounts. Dennis divided the district managers into three subteams, asking each to consider what else they could do to help the region find solutions to these problems. Each subteam worked independently to find solutions to the problems in the three buckets and then reported back with a plan on how they would communicate and implement necessary changes throughout the region.

The eventual plan, distilled from those offered by the three subteams, included a clear definition of why they needed to change and what they needed to achieve. As a team, they established the following goals for their region: to become the number one region in the company, to place all seven districts in the top ten districts at Builtwell, and to achieve promotions for each of the key people in the region, all within the next twelve months. The district managers, feeling personal ownership to achieve these objectives and recognizing what would happen if things did not go well, embraced the goals. After Dennis first communicated the "why," and then determined with his team the "what" and the "when," he began to see a very different team, one fully engaged and committed to the successful implementation of their regional plan.

It took a bit longer than twelve months, but Dennis's region got it done. At the annual awards banquet, with everyone decked out in tuxedos and formal gowns, Dennis accepted the President's Trophy for his region's performance as the top-producing region in the company. All seven of his region's district managers ranked in the top ten. Over time, people throughout the region won promotions to positions of greater responsibility and opportunity. As the region accomplished every goal it set for itself, Dennis came to value the power of communicating expectations with the Why-What-When approach, understanding that you can't succeed without driving home the "Why" behind expectations. Without it, you cannot hope to capture people's imagination and harness their collective energy to achieve key expectations.

WHY-WHAT-WHEN

The Why-What-When approach to communicating your well-formed expectations provides a powerful tool for taking the next step in the Outer Ring of the Accountability Sequence. This tool helps you convey an expectation so clearly and compellingly that it engages people's minds and hearts. It all starts with an explanation of the "Why" behind the expectation. This explanation must spark the imagination and strike a nerve, and it must precede any statements about what you want to see happen and when you want to see it happen. Take a look at the two-way Why-What-When conversation below. Note the progression of steps, from a compelling "Why" to a "What" consisting of three elements (sharing the expectation you have crafted with FORM in mind, explaining the boundaries that exist, and describing available support) and, finally, to a "When" that specifies a target date for fulfillment.

WHY - WHAT - WHEN

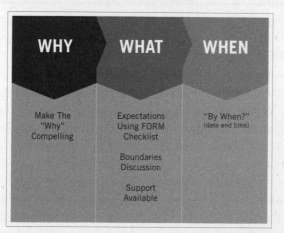

As this model reveals, effectively communicating expectations involves much more than merely tasking people with assignments. The Why-What-When approach, correctly implemented, not only helps people understand the scope of an assignment, it also helps create the buy-in needed to ensure a successful outcome. For key expectations, anything short of complete understanding and buy-in can result in disappointment and failure. Let's take a closer look at the process.

Making the "Why" Compelling

To be most effective, the "Why" needs to speak to people as individuals and convince them that accomplishing the "What" and "When" matters to them on a personal level. One of our successful executive clients, "Dave," works for "Silverstones," one of the largest retailers in the world. One day, during an interview with us, Dave recalled a pivotal point in his career when he fully grasped the importance of the "Why" behind the "What and When." Silverstones was rolling out an initiative on working capital, and "Jeff," the VP heading up the project, hit the trail, traveling throughout the company to explain, "Here's how you are going to do it, and this is when you are going to do it." He provided all the necessary logistical facts, and he answered all the questions that popped up.

Our friend, Dave, said, Jeff did a very good job defining what the change was going to require operationally. In fact, Dave had chatted over lunch with people who had attended the big rollout meeting one morning, and he concluded, "There was no doubt that people were going to do this. It was clear they had no option concerning their implementation of the new plan on working capital." Then something strange happened. The president of Silverstones, "Russ," was scheduled to speak later that afternoon at the same rollout meeting. Everyone, including Dave, expected Russ to put his personal stamp of approval on the initiative. To Dave's astonishment, Russ did not say a word about anything Jeff had said. Instead, he spoke only about the "Why": why it was important to the organization and to their division, and why it was important to the people sitting in that room. The value the initiative would create would not only benefit everyone financially, it would enhance their job satisfaction and pride in the company. As Dave himself put it, "That was a huge 'aha' moment for him." As he listened to his peers talking excitedly among themselves after the meeting, he found them equally impressed by Russ's comments. They all said something like, "Hey, when Jeff said this is what we had to do, we knew we were going to do it. But when Russ got up and talked about 'why' it was important, both to the company and to us individually, I couldn't wait to go out and get going on its implementation." Understanding the importance of the task transformed the group from willing participants to eager go-getters. From that point on in his career, Dave knew that if he really wanted to capture people's hearts and minds, he would need to explain up front the compelling reasons as to "why we need to do it" and "why we need to do it now." As you consider communicating your own expectations, mull over these six ways to craft a compelling "Why":

SIX WAYS TO CRAFT A COMPELLING "WHY"

1. Tailor the why to your specific audience.
2. Make it short, simple, and clear.
3. Be candid, honest, and forthcoming so people believe it is real and genuine and not just the "company line."
4. Make it a dialogue, not a monologue.
5. Create "the hook" that catches people's attention and persuades them to "buy in."
6. Frame it in a strategic context (how the expectation fits into the big picture).

Communicating the "Why" does more than explain the rationale behind a task or mission; it sends people a signal that they are worth the time and effort it takes to enroll and engage them in the mission, to persuade them to own it and make it happen. It tells people that you respect them, that you value them as key contributors to the process of getting things done, that in a "need to know" situation, you see them as people who "need to know." This approach boosts morale and ownership and supercharges everyone's effort to achieve the results you expect. We often tell people that most leaders spend 95 percent of their effort on the "What-When" and only 5 percent on the "Why." When you reverse that approach and spend the majority of your effort on the "Why," you'll begin to see your teams aligning more completely around what they need to achieve. To illustrate this point, let's take a closer look at the six ways to craft a compelling "Why."

First, tailor the "Why" to your specific audience. Common sense argues that the more personal you can make the "Why," the more compelling it will be. When it comes to expectations, this is not a luxury, but a necessity. The Institute for Healthcare Advancement (IHA) estimates that $73 billion is unnecessarily spent every year on health care expenses simply because patients do not understand what health care providers are saying to them. The IHA has come up with a list of common errors that occur when communicators fail to adjust their message for their given audience. First of all, they observed that the literature accompanying medications was usually written at the eleventh-grade reading level, whereas patients who needed to understand this literature read at the sixth-grade level (ninety million U.S. citizens read at between a third- and fifth-grade level). They also observed that patients could not easily read materials printed in a 10-point font size, as it was too small. Lastly, patients' eyes glazed over when they saw medical jargon instead of simple English, like "otitis media" instead of "earache." As a result, in far too many cases, patients who were not asked to repeat explanations or instructions simply nodded politely in response to their doctors' instructions when, in reality, they walked away in complete bewilderment. Tailoring "Why-What-When" to the various audiences up and down the Expectations Chain will help you communicate in a way that all the people who need to understand the message hear it loud and clear.

Second, make it short, simple, and clear. If a doctor wants a patient to understand her message, it probably will not work to say "the encapsulated medication should be ingested with generous quantities of a hydrating liquid." Rather, she should say, "Take the pills with plenty of water." Keeping it simple and clear is the best way to get your message across. That's not always easy to do.

On one occasion, Mark Twain received a telegram from a publisher: "NEED 2-PAGE SHORT STORY IN TWO DAYS!" Twain replied: "NO CAN DO 2 PAGES TWO DAYS. CAN DO 30 PAGES 2 DAYS. NEED 30 DAYS TO DO 2 PAGES." Keeping it simple takes time and requires more work. But when your message is brief and clear, you greatly improve the chances of making sure everyone in the Expectations Chain understands your point.

Third, be candid, honest, and forthcoming. Who would you believe, the doctor who seems reluctant to tell you the unvarnished truth about her diagnosis or the one who gives it to you straight? Most people dislike evasive double-talk and much prefer an honest dose of reality. People in organizations are skeptical and can see through a veiled attempt to sell what most would consider to be bad news. In the long run, "honest and candid" will go further in securing the hearts and minds of those upon whom you depend.

Fourth, make it a dialogue, not a monologue. Good doctors talk with their patients, not at them. The wife of one of the authors of this book went to a much-anticipated meeting with their son's doctor after an important test, knowing full well that the results might indicate that the young boy might need major back surgery. After the doctor made them wait for over an hour in one of the treatment rooms, he finally walked to the door, without stepping over the threshold, and said, "No need to worry, everything is fine. I will set you up with a physical therapist, and I won't even charge you for the visit." Then he dashed away. He left behind him a stunned patient with a lot of unanswered questions. When you don't give people the information or dialogue they need, it often leads to resentment and misunderstanding. Creating a dialogue that allows people to ask questions and hear the answers may do more to address their buy-in than all of the information you have carefully prepared.

Fifth, create "the hook" that catches people's attention and persuades them to buy in. A nurse once told us, subsequent to a physical, "Take two of these pills every day for the next year." She offered no other explanation than that a test had revealed elevated cholesterol and our doctor wanted us to take the medicine. Would that inspire you to do so faithfully? Maybe, if you completely trusted your doctor. But when you don't, it just raises questions and obstacles and leads to inconsistent conformity to a prescribed action. What if the nurse had said, "Your doctor is recommending this medicine for you because it has extended the lives of hundreds of thousands of people with your condition." A longer, healthier life? That's a sharp hook. Making sure you present the hook that speaks to the individual's needs will help them buy in to what you want.

Sixth, frame it in a strategic context. We all appreciate a doctor who takes the time to understand how our bumps and bruises, and the doctor's resulting recommendations, affect the big picture of our everyday life. People need to know how their work fits into the big picture, how it meshes with the overall mission of the organization, and why it is important right now. Understanding this strategic fit gives people an understanding that will help them better assist the organization. In this context, a "strategic" picture is worth a thousand words.

When you craft a compelling "Why," you create a dialogue that draws people into the cause. They become motivated, and can't wait to start making it happen. Recently, while one of our own firm's account managers was calling prospective clients, he reached an account in Florida and began explaining to the person on the other end of the line who he was and that our company specifically helped organizations create greater accountability. The prospect replied that her company did not have an HR department and only employed forty people. Accountability? Who needs it? "When they hire us, they just tell us what to do, and we do it." When we heard that story, we smiled, because sometimes people fall under the illusion that they don't really need or want to know the "why," and can get along just fine with the "what" and the "when." However, in all honesty, if the "why" is important to you, wouldn't it be just as important to anyone else with whom you work?

Making the "What" Clear

Once you have communicated the "Why," you can prepare to talk about the "What." Making the "What" clear involves three discussions: communicating the expectation you have formed, clarifying the boundaries, and establishing available support. By conducting these three discussions, all for the purpose of clarifying the "What," you create the conditions necessary to make success more predictable and failure less likely.

However, you should note that you might need to conduct these discussions more than once. We once heard the chief pilot of a respected international airline explain that when the company instituted a new policy or procedure for pilots in the cockpit, they always explained it "seven times, seven different ways." Given the life-or-death importance of such procedures, the company expended great effort to make sure everyone understood just exactly what was expected. Pilots are smart, highly trained professionals. Why would they need to hear something seven times seven different ways? It turns out that no matter how high your IQ and no matter how extensive your training and experience, repetition drives home an important lesson the same way that "practice makes perfect." When it comes to key expectations, you just can't spend too much effort clarifying the "What." If you don't want to end up disappointed, you must invest the time and effort not only up front but time and time again.

Effectively forming your expectations makes it a lot easier to clearly communicate those expectations. Jack Welch, in his book *Jack, Straight from the Gut*, shares the story about his surprise when he received a financial summary with a great fourth-quarter revenue line with no net income to go with it. He asked how that had happened. Well, the group had held a sales contest in the fourth quarter, which inspired everyone to do a great job. So, where was the margin? Welch wondered. "Oh, we didn't ask for margin," he was told. Welch goes on to say that he then realized, "What you measure is what you get—what you reward is what you get." We would add to this understanding our own realization that what you communicate is what you get—what people think you expect is what they give. Communicating the expectation you have formed is the first step when talking about the "What."

Successfully communicating the expectation you have formed often requires some preparation. In most cases, you will find it helpful to reinforce what you say with the written word, particularly when it comes to key expectations. This enables all concerned to reaffirm what they thought they heard you say. Letting those you are going to hold accountable know the "What" as clearly as you can will facilitate all additional conversations. Most conversations about "What" quickly turn to "How." While we don't usually encourage you to spell out the "How" to capable people, we do suggest you conduct the important "boundaries" and "support" discussions that address the way people go about getting the job done.

The Boundaries Discussion

Boundaries can be real or imagined. Understanding the boundaries up front can help everyone avoid unpleasant surprises and costly mistakes. Making sure that people are not inhibited by boundaries that don't really exist may be as important as spelling out those that do. From countless interviews with people at every level in our client organizations, we have learned that people often do not clearly understand existing boundaries, even when you might think there's no chance of confusion.

The French company Société Générale experienced the tragic results of not managing boundaries when Jérôme Kerviel, a trader authorized to take positions up to 125 million euros, apparently caused a loss of 4.9 billion euros. The company has claimed absolute bewilderment as to how a single trader could have lost so much money. Kerviel himself contends that he committed no fraud, but merely got careless when he crossed certain boundaries established by the bank. He just got "carried away," he insists, and management knew all about his overeagerness to trade beyond his authorization. When Kerviel's unauthorized positions showed 1.4 billion euros in profit, it appeared to him that management had suspended the boundaries, looked the other way, and said nothing. They only accused him of improperly crossing the boundaries, Kerviel asserts, when his positions turned negative.

In another example, Patricia Dunn lost her position as chairman of the board at Hewlett-Packard when she authorized an investigation into leaks of private company information. Later, Dunn admitted that her authorized investigation included "certain inappropriate techniques." Others called it "spying." After the incident, Dunn confessed that the techniques "went beyond what we understood them to be, and I apologize that they were employed." Taking her at her word, we imagine that when she tasked others to plug the company leaks, the boundaries discussion about what was and was not appropriate never occurred. This failure to establish her expectations effectively led to her resignation from HP and the subsequent filing of criminal charges against her.

All too often, people only become aware of boundaries after they cross them. Since an ounce of prevention is always worth a pound of cure, it makes sense to communicate all the real boundaries up front. Defining boundaries builds and sustains trust by clarifying important aspects of the "how," removing imagined boundaries that can serve as obstacles, and giving people a greater sense of freedom. As you prepare to communicate the "What," consider the following boundary questions:

- What are the acceptable and unacceptable business practices in our culture?
- What are the budget, resource, and time constraints?
- What legal and ethical considerations must we take into account?
- Have we clarified existing priorities and their impact on this specific expectation?
- What do our strategies, tactics, branding, and current practices suggest?
- Do we harbor any inaccurate assumptions concerning (imagined) boundaries?
- Have we identified all pertinent "operational" boundaries?
- What external factors must we keep in mind?
- Can we define unacceptable "scope creep" (evolution of the mission's parameters)?

A quick review of these questions before you conduct any boundaries discussion should help you create a full and accurate understanding of the boundaries that will affect the project's outcome.

The boundaries discussion will help build a sense of trust and confidence that the "How" will not jeopardize accomplishing the "What." This conversation builds trust because it ensures that everyone knows what they can and can't do in the grand scheme of things. It strengthens confidence because people realize that what you expect will not require them to do something beyond what you intended, violate standards that will get them into trouble, or jeopardize the viability of the organization itself. The conversation also allows you to manage the natural human tendency to allow "scope creep," an expansion of a task that can cause people to lose focus on delivering what you really want.

The boundaries discussion can go a long way toward removing imagined boundaries that only obstruct someone's path to getting things done. Asking people about such obstacles and boundaries will help move the conversation in a direction that further empowers people to take accountability for finding creative "out of the box" solutions and for not limiting themselves with imaginary restrictions. When you remove such limitations on the front end, you empower people to achieve more results on the back end, particularly when a problem demands creativity and innovation.

No one is immune from the effects of imagined boundaries. Not long ago, our own IT department at Partners In Leadership experienced this firsthand. With more and more client companies looking for high-quality Webinars over the Internet, including state-of-the-art video streaming, we wanted to lead, not just follow, the trend. Our IT specialists found our expectations a bit unrealistic and quite difficult to achieve. In fact, had we adhered to the once-real boundary about doing everything in-house, we would have agreed that they could not possibly fulfill our Webinar expectations. However, we had redrawn the boundaries and had already budgeted for outside help, a fact that required many conversations to convince the IT department that they really could look to outside vendors to help them get our Webinar program up to speed. Even after accepting this new reality, they had grown so accustomed to operating in an environment where they relied only on in-house resources that it took longer than anyone expected for them to abandon the obsolete boundary. When they finally did, they tackled the problem with a higher level of creativity and delivered on the expectation. This situation reminded us that a candid, truthful discussion about boundaries can unleash people's creativity and motivate them to ask themselves what else they can do to meet expectations. It takes confidence to do that. It takes trust to do that. When you take the time to establish a mutual understanding around existing and appropriate boundaries, you build both confidence and trust.

The Support Discussion

The next discussion speaks to the support available to those who must deliver on the expectation, another important consideration when it comes to "how" it will get done. One business leader, whose success we greatly admire, told us, "Too often we tell our folks, 'here's what we need you to do' and then we leave them to sink or swim. We fail to provide them with any understanding as to what we can do to help. We fail to communicate to them just what is available to them to help them meet the expectation. They are often off and running before they know what they might receive in terms of training, coaching, mentoring, or a variety of other important resources." The support discussion should clarify exactly what support people can count on. That knowledge also boosts trust and confidence.

To underscore the need for the support discussion, we often share an interesting story that one of our clients, a health care management company, likes to tell about a woman who handled the laundry in one of their hospitals. Due to a recent injury, the laundress could no longer lift a full bag of laundry because trying to do so put a real strain on her back. Unaware that she could seek help from anyone else, she solved the problem on her own by placing a note in every laundry bag that read, "Please do not fill to the top! I have a bad back and I cannot lift it." Imagine her shock when, the next day, rather than finding the bag lighter and easier to lift, she found it overflowing with laundry. Apparently, her note had offended more than one person. As she wrestled with the now overstuffed bags, one of the hospital's managers happened to walk by and observe her difficulty. After discussing the situation with her, he suggested that they might give her two more laundry bags, thus reducing the weight of each bag by two-thirds. It was a clever solution that cost little to implement, and it made the woman's job manageable. Clearly, when people know about available support, including your encouragement to seek input on what more they can do to overcome obstacles, they can save you time and money in the long run by more easily and quickly fulfilling your expectations.

On a larger scale, we saw this happen for one of our clients in the banking industry. The retail administration of this well-known national bank was implementing a key component of the bank's strategy, improving revenue by increasing teller referrals. Typically, the bank would have focused its effort on simply getting the tellers to implement the needed strategy, but the leadership wisely chose to begin with a careful discussion of support, a decision that would propel the effort onto a more efficient and profitable track. Branch managers, teller supervisors, along with group operations, retail administration, and other business partners engaged in a series of brainstorming sessions about how best to implement the new program in all branches. As part of their brainstorming efforts they concentrated on the support people would need in order to get the job done. At the conclusion of these sessions they developed a plan that would allow branch managers and teller supervisors to manage the branch as a team, with joint accountability for coaching. With the entire division working together, HR conducted workshops to teach managers how to write an effective review, IT developed a tracking system to provide weekly updates on the teller referral initiative, and retail administration adjusted weekly meeting agendas to allow time to review coaching successes and challenges in the branch. With this support, referrals increased by 145 percent, and the number of booked sales from those referrals rose by 155 percent compared to the previous year. Conducting the support discussion up front made all the difference between routine and spectacular results.

Making the "When" Concrete

With the "Why" and the "What" clarified, you can set about framing your expectations in terms of time. You should attach a "By When" to every key expectation; otherwise, people may either approach their work too casually or rush it too much, both of which can lead to disappointing results. Never assume that people grasp the urgency of a particular expectation. As soon as people hear the words "as quickly as possible," they will almost invariably end up letting you down. That's why it's essential to attach, or negotiate, a well-thought-out "By When" to all of your key expectations. Every key expectation requires a specific timeline.

Since deadlines are a basic fact of life, you must stress them anytime you communicate expectations. A "By When" deadline specifies both "date" and "time." Even the origin of the word *deadline* emphasizes its importance.

During the Civil War, prison guards drew actual lines on the floor of the prisons, marking a point past which prisoners could not venture without getting shot, hence the term *dead*line. Now, we're not suggesting you shoot people who miss their deadlines, but we are emphasizing the point that you should "draw your lines on the floor" so concretely that people can easily see and heed them.

Sometimes, an organizational culture emphasizes the complete opposite idea. As a manager at "Dollinger Graphics," our client "Amy Gooden" ran smack into just such a culture. With her first major presentation to the senior management team due in two weeks, she was afraid that her team was about to go "off the rails." With extreme earnestness she told her team, "I'm very concerned. We are two weeks out from this first major deadline, and it just doesn't seem to be coming together. You're still changing things, you still seem unsure. You've got the right concept, but you don't seem to have a good plan. Help me understand what's going on around here." Her team responded, "What do you mean, the deadline is in two weeks? We didn't know that." That shocked her. "Are you serious?" They were serious. "Yes. We're not used to sticking to deadlines at Dollinger." Amy quickly and curtly shot back, "But I am! I've committed to the executives that we are going to meet this date, and I expect to meet it!" The team didn't buy it. "Amy, you don't really understand, the dates are really quite fluid around here." Amy got even more agitated. "Well, these dates are *not* fluid for me, and from this point on they are not fluid for *you* either." Amy went on to explain to us that more than one person at Dollinger had told her in no uncertain terms that she just "doesn't get it." In their minds, her preoccupation with hitting hard and firm dates ran against the culture of the organization. Her commitment to deadlines, of course, sent all the dominoes toppling up and down the entire Expectations Chain.

Creating an environment in your team, your department, your entire organization, and even with outside stakeholders, where concrete deadlines really matter, greatly facilitates everyone's ability to deliver on expectations.

COMMUNICATING THE "WHY-WHAT-WHEN" WITH STYLE

Your Accountability Style will also affect how you communicate Why-What-When and how people receive your message.

Those who tend to use the Coerce & Compel style can mistakenly think one communication will suffice. As we were reminded by the example of the airline pilots, most of us need more than one shot at getting the message before we clearly understand exactly what we are being asked to do, particularly when we face changing circumstances and challenging obstacles. You will benefit from always assuming that people will need to hear and discuss the message more than once.

This style also has a tendency to set unrealistic expectations around the "By When," setting aggressive deadlines, bordering on unachievable, that may be doomed from the very outset. The attitude of "just find a way to get it done" is a two-edged sword that may work for some people but not others. For those in the Coerce & Compel style, remind yourself of the old saying, "Nothing is impossible to the person who doesn't have to do it themself."

This style also tends to foster impatience with the process. Taking the time to dialogue about the expectation, the boundaries, the support, and the buy-in may seem cumbersome to those with this style because it requires spelling out a number of details up front that they would just as soon let people figure out on their own. Here, again, it is important to recognize that the time spent up front is a good investment that will save time in the long run and go a long way to ensure delivery on your expectations.

For the people with Wait & See style tendencies, they can fall into the "sympathy trap," becoming so sensitive to others during the Why-What-When conversation that they start feeling obligated to provide support they really don't need to provide. If you think of yourself as a Wait & See person, you may fail to steer the conversation in a direction that will allow others to work through their concerns and issues in their own way until they can effectively deliver on expectations. The last thing you want to do is walk away from the discussion with your plate full of problems to solve, especially when it gets to the point that others feel they cannot move forward until you have done your part. Try to keep bringing the conversation back to the question, "What else can you do to move forward, overcome the obstacle, and achieve the result?"

Someone with this style may also feel inclined to skip the "By When" step altogether. If you like people and respect and trust them, then why hold them accountable for a hard and firm deadline? Because you're not helping them if you set them up to fail just because they did not know about a due date. You may find it helpful to adopt the practice of setting deadlines with your people, asking them to make sure you always set a "By When" date. That way, no one tries to crash forward too hastily or meander at a leisurely pace, falsely assuming they have all the time in the world to get the job done. Adjusting your approach to capitalize on the strengths of your style and to compensate for your weaknesses will allow you to use the Why-What-When approach much more effectively.

ACCOUNTABILITY REALITY CHECK

Take some time during the next few days to apply what you have learned in this chapter. Choose someone from the Accountability Connections List you put together in Chapter Two. Preface the conversation by affirming your desire for candid, honest, truthful feedback. Focusing on a recent situation where you communicated an expectation to this person, ask how well he or she thinks you did. Use the "Six Ways to Craft a Compelling 'Why'" and the Why-What-When framework as a guide.

- Did you tailor the message to this individual?
- Did you make it short, simple, and clear?
- Was it perceived as honest and real, not just the company line?
- Did you engage in a dialogue, rather than a monologue?
- How fully did this person "buy in" to the mission?
- Was it presented within a strategic context?
- Did you communicate the expectation using FORM?
- Did you conduct discussions about boundaries and support?
- Did you set a specific and reasonable deadline?

Don't just do this with someone you think has already heard the message loud and clear. Rather, talk it over with someone who doesn't "get it" and you will learn much more about how well or how poorly you communicate your key expectations.

WHY-WHAT-WHEN-AGAIN

In this chapter we have suggested that the Why-What-When conversation should take place more than once. Just as the chief pilot of the international airline observed, you should communicate important topics seven times, seven different ways. Finding a way to conduct the dialogue more than once at the outset will help you make sure the communication sufficiently creates full understanding: the kind of understanding that captures people's hearts and minds.

Implemented effectively, Why-What-When puts in your hands a powerful tool that sets the stage for getting people aligned with what you want to accomplish. Alignment is essential to the fulfillment of key expectations and getting results. The next step in the Outer Ring of the Accountability Sequence will show you exactly how to do it.

Chapter Three

THE POSITIVE, PRINCIPLED WAY

A quick review of the main points presented in this chapter will help you put them to work in your own organization. Remember, the best way to become proficient in these steps and methods is to select something you can use in your daily work right now and apply it.

Command, Control, and Fail
When it comes to fulfilling key expectations that require significant effort and a full personal investment, the old What-When approach does not generate enough "hearts and minds" effort.

Why-What-When
You need to engage in a two-way conversation that conveys what you want to have happen so clearly that people buy in to making it happen.

- **Make the "Why" Compelling:** You frequently need to present the "Why" in a way that speaks to people as individuals and convinces them that accomplishing the "What" and "When" matters on a personal level.
- **The "What" Discussion:** The first step in clarifying the "What" involves effectively communicating the "key" expectation after applying FORM.
- **The Boundaries Discussion:** Next, you want to clarify right up front what people can and can't do to fulfill the expectation, addressing both "real" and "imagined" boundaries. This conversation should build trust.
- **The Support Discussion:** This final "What" step clarifies, at the outset, the support that is available to help others fulfill your expectations of them.
- **Making the "When" Concrete:** You should accompany every expectation with a "By When" that specifies the date and time the expectation will be fulfilled.

Chapter Four

ALIGN EXPECTATIONS

COMPLETE ALIGNMENT MEANS AGREEMENT

Now that you have progressed through the first two steps on the Outer Ring, the next step is to ensure alignment around your expectations with everyone in the Expectations Chain. Your efforts at carefully forming and thoughtfully communicating your expectations can be entirely undone unless you create and maintain alignment around those expectations with everyone in the chain. Unfortunately, we too often assume people are aligned simply because we felt we did a good job communicating with them, only to wake up one day to see that the results we expected are nowhere in sight.

When it comes to achieving key expectations, it is important to recognize that there are different levels of alignment. The highest level, the level that brings full ownership and personal investment, is what we call "Complete Alignment." All other levels of alignment, with their lower levels of buy-in, fall into the category that we call "Complyment."

Complyment occurs when people decide to move together toward a destination, not because they agree with the course of direction, but because they have determined that moving forward and complying with what you want them to do will satisfy their own best interests. Complyment rules most organizations today. While it may get the "hands and feet" moving, it usually fails to generate the kind of investment and ownership necessary to ensure success. In contrast, Complete Alignment brings people to a level of agreement where they believe in, and completely commit themselves to, fulfilling expectations. When you bring people into Complete Alignment, they not only invest their "hands and feet" in the undertaking, they also invest their "hearts and minds" in getting it done. When people fully agree with the mission—when they want to fulfill the expectation just as much as you do—they will meet or surpass your expectations far more often than they ever would by merely complying with the request.

Accomplishing Complete Alignment is never easy. Wilco van Rooijen, the leader of the Dutch mountain-climbing team, recalled from his hospital bed in Islamabad how a climbing accident on K2, the world's second-highest mountain, led to the deaths of eleven climbers. Skilled climbers view K2 as one of the most dangerous mountains to scale because the slopes are steeper and rockier and more prone to sudden changes in weather and severe storms than those of Everest. The record books show that more than seventy people have died attempting to summit K2.

Imagine yourself in the midst of climbing a dangerous and potentially deadly mountain like K2, only to find that a teammate had brought just half the length of rope you expected him to bring. In the case of the Dutch mountain-climbing team, one might be tempted to think that this was a simple oversight. But when you consider the fact that the Dutch climbing team had additional time to prepare, with bad weather forcing them to wait for more than a month beyond their scheduled ascent of K2, it becomes unthinkable and utterly unacceptable. It is important to understand how the misalignment around the amount of rope needed for the summit became so costly. Not long after the climbers began the ascent, they saw a huge column of ice sheer off in one of the most treacherous sections of the climb known as "Bottleneck." The ice tore away the ropes the team had fixed to guide and assist the climbers.

Trying to explain this tragedy, van Rooijen stated, "The biggest mistake we made was that we tried to make agreements. Everybody had his own responsibility, and then some people did not do what they promised." Van Rooijen thought he created Complete Alignment around not only what people needed to do, but around why it was so important for them to follow through and do all that they had agreed to do. Van Rooijen's frustration arose from the fact that, in spite of the life-or-death circumstances they would surely face on the mountain, he did not achieve the level of alignment necessary to make sure that simple, avoidable mistakes, such as bringing insufficient rope, would not occur. Because of their insufficient rope, van Rooijen recalls the team "wasting precious time by cutting rope from the bottom and bringing it up." Ultimately, despite all the additional time they had to prepare, their lack of Complete Alignment around their preparations set the stage for perhaps the most devastating mountaineering disaster in history.

THE COMPLETE ALIGNMENT CHAIN REACTION

Not only does Complete Alignment energize people in a way that engages their hearts and minds to deliver on expectations, it ignites a chain reaction, because the presence of completely aligned people improves everyone else's alignment. Mark Katz, senior vice president in the building efficiency division at Johnson Controls (JCI), and his management team experienced the powerful impact of such alignment in their organization. JCI, a Fortune 80 company, earned the number one ranking in its category among *Fortune*'s America's Most Admired Companies for three years in a row. The company's excellence comes from the performance of teams like Mark's, which formed, communicated, and created alignment around safety expectations in JCI's services division. Few factors influence workforce morale more than a safe work environment. Over the past year, the building efficiency division reported 102 safety incidents, each of which resulted in lost workdays. Not only Mark and his management team, but also everyone up and down the Expectations Chain, wanted to see that number drop. Using the principles associated with the steps in the Outer Ring, the building efficiency division was able to create Complete Alignment around the importance of reducing safety incidents throughout the Expectations Chain, and as they did the team got the job done: in one short year safety incidents, measured in workdays lost, declined from 102 days to just 19 days, a whopping 81 percent reduction!

In addition to focusing on safety, the building efficiency division formed and communicated expectations around customer satisfaction. They worked in the entire organization to create alignment in each branch around these expectations, until everyone, most especially frontline workers, understood both what was expected of them and how they could help. The team enlisted branch managers to lead discussions designed to produce alignment with the technician workforce, the front line of the organization. Initially, these conversations provoked some astonishment, with the technicians wondering, "You are going to hold *me* accountable for customer satisfaction? What do I have to do with customer satisfaction?" Troubled by this apparent incongruity, many wondered aloud, "What if everyone else fails to do their job?"

However, with robust dialogue and honest discussion, the team began to gain some agreement around what the organization wanted to accomplish and why it needed to do it. In the end, one technician aptly summed it up, saying, "If we are all working together, we are more likely to make the customer happy." Here, again, as with safety, the division created Complete Alignment and, with it in place, dramatically improved customer satisfaction.

Of course, Complyment can and does work when all you need is a "hands and feet" effort to get the job done. For the majority of day-to-day tasks, Complyment will suffice, but when it comes to fulfilling those all-important key expectations, the work requires a greater level of personal investment in order to gain people's hearts and minds and thus ensure everyone follows through. And with that investment, you stand a chance of reaping a huge return on the time, energy, and effort you took to establish Complete Alignment. This alignment does not come from performing some sort of charismatic magic, but rather from a deliberate, step-by-step approach to capturing the hearts and minds of the people you will ultimately hold accountable for results.

People who invest their hearts and minds go beyond the basic requirements of their jobs and work to make things happen in a way that may even surpass expectations. One of our clients, a major international hotel chain that had invited us to assist in their effort to foster accountability at all levels of their organization, offers a good example. When one hotel employee asked a guest about the quality of his stay at the hotel, the guest replied that everything was fine but that he needed to attend an important dinner that evening and had forgotten to bring his dinner jacket with him. The employee took it upon himself to contact the restaurant's night manager at home before the manager came in to work and asked if he could bring along his own dinner jacket, since the manager and the guest were about the same size. The night manager showed up with not one but two jackets for the guest to choose from. The guest, thrilled by this act of service above and beyond the call of duty, made a point of praising this behavior to the hotel's general manager before he checked out and has probably told this story on more than one occasion to amaze his friends and colleagues about the results people can get when they are fully invested. That's what always happens as a result of a "hearts and minds" effort: you get the kinds of results that people just can't stop talking about.

Of course, when we talk about people's "hearts and minds," we are not talking about people making personal sacrifices to the detriment of themselves and their families. No, we are talking about a deep level of professional commitment to fulfilling an expectation. In a *USA Today* interview, reporter Del Jones asked Kerry Clark, CEO of Cardinal Health (the nineteenth-largest company on the Fortune 500), this alignment question: "There are 45,000 Cardinal employees who hardly know you. Would you expect them to jump in front of a train for you?" Clark answered, "I look for people who can build their business and build their organization. It's not about personal loyalty per se. It's about facing reality, accountability, and doing the right thing. . . . So, it's not about jumping in front of the train, but maybe realizing that the train is coming and doing something about it." Capturing the hearts and minds of the people you work with is another way of saying you have gained "Complete Alignment."

CLUES FOR DETECTING COMPLETE ALIGNMENT

How do you tell the difference between Complete Alignment and mere Complyment? You look closely at what people are saying and doing as they work to fulfill expectations. In the table below, we provide some hints that will help you recognize the difference.

Complyment versus Complete Alignment

COMPLYMENT	COMPLETE ALIGNMENT
1. People need constant reminders about "why we are doing this."	1. People talk about the importance and positive impact of what they are doing.
2. People don't give a 100 percent effort.	2. People give it 100 percent.
3. People go through the motions and focus on just doing enough to get the job done.	3. People invest themselves and work to get the job done, adding their own personal touch with an obvious sense of ownership.
4. People exhibit no visible enthusiasm for the task when they discuss it with others.	4. People speak with conviction about the importance of what they are doing.
5. People get stuck quickly and don't know "what else to do" to overcome tough obstacles.	5. People think creatively and stretch themselves to overcome all the obstacles they encounter.

As you can see, Complyment may "get it done," but Complete Alignment gets it done better.

MOVING THE BOULDER

The chain reaction of Complete Alignment displays its greatest power when someone faces a particularly daunting challenge. Toward the end of the 1999 Phoenix Open golf tournament, Tiger Woods blasted a tee shot that sailed wide left and landed in front of a boulder nestled fifteen yards beyond the fairway. To the surprise of spectators and commentators, an official responded to a query from Tiger that, yes, the boulder was a loose impediment, meaning the player could move the obstacle without suffering a penalty. It may have been "loose," but that boulder weighed a whopping one thousand pounds. About a dozen men from the gallery volunteered to get behind this half-ton impediment and, with everyone pushing in the same direction, moved it forward just enough to allow Tiger to hit his shot. That image on the television screen reminded us of the power of Complete Alignment, when enthusiastic people come together to move forward and achieve the seemingly impossible. The result? Tiger Woods went on to birdie the hole, inciting enough controversy that officials changed the rules of golf as a result: today it's considered a loose impediment only if you and your caddie can move it.

If everyone in the Expectations Chain, even just one person, pushes in a different direction to "move the boulder," that boulder won't budge. Take "Chris Solomon," for example. A major contributor to his company's success, Chris had left "Bridgeport Health Corp" (BHC) to pursue other dreams, but after one short year away from his old job, he could not refuse when BHC's CEO passionately recruited him to come back and help the organization through the next crucial step in their plan: revenue generation in the company's clinics. When Chris returned, he rolled up his sleeves, and within a year and a half he had made another huge impact on the organization. The new lean manufacturing process he introduced to the entire hospital system had generated great improvements in performance. Patient satisfaction scores had soared, wait times in the clinics had fallen sharply, and overall business performance had risen to unprecedented levels. In fact, Chris's initiatives had proven so successful that BHC's leaders asked him to travel around the country and share his success with other companies. Everyone in the company knew that BHC was "rock-starring" Chris and promoting BHC as he shared the secret of his success, performing "peer reviews" and "black belt" training on lean manufacturing. What he had accomplished in the clinics became the benchmark of excellence for many organizations. With all this attention, Chris had every indication that he was right on track and assumed, quite naturally, that senior management was happy with his performance.

Then, in a public forum with the management team, the CEO declared that Chris and his team were "not moving fast enough" and that he thought Chris would have accomplished a lot more by now. This criticism stunned Chris. He couldn't believe his ears. In essence, the CEO had dismissed all of the progress that Chris and his team had made in the clinics. Why had he busted his tail, only to get hit between the eyes with a two-by-four? On Monday morning, an angry and frustrated Chris met with the CEO, the chief operating officer, and the chief medical officer. He expressed how thoroughly the CEO's comments had demoralized him. "Do you want me to believe that what I have done in the last year is poor performance?" He explained that even other major hospitals were adopting his lean manufacturing concepts as their benchmark. Chris wanted to know, "How could this have happened?"

Defending his position, the CEO said to Chris, "I don't understand why you are so offended." He thought Chris would see it the same way he did. Everyone knew the board was pressuring the CEO for bottom-line improvement and that Chris was the one primarily responsible for moving that boulder forward. Without a doubt, Chris had done a tremendous job producing productivity gains three or four levels down in the organization, but his efforts were not getting revenue to the bottom line fast enough. Why, the CEO wondered, had he not aligned with him on the real bottom-line goal? Why was Chris pushing against one side of the boulder, while the CEO was pushing against the other? Completely frustrated, rather than completely aligned, Chris ultimately left the company. In the wake of his departure, BHC suffered a downturn in patient satisfaction and is still losing market share today. A serious lack of alignment left everyone disappointed and expectations unfulfilled. Ensuring that you have Complete Alignment, with everyone moving in the same direction, depends, more than anything else, on conducting the right dialogue about your key expectations.

THE ALIGNMENT DIALOGUE

The Alignment Dialogue eliminates the danger mere Complyment poses to key expectations by ensuring that everyone up and down the Expectations

Chain commits their hearts and minds to fulfilling the expectation. Consisting of three simple steps, this dialogue helps you determine the current level of alignment (or Complyment) and to determine what else you can do to gain Complete Alignment. Had Chris and the CEO taken these steps, they probably would have avoided the crushing impact of being on opposite sides of the boulder. Take a quick look at this chart before we discuss how you can use it in your own work.

ALIGNMENT DIALOGUE

SCORE IT	Restate the expectation, agree to use the Alignment Dialogue, and then have them rate their alignment with this key expectation (on a scale of 1-10)
EVALUATE IT	Determine what else is needed by asking, 1) Is it Clear? 3) Is it Needed? 2) Is it Achievable? 4) Is it Linked?
RESOLVE IT	Resolve concerns and confirm the original expectation, or Revise using Why-What-When

Step One: Score It

When you sense any misalignment, you begin the dialogue by restating the expectation and agree to use the Alignment Dialogue. By getting people to agree on applying this tool, you give everyone permission to work within the parameters of the device to achieve Complete Alignment. With that understanding, you engage in a candid conversation with people about the extent to which they agree with your expectation (we assume, of course, that you have formed and communicated it effectively). We suggest having them assign a number to the level of agreement because that gives you a more concrete sense of any gap between their current level of agreement and the level you want to achieve. A low number suggests that you have a lot of work to do. A high number, especially a 10, lets you take some comfort from the fact that you've gotten the people in the Expectations Chain on board and that they will invest their hearts and minds in the task at hand. Use the following chart to interpret your results:

IF THEY RESPOND . . .	THEN THEY PROBABLY . . .
1–2	disagree with the direction you have asked them to go. It will take some significant work and real understanding to move them. Requiring them to move forward without resolving their concerns will most likely lead to resistance and then resentment.
3–4	agree to some extent with the "Why," but probably don't really get it. They most likely worry about the "How" and find the expectation difficult to achieve. You can convince them to change their minds, but you need to speak directly to their concerns.
5–6	hold some doubts about what they are being asked to do. They may understand the "Why," but not the "Why Now." Getting to the bottom of their issues and resolving them will help get them on board quickly.
7–8	agree, but after some additional dialogue will most likely move forward with both their hearts and minds invested.
9–10	support the direction enthusiastically and are ready to move forward.

In this Alignment Dialogue, you want to stimulate forthrightness, encouraging people to give you completely candid answers. Make it abundantly clear that you want to hear what they *really* think, not what they think you want to hear.

Step Two: Evaluate It

Once you have gained some understanding of current levels of agreement, you are ready to determine what else is needed to achieve Complete Alignment. People may be unaligned for a variety of reasons, but you can generally group them into categories by asking four key questions:

1. Is it clear?
2. Is it achievable?
3. Is it needed?
4. Is it linked?

These questions can guide the conversation about what is missing. As we stressed in our book *Journey to the Emerald City*, "alignment is a process, not an event." Certain natural forces constantly conspire to drive people out of alignment. Over time, an expectation can once again become unclear or begin to appear disconnected from the company's vision—circumstances in the marketplace may take a dramatic turn or a change in company resources may make it harder to get the job done. Whatever the cause, these four questions offer a handy tool for determining the source of any misalignment. Even if you rated initial alignment a perfect "10," a whole host of normal business fluctuations could radically shift your level of agreement no matter where you find yourself in the Expectations Chain.

"Is it clear?" This question allows you to assess just how well someone understands the expectation. The answer may reveal that you did not form or communicate your expectation properly. One of our clients, the director of a service department in a large organization, began asking the firm's fifty vice presidents if they felt satisfied with the experience and the results they were getting from her department. Since this group included people who oversaw the company's subsidiaries, the director wanted to make sure everyone was "clear" about her team giving people the support they wanted. Everyone politely responded that, "yes," her team was very nice and always willing to help. This feedback delighted the director, until she heard an unsettling comment: "But, if your team went away tomorrow, it would literally have no impact on us."

When the director shared this feedback with her team, they strongly disagreed. "They can't be unhappy with what we're delivering. We always do what they ask us to do. You must be talking to the wrong people. Try talking to the people who report to the VP's. We know they're happy because they tell us that all the time!" This reaction prompted the director to clarify for her people that the company's executive team funded their department, and if they were not delivering anything of real value from the point of view of the executive team, their funding could stop on a dime. While the team was working hard to implement the service department's support efforts, they were not "clear" about whose expectations they needed to meet. The moral of this story: you should never assume clarity until you receive good, candid feedback from everyone involved in fulfilling the expectation that they do, in fact, clearly understand it.

"Is it achievable?" In other words, can people actually execute and deliver on a specific expectation? As they consider their skills, available resources, competing priorities, and existing obstacles, do they feel they can actually do what is being asked of them? If not, Complete Alignment will remain entirely out of reach. This question can sometimes be a matter of life or death. In 1944, the Allied forces developed an aggressive plan to secure a line of bridges in eastern Holland that would provide a route for the Allied army where they could advance without encountering the German lines of defense. The northernmost bridge in this line crossed the Rhine River in a town called Arnhem. The plan called for dropping paratroopers around the target bridges. These paratroopers would receive support from ground forces that would make their way north on the only available highway, one that intermittently crossed the secured bridges. If the soldiers captured the bridge at Arnhem, they would remove the last natural obstacle blocking entrance to Germany, the Rhine River.

During a planning meeting, British Lt. Gen. Frederick Browning, deputy commander of the First Allied Airborne Army, raised the issue of "achievability" with Field Marshall Bernard Montgomery when he remarked, "I think we may be going a bridge too far." Last-minute reconnaissance photographs supporting this view showed that the German command had positioned panzer forces where they would block the advancing Allied forces. The British had dismissed these reports, claiming that the tanks in question were inoperative. Even reports from the Dutch underground verified the threat, but the warning went unheeded. It later turned out that, in fact, one of the top German field marshals, commanding veteran German forces, had placed his troops in the area and could easily provide a strong defense.

To make matters worse, the Allies possessed insufficient aircraft for both equipment drops and paratroop deployment. No one knew for sure if vital communications equipment would work over the long distances the Allied troops must cover. On top of all of this, securing the bridge at Arnhem required that paratroopers deploy eight miles from the bridge and then traverse open fields under enemy fire. The entire plan to take this bridge hinged on the ability of the Allied ground forces to make their way to Arnhem within two to three days over a single, narrow highway in time to reinforce the paratroopers holding the bridge. Unfortunately, the "achievability" conversation initiated by General Browning went nowhere. History shows that, while the paratroopers made it to the bridge, reinforcements never did. The defeat cost valuable lives and time. More than six months elapsed before the Allies crossed the Rhine over the Ludendorff Bridge at Remagen, Germany.

"Is it needed?" Do people find the "why" sufficiently compelling? Exploring this question may reveal unanticipated issues along the Expectations Chain. The CIO of Cedars-Sinai, a major organization in its community, communicated throughout the information technology department the expectation that they would complete "100 percent of their projects on time." When his top team heard this requirement, they expressed their skepticism. Not only did they find that an impossible dream, they couldn't see the need to do so, since no one in their industry expects to complete every project on time. When the conversation turned to getting the external vendors on board, a variable many felt lay outside their control, the objections grew fierce. It would never happen. However, as the CIO more fully detailed "why it was needed" and made a compelling case to his team, people began to come around. "Why," they began to wonder, "are we using vendors that don't deliver in the first place?" As the CIO had looked down-line in the Expectations Chain to the vendors, he saw clearly that the "on time" objectives could depend on them more than anyone else. That meant presenting vendors with the same compelling case he had offered his own people.

"Is it linked?" Do people perceive a strategic fit between your expectation and the priorities of the organization? If they do not, they will not completely align with your expectation due to their perception of conflicting priorities. Paul Everett of Ceridian Corporation ran the company's HR Payroll call center. His boss expected two results from Paul's group: improved service and improved operating margins. This came as no surprise to Paul, since he had been focusing on these two objectives already and felt the group was making good progress on both. Over the past year, average speed of answer (ASA) had decreased 12 percent, from 4.44 to 3.91 minutes, and costs had dropped a full 7 percent. Then Paul's boss set goals for the New Year: "I want a minute on ASA, and I also want another 8 percent improvement in operating margins." This concerned Paul. The group had already picked all "the low-hanging fruit," the most easily accomplished improvements in ASA and expense reduction. As much as he wanted to make his boss happy, he just could not see a way to do it all. They might be able to reduce the ASA to one minute, but not with fewer resources. As he pondered the dilemma, he saw only one solution: further investment in technology and training.

With that in mind, Paul engaged in an Alignment Dialogue with the management team about what they really wanted. While everyone wanted to fulfill both expectations, Ceridian's current strategic direction required capital, and that meant budget cuts. It seemed to Paul that this argued for providing satisfactory service with fewer resources. But he wasn't sure. In the conversation with his boss, he said, "I can't get to a minute and lose 8 percent of my budget, because I need a portion of the budget to get there. To get to a minute, I need to invest more in the effort." Then he offered his solution: "I feel comfortable that I can get to the two-minute range with the initiatives we already have in place and meet the financial performance objectives." In other words, he was asking, "What does the management team really want?" His boss agreed that the strategic objectives linked first with hitting the financial numbers, second with reducing ASA. They quickly settled on the two minutes and 8 percent.

When your boss asks you to do something, you naturally want to say "Okay, I'll do it." But Paul knew that doing so in this case would doom him to failure. Did his forthright response to his boss get him fired? Far from it. The HR Payroll call center had never recorded a two-minute ASA in any month during the preceding year, but throughout the next year it reported a monthly average of less than two minutes. The 8 percent reduction in expenses? Mid-year, corporate came back to every division, including Paul's call center, asking for additional budget reductions. Paul's team, now 25 percent smaller, because Paul had not replaced the people who left, continued to maintain an average answer time below two minutes. Not surprisingly, having success-fully linked his efforts in the call center with the company strategy, Paul now oversees a number of customer service platforms throughout the nation.

Linking the expectation can prove especially difficult in a matrix environment where the people you depend on are asked to do things by others who are pursuing a different set of priorities. In this situation, the Alignment Dialogue becomes even more important because it will help everyone avoid or resolve problems that could arise from conflicting expectations.

Step Three: Resolve It

Once you pinpoint what is missing, you can set about resolving any concerns. Complete Alignment requires you to persuade and convince, not coerce and compel, as you work to resolve issues. The latter may force Complyment, but it will not get people moving forward with the high level of energy and enthusiasm they will need in order to succeed. Forcing people into align-ment may get them moving, but it won't necessarily get them thinking. Understanding people's concerns and working to capture their hearts and minds takes more time and effort, but it always pays off in the end.

This phase of the dialogue requires that you seek input from people about all their concerns, especially their worries about both real and perceived obstacles, so that you can address them head-on. You do this by providing information, coaching, and feedback. If you really want Complete Alignment, and not just Complyment, then you must commit yourself to persuading and convincing people to invest their hearts and minds in the effort. What we call "position power" can get people aligned, but that approach most often results in mere Complyment. "Persuasion power," on the other hand, can result in enthusiastic agreement, provided you engage people in a forthright dialogue that honestly addresses their needs and concerns. This chart highlights the difference between the two approaches.

POSITION POWER	PERSUASION POWER
You tell people what you are thinking and then ask them to share their views, looking more for validation of your opinion than constructive disagreement.	You encourage people to speak up and tell you what they really think, waiting to express your own views until after you have heard theirs.
You keep information to yourself and don't try to persuade people.	You provide information that will help convince people of your expectation's validity.
You truncate the process too quickly, wanting to move on, whether people are ready or not.	You display appropriate patience with the process, allowing people to work through the issues.
You tell people, "This is the way it is."	You give people a chance to buy in to where you want them to go.
You say you want to know what people think, but then find ways to remind them that you're the boss and this is your call.	You invite candid comments in a variety of ways—private consultations, e-mails, and so on—in order to understand what people really think.

You will find the power of persuasion especially valuable in situations where you are trying to create Complete Alignment around key expectations. Certainly, you could just "require" everyone to fall into line, and, most likely, they would. But you can't require them to get excited, to buy in enthusiastically, to bring their utmost creativity to the undertaking. No, you must earn that. The best way to earn it? Through the power of persuasion.

Once you have resolved any concerns, you can either confirm the original expectation or revise it, based on any new information you gleaned from the dialogue. If you enjoy complete agreement, you may not need to tinker with the original expectation. If, however, the dialogue causes you to re-form the expectation, then apply the Why-What-When process to reconfigure and recommunicate it. Think back to Paul's dilemma. His honest reaction to senior management's expectation caused them to revise it and make it more achievable, thus allowing everyone to push against the same side of the boulder.

Alignment with challenging expectations often requires a discussion of the "How," a conversation that naturally occurs when we are resolving concerns. Some people need to talk through the "How"; others don't. This is a fact of life. However, do not assume one type of person will do a better job than the other. If you want alignment with everyone in the chain, then you should know if they are going to need the "How" conversation to move the ball forward. Of course, conducting a "How" conversation does not mean you must tell people exactly what to do. It simply means that you hear their concerns about "How" they will get it done and help them see that they can figure it out for themselves. You may feel that you pay people to figure out the "How" and that you shouldn't have to deal with that. That might be true in a perfect world, but if someone needs that conversation to get on board, spend a bit of time helping them see that they can fulfill the expectation.

Will a time ever come when you just can't get agreement and must grit your teeth and move forward without it? Of course. But, in that case, you settle for Complyment. That's not necessarily the end of the world. However, we suggest that you ask yourself this question: "If the people I am counting on are in Complyment, will that be enough to get the job done?" Nine times out of ten, you will reap far greater dividends by resolving concerns and moving forward by creating Complete Alignment when it comes to fulfilling key expectations.

One of our clients recently reminded us that people's ability to get aligned with a specific expectation depends to a large extent on how overloaded with work they feel. In his monthly one-on-ones with his direct reports, he devotes a section of time on his standard agenda to what he calls "Your Time." At this point, people can raise any personal issues and concerns. Predictably, he says, at least 25 percent of people seize this opportunity to say something like, "Hey, I have more on my plate than I can handle." When they feel that way, our client contends, their opinion will erect another obstacle to creating Complete Alignment around anything else that might come up in the near future. With this in mind, you should routinely explore how well people are "keeping up" with the work. To help you identify when the workload might affect alignment, we suggest you pose these questions, first to yourself, and then to the people you work with, so that you can gauge how well they are keeping up. For each question below, select the response that best describes how you feel.

The Keeping-Up Quiz

For each question, select the response below that best describes how you feel.

	DO I . . .	COLUMN ONE	COLUMN TWO	COLUMN THREE
1	find myself feeling overwhelmed with the amount of work that I have to do?	All the time	Often	Never
2	feel I am in a no-win situation?	Yes	Maybe	No
3	think I will miss some deadlines?	Yes	Maybe	No
4	believe things will stay pretty stressed in the future, with no "relief" in sight?	Yes	Not Sure	No
5	feel stressed about the mounting priorities and my ability to complete them?	Totally	Somewhat	Not at all
6	feel that I am unable to succeed because of my workload?	All the time	Sometimes	Never
7	get frustrated because people do not see the impossibility of what I am being asked to do?	Yes	Sometimes	No
	Column Score			
	Total Score			

Now, score the quiz by awarding yourself three points for every answer in column one, two points for every answer in column two, and one point for every answer in column three. Total your points, then interpret your score using the scorecard.

YOUR "KEEPING-UP" SCORECARD

Your Score . . .   *Means You Are In . . .*

18–21 Points   "BURN OUT" mode. You need to make some changes that will work in the long run because you cannot maintain this pace.

Potential prices you may pay if you don't make changes: personal problems such as a decline in health and family stress and a potential "disaster" for your company. Your increased inability to get aligned with key expectations will prove to be an obstacle to fulfilling them.

14–17 Points   "OVERWHELM" mode. You feel swamped with more work than you can handle. You may be keeping all the balls in the air, but you can easily drop one or more at any time.

Potential prices: you will either progress into "burnout" mode or move on to another job working for someone else. Your workload reduces your ability to get aligned.

10–13 Points   "MAKE IT HAPPEN" mode. You are busy, but not so busy that you feel overwhelmed or burned out. You know you can handle all your work, and you feel confident you can fulfill everyone's expectations. Your ability to maintain the pace and remain aligned make it quite likely you will fulfill all key expectations.

Potential prices: you know you can offer your organization or team even more. A greater investment on your part could assist the organization in fulfilling key expectations.

7–9 Points   "I CAN DO MORE" mode. You're doing your job, but you could do much more to help the organization reach a higher level of performance. You have invested your hands and feet, but probably not your heart and mind.

Your ability to get aligned with key expectations may actually diminish if engaging at a higher level makes you uncomfortable or requires more change than you want to make.

Potential prices: the organization or team suffers from too little of your heart and mind investment in improving performance and going beyond the expected. You may lose interest in your current work and move on to another more challenging and rewarding opportunity.

ALIGNMENT MEETINGS

Continual diagnosis of whether or not you have Complete Alignment involves an ongoing conversation. We find that most teams and organizations benefit greatly from integrating Alignment Meetings into coordination meetings that already take place, especially when they sense there is any misalignment that threatens the success of the undertaking. These short meetings, held on a regular basis with the appropriate people in the Expectations Chain, can help you understand the degree of alignment within your organization and ensure that all the links remain lined up in the same direction. When you do hold an Alignment Meeting, make sure you include these items on the agenda:

1. Identify your key expectations for a given individual or team.
2. Apply the Alignment Dialogue to these expectations.
3. Periodically use the "Keeping-Up" Quiz to check in.

This meeting works best when you make it a two-way conversation. We all expect things from others, and they also expect things from us. It's not a one-way street. In our experience, people look forward to these meetings because they appreciate the opportunity to talk about their work. The routine nature of this meeting lets people anticipate the opportunity to discuss issues that they might otherwise bury, issues that are preventing them from truly getting aligned to fulfill your expectations.

A word of caution! We can all fall prey to the illusion that the closer people are to us in the Expectations Chain, the more aligned they will be.

However, there is no such thing as "alignment by proximity." If you want to ensure Complete Alignment all along the Expectations Chain, you must consider the weakest links in the chain and engage in Alignment Dialogues at all crucial points in the path. The weakest link in the chain might be someone you work with every day, or it could be someone with whom you have minimal contact down-line in the Expectations Chain. Take note of the fact that anyone can conduct an Alignment Meeting. You might do it with your immediate team, your manufacturing people might do it with suppliers, and service personnel might do it with customers. Just remember that those in your own immediate vicinity and those further down-line all need periodic assessment and reinforcement.

ACCOUNTABILITY REALITY CHECK

Try adding an alignment check to the agenda for your next three regularly scheduled one-on-one meetings, whatever their original purpose. Suppose you are getting together with your executive assistant to go over their work on an important monthly report to your boss. Instead of just asking them how it's going, use the Alignment Meeting agenda presented above. Be sure to work with the expectations that are most in jeopardy of not being fulfilled. Make sure you consider the entire Expectations Chain and choose the weakest link as your main focus. With practice, this sort of reality check can become an ingrained practice, one that can do a lot to eliminate surprises and make things happen just the way you want them to happen.

ALIGNING WITH STYLE

As with all of the steps in the Accountability Sequence, your Accountability Style comes into play when you conduct an Alignment Dialogue. Those with a Coerce & Compel style tend to rely on position power to get people aligned with their expectations. They may do so overtly or subtly. To them, "Position Power" represents a natural default behavior designed to save time and speed up the decision-making process. Their impatience with others with whom they wish to get aligned can actually backfire and cause people to spend less effort and energy getting things done. They need to guide the discussion with a commitment to process and timelines. Keep in mind that important timelines are best set with input from others who may not have yet bought into the desired outcome.

Another danger for this style arises when coercion causes people to comply with the request by falling victim to the "tell-me-what-to-do" mode. When this happens, people who have not fully committed to the outcome may go through the motions of Complete Alignment when in reality they are in Complyment. Without the enthusiastic ownership necessary to guarantee that they will do everything they possibly can do to fulfill the expectation, they may move forward, but their progress will falter. Facilitating an honest discussion, rather than trying to solve all the problems, will help avoid this common trap.

Those with Wait & See tendencies usually rely too much on relationship power. Rather than persuading, they assume automatic loyalty and trust, hoping others will just naturally get aligned for those reasons. If people don't do that, they sometimes take it personally. This style would get better results by using persuasion power. While loyalty does serve as a strong motivator, exclusively relying on it can set people up to feel betrayed when things go wrong. Letting people know that you appreciate their trust, but that you do not assume they will want to move forward on that basis alone, will help create the sort of open dialogue that makes a big difference in the end.

In addition, someone with the Wait & See style may pay less attention to the details when working through the "resolve concerns" phase of the Alignment Dialogue. By not digging into the issues and really working with the details, they may incorrectly assume resolution on certain issues when, in fact, none really exists. Providing detailed information that convinces others of the direction's value can prove invaluable in engaging their hearts and minds.

HEARTS AND MINDS

Throughout this chapter, we have talked a lot about the difference between "hands and feet" and "hearts and minds." This step in the Outer Ring of the Accountability Sequence is all about helping people take ownership of the expectations as if they had come up with them themselves. By engaging the heart, you engage the most vital part of a person's conviction to get things done. By engaging the mind, you ignite their most creative thinking, as they devise solutions that may never have occurred to you or them. The power of gaining people's hearts and minds in getting things done may seem obvious, but the price you pay when they only apply their hands and feet to a task, while not so obvious, is nonetheless real. You can easily see the heart and mind at work, but you cannot so easily see what might happen without them. The next step in the Outer Ring, Inspecting Expectations, will help you determine whether you have that commitment or not.

Chapter Four

THE POSITIVE, PRINCIPLED WAY

Before you move on to Chapter Five, pause for a moment to think about the key concepts we have introduced in this chapter. Following these steps and implementing these principles will help you create positive accountability connections and get better results throughout the Expectations Chain.

Complete Alignment Means Agreement
While there are many levels of alignment, for the purposes of talking about the kind of alignment that makes key expectations happen, no matter what, there are two kinds: Complete Alignment and Complyment.

The Complete Alignment Chain Reaction
Complyment brings the "hands and feet" to the task, while Complete Alignment engages the "hearts and minds" and affects everyone else throughout the Expectations Chain.

Moving the Boulder
As you saw with Tiger Woods at the Phoenix Open, the alignment process depends on getting everyone in the Expectations Chain pushing in the same direction, from the same side of the boulder.

The Alignment Dialogue
Use the Alignment Dialogue to gain Complete Alignment: Step One—Score It by restating the expectation, agreeing to use the Alignment Dialogue, and getting people to rate their level of alignment (on a scale of 1 to 10); Step Two—Evaluate It by asking, "Is it clear, needed, achievable, and linked?"; and Step Three—Resolve It by addressing concerns (remember to favor persuasion power over position power) and then either confirming the original expectation or revising it with Why-What-When.

Alignment Meetings
Integrate an Alignment item into your existing meetings so you can routinely identify your top expectations, conduct the Alignment Dialogue, and periodically apply the Keeping-Up Quiz.

Chapter Five

INSPECT EXPECTATIONS

INSPECT WHAT YOU EXPECT

Now you can take the last crucial step in the Outer Ring of the Accountability Sequence and "inspect what you expect." Getting the results you want depends on performing this step well. If you don't, all the hard work you put into forming, communicating, and aligning key expectations will go unrewarded. Implement the inspection process properly and you may actually see people exceed your expectations, which is exactly what happened for Perry Lowe, president and CEO of AXIS Dental Corporation.

Perry's company supplies dental equipment exclusively to other distributors who, in turn, sell the products directly to dental offices. For six years, AXIS had consistently produced 33 percent compounded growth. Their success made everyone feel comfortable, especially the sales force, which had grown accustomed to receiving generous commission checks. Then, almost without warning, AXIS experienced a year when sales growth plummeted to nearly zero. To Perry, it felt as though his high-performing racing machine had unexpectedly broken down during the middle of the race and needed a quick fix. The annual business meeting that year was unusually short and not so sweet; for the first time AXIS recognized only one person in the field for performing at 100 percent of plan. The organization reeled in shock. To Perry's credit, however, he did not despair but seized this opportunity as a wake-up call to make some major changes, and to make them quickly.

Initially, Perry's analysis attributed the decline in performance to the sales reps' failure to pay enough attention to the sell-through of the product to the ultimate end user, the dental offices. However, as Perry drilled down further, he found deeper causes. Yes, the reps were not properly focused on end-user results, but whose fault was that? Somehow, the management team had failed to get the message about the importance of sell-through to everyone along the Expectations Chain. Too many people were unaligned and out of the loop. Perry acknowledged to us, "At some point, I simply quit paying attention to what my management team really needed in order to focus on sell-through, and when that happened, things began to crash really fast."

Working with the field force, Perry redirected the focus beyond distributor invoices to ultimate end-user orders. He so skillfully formed and communicated this expectation that he easily got everyone aligned with it. Still, Perry knew that in order to effect real change as quickly as he needed it to happen, he would need to keep a close eye on the execution of this initiative. As he began his inspection, he was pleased to see the sales group walking the talk, but he was displeased to find that the rest of the organization continued to concentrate on the front end of the pipeline. As he delved into this further to isolate the cause of the misplaced focus, he found that the problem stemmed, in part, from the report AXIS used to update progress for the company. Specifically, every department had to wait thirty days to get the report and the feedback they needed before they could decide what, if any, changes to make in order to hit plan. When, after thirty days, they received the vital numbers, it was too late for any of the departments to react in a way that could affect the outcome. Perry recognized that he needed to get the entire organization inspecting progress on a real-time basis and in such a manner that his people could react to the data and take the required additional steps needed to achieve their expected sales growth.

Thinking outside of the box, AXIS Dental asked their distributor to submit weekly reports summarizing the numbers coming through the pipeline all the way down to the end users, thereby allowing them to see dental offices actually placing orders. At first, this request did not sit well with the distributor because they usually provided this information only to the "biggest of the big," a status to which AXIS aspired but had not yet reached. However, after some compelling negotiations, AXIS persuaded the distributor to comply with their request. Soon, all the departments were receiving the right information every week. They now knew their distributors' order quantities and were equipped to respond quickly when they saw orders falling below expectations. Consistent reviews of these new reports opened up the floodgates of dialogue, and e-mail chatter expanded exponentially. Everyone began to look for success, and when they failed to detect it, they began asking what else they could do to achieve it. Interestingly, before this new report came into play, people could not name their ultimate customers. Now, armed with that knowledge, they took action to help pull demand through the pipeline.

By inspecting what he expected, Perry propelled the AXIS field force well on their way to regaining their former glory, with over half the field force soon achieving 100 percent of plan. AXIS put itself back on track to capture the market growth the company desired. Perhaps, even more important, Perry was no longer the only one looking to see if his expectations were being fulfilled; he now had all eyes in the company focused on sales throughout the pipeline. The AXIS example is but one of many we could share that convincingly demonstrates the importance of consistently inspecting what you expect and the corresponding impact of this leveraged activity on results.

Too often, people operate under the illusion that "just because I said it will happen, it will happen" or "just because I told them what I needed, people will get it done." In fact, we'll bet that your own experience proves the opposite. In reality, many different pressures and problems always pop up along the way, including conflicting personal motivations, changing requirements, and serious roadblocks, all of which conspire to derail the effort to get things—especially difficult things—done on time. Under all these pressures, people can easily wander off track and fail to fulfill the expectations we have of them. It takes conscientious effort to keep people on track all the way up and down the Expectations Chain. The Inspect Expectations step helps ensure that you maintain this focus.

A positive and principled inspection is a thoughtful and planned activity with the following purpose:

> To assess the condition of how closely key expectations are being fulfilled, to ensure continued alignment, to provide needed support, to reinforce progress, and to promote learning, all in order to bring about the delivery of expected results.

During the inspection step people clearly begin to see accountability at work. As you begin to inspect how closely expectations are being fulfilled, people begin to validate that you are entirely serious about holding them accountable. At the same time, you manifest your own accountability and your personal dedication to doing everything you can do to get the result. Like most endeavors, getting people ready for the experience, and making sure they know what to expect from it, will make the whole experience all the more productive.

GETTING PEOPLE READY TO BE INSPECTED

Your own experience should tell you that the people you inspect will, most likely, view the inspection negatively if you don't prepare them for it in advance. Think about it. Did you look forward to tests and exams? Does it ever make you nervous when you know someone will be checking on your progress? It's only natural for people to feel that way. Consider the following list of reasons why people *don't* want to be inspected.

Reasons People Don't Want You to Inspect

- They think your follow-up means you don't trust them to do their job, and to do it well.
- They want to be "empowered" and don't want to be "second-guessed," having to run things by you in a way that slows them down.
- They don't want to disappoint you and fear you will discover that they cannot live up to your standards.
- They want full credit and do not want you to force them to share *their* rewards for fulfilling *their* responsibility.
- They take pride in not needing your time or attention, further establishing their credibility and value to the organization.
- They don't think your inspection will add any value to their ability to get the job done.

If you don't appreciate and deal with these natural concerns up front, don't be surprised if people resist your inspection efforts. However, as you obtain a mutual understanding and agreement about how the inspection process will occur, you will generally find that the inspection process not only helps you develop positive accountability connections, but also facilitates the delivery of the results you desire. We recommend applying all four of the steps in the Outer Ring to how you will inspect others. As you follow these steps, you will tend to find people much more receptive and sometimes even eager to participate in the process. Forming an expectation around how you will inspect, communicating that expectation using Why-What-When, and ensuring you have alignment about doing it will help get everyone invested in the inspection process. Additionally, from time to time, you should inspect the inspection process itself. You may not have used a fully deliberate and conscious inspection process in the past, but if you start doing it now, you will soon come to appreciate that this effort upfront will save you a huge amount of time correcting problems later.

An effective inspection process extends all along the Expectations Chain, not just to those closest to you. Getting everyone in the organization to look all the way down-line in the chain, just as Perry did at AXIS, past their immediate customer to the end user, helps everyone understand what they need to do to fulfill the expectation. Of course, your inspection methods will vary as you move through the chain. In many cases, you need only make sure that everyone is inspecting everyone else in some appropriate manner. Again, the purpose of the inspection, an act of accountability on your part, is to ensure that you are doing everything you can to help people succeed in fulfilling your expectations. Let's take a look at each of the elements of the inspection purpose statement; they prepare you to do it with others the positive, principled way.

Assess the Condition

Just as your doctor schedules a routine physical to ascertain the condition of your health and to make sure everything is functioning as it should, and that there are no hidden problems, an inspection aims, first and foremost, to assess progress. At this point, you make sure everything is on track and that surprises are not lurking around the next corner. Regular check-ins to assess the condition of things can go a long way toward preventing those surprises that so often delay results. For example, we watched as one organizational leader with whom we were consulting gathered 150 branch managers from all over the country in a WebEx conference. During this conference he talked about the importance of using a certain procedure that everyone should have integrated into their safety meetings throughout the United States. Although relatively easy to implement, this important procedure nevertheless required everyone's conscientious effort to add it to the existing safety protocol. Walking into the WebEx conference, the leader seemed assured and excited that the branch managers were consistently following that protocol. However, as the dialogue proceeded and branch managers shared anecdotes about the existing program, we began to get the feeling that maybe they had not yet fully implemented the procedure in their branches.

At that point, we encouraged the leader to take a few minutes to check in with the branch managers by using the WebEx feedback feature that allowed them to place either a green or red checkmark beside their name (green if they had successfully incorporated existing protocol into their regular branch safety meetings, red if they had not). When the organizational leader asked everyone to check in, he immediately saw so many red "x's" flashing on the screen that it became apparent that over 50 percent of the branch managers had failed to implement the new procedure. The result surprised all of us and, most especially the organizational leader. Once again, it was painfully clear to us that when you fail to take the time to inspect and check in along the way, you often find yourself surprised at some point down the road.

One measure of your effectiveness at inspecting is just how often those big surprises pop up in your business life. The assessment below will help you evaluate the degree to which you get surprised in your daily work.

"How Often I Get Surprised"

Respond to each statement with "Almost all the time,"
"Frequently," "Sometimes," or "Rarely."

	ALMOST ALL THE TIME	FREQUENTLY	SOMETIMES	RARELY
I am surprised to learn that people have not made the progress I thought they should have made.				
I find myself wondering, "How did that happen?"				
I feel as if I am the last to know about important setbacks that interfere with the ability of others to achieve my expectations.				
I worry that people misunderstand my expectations and what I need them to do.				
I do not see people proactively reporting on their progress.				

To tabulate your score, give yourself four points for every "Almost all the time" response, three points for every "Frequently" response, two points for every "Sometimes" response, and one point for every "Rarely" response. Use the Surprise Meter to understand what your total score says about your effectiveness at inspecting.

The Surprise Meter		
IF YOU SCORE	**YOUR SURPRISE LEVEL**	**OUR ADVICE IS . . .**
18–20	*Stupefaction*	Off the charts! There is a disaster in the making. You desperately need to take the element of surprise out of your business practice by inspecting exactly what you expect.
15–17	*Bewilderment*	You are just not sure what the problem is. Most likely, you have identified it as the people you are working with, and not the way you are working with them, that is leading to the surprises.
13–14	*Disbelief*	You hope to see a different result, although you know you probably won't, in situations where people, including yourself, keep making the same mistakes.
9–12	*Confusion*	Surprises happen to you often enough to make you wonder if things could still be significantly more efficient.
5–8	*Unaware*	You either establish really low expectations, making it hard for people to surprise you, or you are simply unaware of what is really going on. In either case, you will benefit from learning how to improve your inspections.

Obviously, these categories reflect a generalization, but they do give you some idea about whether your current inspection practices effectively minimize surprises. Can you totally eradicate surprises? Of course not. No one can completely control every single variable that affects them in business. But you can do a lot to eliminate the big ones by taking the Inspect Expectations step we describe in this chapter.

Ensure Continued Alignment

As we discussed in the previous chapter, you can best maintain alignment through an ongoing series of checks, and not just a onetime dialogue. We recommend that this be done through what we call Alignment Meetings. The inspection process affords opportunities to check for that alignment and make sure everyone remains on the same page, thus allowing you to correct any misalignment before things get too far off track.

Several years ago we watched a seasoned Scout leader teach a valuable lesson to his peers during a high-level training meeting at the Philmont Scout Ranch in New Mexico. In the very first session of this important weeklong training, this veteran instructor stood up and said something that we have never forgotten. He said, "Remember, the main thing is to keep the main thing the main thing." At first we all laughed at this bit of homespun wisdom, but the dead-on accuracy and universal applicability of that statement has resounded in our ears for years. Inspections can help you apply that advice so that everyone throughout the Expectations Chain keeps "the main thing the main thing."

We appreciate the well-known story about the rescue of the *Apollo 13* crew because it shows the power of keeping everyone focused and aligned around what you want to have happen. Recall the incident when the oxygen tank exploded in the service module. When the explosion took out power to the spacecraft, the lunar module, with its larger-capacity batteries, became the astronauts' lifeboat. The "lifeboat" was designed to support two men for two days but was now being asked to support three men for four days. Flight Director Gene Kranz's team was evenly split on whether to continue with a mid-orbit return to Earth or, to try a bold move, shooting around the moon in a slingshot effect that might pick up the momentum needed to return to Earth. Director Kranz opted for the latter, unconventional and unproven solution. Would the slingshot effect produce enough momentum to put the lunar module on the right trajectory? No one knew for sure. But one thing was for sure, it stood a much better chance of success if people both up-line and down-line the Expectations Chain got aligned around this new expectation. Everyone went to work, calling on both internal NASA resources and external vendors. The race to save the astronauts was on. Every minute counted. There was only a tiny window of time for making key decisions, such as powering down the command module and then powering it back up just before re-entry, and reversing the flow of power from the lunar module to the command module, a tricky and untried maneuver.

In an effort to align the team, Kranz pulled everyone into one room to discuss what many viewed as an almost unsolvable problem. As he recalled, he needed to convince people that they "were smart enough, sharp enough, fast enough, and that as a team, good enough, that they could take an impossible situation and recover from it." Standing at the front of the room, he told the team, "This crew is coming home. You have to believe it! Your people have to believe it! And we must make it happen!" With that, people began brainstorming ways to get it done. With the kind of alignment that keeps the "main thing the main thing," they tapped an amazing amount of ingenuity. However, just as everyone took accountability to solve the problem, another equally serious and dangerous one popped up. Carbon dioxide began building up quickly in the lunar module "lifeboat." Working two straight days on this life-threatening development, one team came upon an ingenious solution. Using parts available in the spacecraft, including large amounts of duct tape, a plastic bag, a sock, the cover of a flight manual, and several other unlikely, pressed-into-service components, they fashioned a makeshift device that allowed the command module filters to interact with the lunar module life support system to successfully reduce the CO_2 levels.

It took hundreds of engineers in California and New York almost three days to complete a power-up sequence that would work. Another team worked to reduce the time for return to the splashdown target. Other teams carefully controlled the use of on-board consumables, such as drinking water. Power usage was reduced from the normal 75 amps to an incredible 12 amps. Incredibly, as we all know, the *Apollo 13* astronauts made it home safely. It happened because, throughout the entire saga, Kranz and his team kept "the main thing the main thing." Kranz perfectly and doggedly kept everyone, up and down the Expectations Chain, aligned around achieving the same goals by making them compelling for everyone involved.

To maintain that degree of alignment, people need to see how achieving the expectation will benefit them personally. Helping people see the compelling "why" behind fulfilling the expectations you have of them, and helping them see how that "why" speaks directly to their own situation, can provide the key to securing Complete Alignment. One leader whom we greatly respect, and who enjoys a reputation as one of the most successful female CEOs in her industry, told us that in order to secure alignment she would often engage people in a conversation at the beginning of any significant effort, stressing what might happen if the expectation went unfulfilled. She would ask, "How would that affect the business, the team, and future opportunities for people in the organization?" This conversation drove home the importance of getting the job done and getting it done well. While raising the specter of failure may seem somewhat fatalistic or even imply some disbelief in people's ability to get the job done, in this case the leader did it correctly, helping her people connect the dots between the outcome of the assignment and each of their personal contributions. That connection helped people maintain a high level of accountability for staying aligned.

Who should assume accountability for making sure the inspection happens, the person who established the expectation or the person tasked to fulfill it? It may seem obvious that the former should inspect the latter's progress, but that can absolve others from their responsibility to report proactively on where things stand. An effective inspection not only creates a joint accountability and ownership for both checking in and proactively reporting; it helps ensure a positive inspection experience. If you are a "chaser," then you are consuming valuable time and wasting energy on a process that probably doesn't feel very good to either the chaser or the "chasee." Do you spend a lot of time trying to track down people to get them to report on how things are going? Try answering "Often" or "Seldom" to each of the following statements:

AM I A CHASER?

Answer "Often" or "Seldom" to each statement:

_____ 1. I find myself having to take the initiative to ask people for a report on progress.

_____ 2. People are not prepared to provide the information I need when I ask them for it.

_____ 3. I spend time tracking people down to find out how things are progressing.

_____ 4. People are not very good about letting me know what is going on.

_____ 5. I find myself asking lots of questions to get the information I need, when I need it.

If you answered "Often" to most of these, then you probably do too much chasing and should try to strike a better balance and establish more joint accountability when it comes to inspections. As the people you work with assume more accountability to let you know how things are going, they participate more fully in the inspection process. It becomes more positive for them and, as a result, they take more ownership in making the inspections happen. Certainly, the best inspections include a sense of shared accountability for keeping everyone up-to-date.

Provide Needed Support

Every good inspection achieves two intertwined goals: making sure that the right things are happening to fulfill the expectation and helping people succeed in getting it done. Rather than a "test" to see if people are doing what you asked and will deliver what you need on time, the inspection should function as a "check-in" to discuss progress, problems, and solutions. There's a world of difference between the two.

THE TEST	THE CHECK-IN
You ask lots of questions that make people feel as if they are being interrogated.	You create a two-way conversation that feels more like a dialogue.
When you are done, people feel that they have passed or failed.	When you finish, people feel that the grade is pending, but will be higher because of the interaction.
You make people feel as if the grades, particularly the bad ones, are posted publicly.	You make people feel as if problems and mistakes are still somewhat private and that there is time to overcome them.
The person testing acts more like a proctor, making sure people don't do anything wrong, but not really providing much help.	The person checking in acts more like a mentor providing needed support and making sure people do the right things to ensure the result.

Predictably, it usually takes more time and effort to conduct a check-in than it does to administer a test. However, as with any of the methods that create a positive, principled approach to holding others accountable, we guarantee that the extra time and effort will pay off handsomely. People will feel supported, they'll get the job done, they'll do it enthusiastically, they'll solve problems that crop up along the way, and they'll delight you with the results they achieve.

When providing support, you focus on facilitating solutions, a positive approach that strives to build on the strengths and successes that have occurred so far. Facilitating solutions means providing coaching, mentoring, training, and resources that can help move things along and make people successful. Ultimately, your people are accountable for figuring it out and succeeding, but your ability to help that process along can often make the difference between success and failure.

Providing support does not fall solely on your shoulders. Getting others enrolled in supporting the cause can be even more powerful. Consider Chicago Bulls basketball player Joakim Noah, a rookie with tremendous potential. During a practice session, Joakim got into a serious confrontation with one of the team's assistant coaches and found himself slapped with a one-game disciplinary suspension. His fellow players, however, went to the coach with their unanimous decision that Joakim's behavior warranted an additional game on the sidelines. They cited other incidents that bothered them: a pattern of showing up late for meetings and just not living up to the standards expected of a Chicago Bull. Did their opinions bother Joakim? Yes, but not in a negative way. As he told a reporter, "They (the team) just told me what I did was unacceptable, and I'm just going to have to move on from here. I've just got to accept it . . . there's nothing I can do about it . . . they felt I deserved more. It was the entire team that felt that way, so I back my team and the decision that they made, and appreciate the leadership that they've shown." In Joakim's case, the entire team held him accountable as they inspected what they expected and held him to the higher standard they required from every player on the team.

In the strongest culture, everyone is accountable to everyone, regardless of position or the ability to influence others. When the Expectations Chain involves a lot of people, and when you don't have the time to follow up on everything personally, getting the culture to help you inspect can make all the difference between success and failure. Inspections like these, where the team as a whole holds each member accountable, can quickly and positively shape behavior and strengthen the organization's ability to fulfill expectations.

Reinforce Progress

Consider this dictionary definition of the word *inspect*: to "look at (someone or something) closely, typically to assess their condition or to discover any shortcomings: *they were inspecting my outside paintwork for cracks and flaws.*" In our opinion, that definition places too much emphasis on discovering shortcomings, a typical goal associated with inspection that often makes people dislike or even dread the experience. It's always easy to see the cracks and flaws in the paint job, isn't it? Instead of inspecting for shortcomings, why not reorient the process to reinforcing progress? The latter will almost certainly lead to better results.

Many businesspeople use the old "management by exception" approach, because it seems easier and more efficient to ignore everything that is going well and concentrate only on what is going wrong. This approach will not create an environment where you can hold people accountable the positive, principled way. Rather, it does the opposite. Focusing solely on a lack of progress generally drives negative experiences, which in the end take their toll on an organization's culture, morale, and capacity.

It's worth repeating. Inspections should hold people accountable for what they do right, not just what they do wrong. When you create positive and supportive experiences over time, emphasizing solutions and reinforcing progress, people begin to anticipate the inspection process and may even look forward to it, rather than dread it. This emphasis on solutions promotes a positive outlook and keeps everyone looking forward and not backward.

Almost without exception over the past twenty years, as we have worked with some of the most admired companies in the world, we have heard leaders, managers, and team members lament the dreaded quarterly update meeting. This meeting gives management a chance to inspect progress in a public forum. Since these meetings usually center primarily on sniffing out weakness and potential hazards, people often dread them; particularly when they know beforehand that things are not going well. These feelings can even cause people to undermine the meeting's efficiency as they hold back information, blame others, misrepresent circumstances, or fail to portray the true facts of the situation. If that happens, the behavior can continue long after the meeting ends, infecting the entire organization and ultimately becoming part of the culture.

While good managers do keep their eyes open for weaknesses, threats, or potential risks, the best ones do that within the context of observing and reinforcing progress. Smart managers know that every time they hold someone accountable they are, in essence, holding the entire organization or team accountable. Word always gets around about what it felt like to undergo the "inspection." Based on the stories they hear, people begin to form beliefs. To make sure they form and communicate the right beliefs, you need to inspect in a positive and reinforcing way. Creating a culture where people expect to be inspected, and where they actually take accountability to make sure it happens, can open up the business process and its associated interactions, and speed up essential communication and decision-making.

Promote Learning

The right kind of inspection process will also facilitate real-time learning and the transfer of that learning into future performance. Some of the most important real-time learning occurs throughout the project, not just after its completion. You will see a lot more learning taking place in your organization if you emphasize that it occurs on a daily basis. Ensuring that it does so requires frequent inspections. Waiting until the very end to inspect often inhibits real-time learning and its associated long-term benefits. You always want to encourage real-time learning because it often translates into improved individual performance and enhanced capability throughout the Expectations Chain.

NASA provides a stunning example of this phenomenon. The hugely expensive *Mars Orbiter,* a valuable scientific tool for exploring Mars, had successfully landed on the red planet and had done its job for ten years before it suddenly disappeared from NASA controllers' screens. When communication with the vehicle stopped altogether, it took NASA officials by complete surprise. Upon investigation, NASA discovered that dead batteries killed the *Mars Orbiter.* The batteries died because a computer ordered the craft to go into "contingency mode," which exposed the battery pack to direct sunlight. The overheated batteries soon stopped working. A second computer command caused the antenna to point away from Earth, entirely eliminating communications with the craft. As it turned out, when NASA engineers transmitted commands to the craft through the Deep Space Network, someone wrote the commands to the wrong memory address in the onboard computer. The upload apparently went awry, because previous updates contained a discrepancy that programmers were trying to fix. NASA concluded that better periodic reviews of the programmers' work—or what we would call timely inspections—would probably have prevented the problem altogether.

Learning depends on a teacher, coach, or facilitator who can help others extract new knowledge and understanding from their own experience or the experiences of others. If you approach the inspection as an opportunity to promote learning, you will automatically confront problems and challenges in a solution-oriented manner. Doing so will also help you to help others capture best practices they will remember and use in the future. By carefully looking at the situation and extracting learning in a positive way, you will discover ways to help people move forward and fulfill your expectations.

THE LOOK MODEL

Since an effective inspection means looking closely at what is happening in a positive, principled way, we have developed a process for doing just that. We call it the LOOK Model.

THE LOOK MODEL

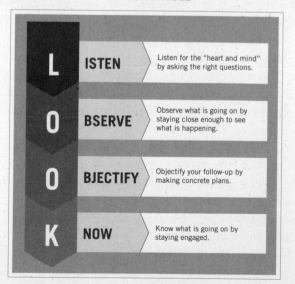

L	**ISTEN**	Listen for the "heart and mind" by asking the right questions.
O	**BSERVE**	Observe what is going on by staying close enough to see what is happening.
O	**BJECTIFY**	Objectify your follow-up by making concrete plans.
K	**NOW**	Know what is going on by staying engaged.

The memorable acronym LOOK captures the best practices that will assist you in designing the most effective inspection process.

Listen

First, *listen* for the "heart and mind" by asking the right questions that help you determine whether people have fully invested in fulfilling key expectations. What people talk about when they answer your questions will either reflect their alignment or reveal a need to do something else to strengthen their level of commitment. The way you ask questions can influence the way people answer them, as one of our clients learned the hard way. "Jim," the vice president of a manufacturing organization, turned in unprecedented results in terms of productivity and efficiency. A very bright man, Jim usually took credit as the "brains" behind the improvements. When we first met him, he proudly told us that he held people accountable "with a vengeance."

As we began working with his team, we could see that he was, indeed, very successful at getting people to account to him for what they did and did not do. He accomplished this rather simply. He just asked a lot of questions. Unfortunately, his questions came across more like an "interrogation" than a polite inquiry and tended to make people feel stupid in front of their peers. People told us that Jim's litany of questions during the morning production meeting always seemed to make other people look dumb and Jim look smart. On occasion, he would even slyly mock people and make jokes that would either cut people to the core or completely embarrass them. Not infrequently during a presentation, Jim would launch his inquisition with something like "Why don't you explain to us why in the world you think that process would actually work?" Some team members found the drama a bit amusing, until they found their own heads on the chopping block. Before long everyone began to dread the meetings and, behind Jim's back, nicknamed him "Darth Vader." The nickname stuck because every meeting brought an accounting, and if you were the person not performing perfectly, he would, as one team member joked, inflict "death by a thousand questions."

After we sat down with Jim and provided some coaching, he began asking his questions in a different way. He eliminated the sarcasm that minimized the person he was inspecting and, instead, focused on helping the team resolve issues. The defensiveness that once characterized his meetings slowly began to disappear as more open and candid conversations became the rule. He actually led this change by learning to ask the "right" questions.

THE RIGHT QUESTIONS...

- Focus on the issue, not the person (they do not get personal and they do not contain sarcasm).
- Are designed to help people succeed, not to reveal their failures.
- Are candid and designed to help people get to the "real" issues.
- Help create an environment where people feel respected, professional, on task, and successful.
- Avoid an egocentric emphasis, which draws more attention to the questioner than to the issue at hand.
- Do not belittle or scold in any way (all issues with individual performance are handled privately).

By sacrificing the "Darth Vader" approach and asking the right kinds of questions, Jim changed the way people felt about his meetings. They actually began to look forward to getting input during the meetings and to hearing things that would help them solve problems and move forward toward specific objectives. People began to enjoy Jim's company and perceived him as a brilliant resource, rather than as an intimidating inquisitor with a deprecating style. Jim and his team went on to accomplish amazing things in their industry, building long-term relationships with team members that he continued to enjoy throughout his career.

When you ask the right questions, in the right way (with respect, patience, and an emphasis on solutions), people become more responsive and forthcoming. Nevertheless you must make sure that you listen not just to what they tell you, but also to what they don't tell you. Ginger Graham, a former senior executive of Guidant Corporation and CEO of Amylin Pharmaceuticals, is a very effective and accomplished business leader. She is a strong advocate for checking in on the level of people's engagement, and she looks for opportunities to ask the right people the right questions in the right way: "What are you trying to get done today? Do you think what you are working on is really going to matter? If there was one thing you needed, what would it be?" And then, after asking her questions, she does what every executive ought to do next: she listens.

Ginger relished reaching out to people at all levels of the organization. On one occasion, during a leadership development exercise we conducted with her team, each member of the management team selected a "coach," someone else in the organization outside of the senior team who could provide a different perspective. Ginger, surprisingly, chose a worker on the shipping dock. He turned out to be a great coach. Ginger's conversations with this worker helped her to take the temperature of the organization and see how things were really going. Her associate from the shipping dock would even go out on assignment and take the pulse on specific issues that concerned her and then return and discuss with Ginger what he had learned. Ginger took great pains to listen dispassionately and to not get defensive so that she could really understand what was on the minds of people throughout the organization.

Observe

By *observe* we mean staying close enough to the situation to actually see what is happening. A good inspection requires you to get around and talk to people throughout the Expectations Chain. Two CEOs, well-known for getting out and observing their organizations at work, were Walmart's founder, Sam Walton, and James Sinegal, founder of Costco. Sam believed so deeply in staying close enough to the organization to see what was really going on that he visited hundreds of stores each year. James follows this same philosophy, purposefully visiting every store at least once a year. While many leaders rely heavily on reports to tell them what they need to know, Amylin's Ginger Graham insists that report cards do not reveal as much as the more prognostic tools. "These tools," she says, "can tell you more about a team's true health and can thereby help you more accurately predict whether they will turn in the performance you expect. You always know something about how the team will do when you walk into a meeting or workspace and simply observe." Ginger made it a practice to "hang out" at team events and watch the team in action. During her observations, she'd ask herself questions like these:

- Are there signs that they are bonding as a team, smiling and laughing in a way that tells you humans are working here and not just drones?
- Have they invented nicknames for each other?

- Can they get "good, bad, and ugly" (i.e. "get real" with each other)?
- Do I see evidence that the team is making progress?

By observing human relationships in action, Ginger could more easily assess whether people have engaged their hearts and minds in their work and are aligned and functioning effectively. In one case, it took a team two to three months to build the relationships that would allow them to talk honestly with each other about timelines. She could actually see them reach that turning point, underscoring the fact that you learn things through observation that you may not learn any other way.

At the same time, there are obvious benefits to finding ways to inspect without being physically present at the scene. The San Mateo, California, police department came up with a creative way to do just that. Operating with tight budgets, the department established a greater presence on the street by placing a mannequin police officer (officer David Coy, also known as officer "D-Coy") behind the wheel of some police cruisers and then parking those cruisers strategically in certain neighborhoods. When citizens spot the cruisers, with Officer D-Coy in the front seat, they adjust their behavior because of the perceived inspection (an effective remote inspection, at least until the citizens catch on to the ruse). Car manufacturers have also found a way to remotely inspect drivers for safety and inspire compliance with seat belt laws. As most of us have experienced, new cars feature an alarm bell that alerts a driver who has not buckled up within the first thirty seconds of starting the car. The bell will drive you increasingly crazy if you don't put on that seat belt. Some clever engineer determined just the right timing for this system to make you want to fulfill their expectation as fast as you can. Remote inspections can work wonders in some situations.

Objectify

Yes, the word *objectify* is a real word; it means you follow up by making concrete plans. This includes all the traditional tools that help you see the results of everyone's efforts to date: dashboards, management reports, update meetings, e-mails, monthly reports, and so on. Whatever tools you select, you want to make sure you specify the key indicators of progress, and then establish a systematic way to watch them.

Take some care with this, however. Efforts to objectify the inspection and create systematic reporting can sometimes become too predictable for everyone involved and deteriorate into "just another exercise." For instance, a large American candy company set a policy that required management to audit retail stores when they traveled. Associates would learn two to three weeks in advance that management would be paying them a visit. That gave them plenty of time to engineer what everyone called the "Milk Run," an activity that made sure, for instance, that all twenty stores in a district looked perfect just long enough to pass the inspection. Sales reps would give free product to all the stores to get their displays up, replace outdated packaging, and create the impression that the company "owned" these stores. Even though management knew this was happening, and had come to expect it, they simply wanted to report back to corporate that everything looked great. Clearly, predictable inspections can generate false or misleading data. Effective inspections reflect reality.

In another recent case, USDA inspectors of meat-processing plants came under criticism after the nation's largest meat recall, which was attributed to meat handler abuses of cattle—practices that went back as far as twelve years. A *USA Today* story reported that the culprit plant had racked up a long history of complaints. Interestingly, the plant had never resolved the issue, despite regularly scheduled daily inspections. As it turns out, the Humane Society of the United States discovered that these plant inspections occurred at the same time each day. Here again, meat processors could accurately predict when the inspector would appear and could thus make sure everything looked shipshape at that particular time. In this case, the inspection was concrete, formally planned and agreed upon, but it became just another exercise, one that lasted for over twelve years and served no real purpose.

When assembling concrete plans to follow up, make sure your inspections serve their purpose and do not devolve into mere exercises: reports that no one really uses; habitual check-in conversations that lack value; observations that can be manipulated; and all of the other routine activities that can make inspections more hurtful than helpful. Fashioning a concrete plan for how you will follow up, a plan that watches the right variables at the right time, will prove beneficial and help you LOOK more effectively as you inspect what you expect. You will most likely need to change the way you inspect from time to time and to build some redundancy into how you inspect so that you do not end up relying solely on one source to know what is going on. This will allow you to be more confident that even if one inspection system turns into an "exercise," other inspection systems can supply the accurate information you need.

Know

To *know* what is going on, you need to stay engaged. This step aims at keeping you "in the know" by making sure you are taking the first three steps (Listen, Observe, and Objectify) often enough. Deciding how often the inspections should take place depends on a number of variables: the complexity and difficulty of fulfilling the expectation, the capability of the people you are depending upon, and the nature of the "uncontrollables" in the environment.

Interim inspections should help you predict the outcome of an undertaking. If it looks good, fine. But if it looks grim, interim inspections using the LOOK Model allow you to make the necessary corrections to ensure success. How often is often enough? Experts at the Centers for Disease Control and Prevention suggest that dieters weigh themselves once a day. Researchers found that those who stepped on the scale every day averaged a twelve-pound weight loss over two years. Those who weighed themselves just once a week lost only 6 pounds in that time. On top of that, the daily weight watchers were less likely to regain the lost pounds. Reporting on this phenomenon, *Prevention* magazine quoted Dr. John Jakicic, director of weight management at the University of Pittsburgh, "The more often you monitor your results, the quicker you can catch the behavioral slip that caused weight gain." Different people slip in different ways. That's why you want to tailor and negotiate the frequency of your inspection with the person or team accountable for delivering the results you expect.

Finding the right balance requires honest conversation, but performing the first three steps of the LOOK Model with the right frequency (Listen for the "heart and mind" by asking the right questions; Observe what is going on by staying close enough to see what is happening; and Objectify your follow-up by making concrete plans) will help you know things are on track, the last step of the LOOK Model. Wondering, hoping, and assuming are the enemies of knowing. These three cohorts can destroy the very best efforts of everyone involved and prevent the needed support from getting to the right people at the right time. When this happens, you pay the price in unmet expectations, and you lose trust all the way through the Expectations Chain.

These are prices you can cancel with the proper approach to this critical step in the Outer Ring of the Accountability Sequence.

TRUST BUT VERIFY

Does inspecting what you expect imply a lack of trust? Is it just another form of that much-abhorred practice of micromanagement? Not at all. Done properly, inspecting builds trust and solidifies a mutual effort that is more about helping each other succeed than about catching others when they fail. Lou Cannon, in his book *President Reagan: The Role of a Lifetime*, recalls that "in signing the INF treaty, Reagan and Gorbachev demonstrated a comfortable familiarity with each other that was a by-product of their meetings in Geneva and Reykjavik. 'We have listened to the wisdom of an old, Russian maxim,' said Reagan, repeating a phrase he had repeated scores of times. 'The maxim is *doverey, no proverey*—trust but verify.' 'You repeat that at every meeting,' Gorbachev said good-humoredly. 'I like it,' said Reagan." We like it, too. To us, "trust but verify" means not only relying on people, but also checking in to make sure we are all succeeding at what we all intend to do.

Consider the difference between "trusting people" and "testing for results." They reflect two different motivations. The latter suggests the gaze of Big Brother; the former conveys wanting to help people succeed in fulfilling key expectations. At the end of the day, you generally get what you inspect. If you do it well, you increase the likelihood of success and you build the morale and capability of the Expectations Chain to deliver in the future.

ACCOUNTABILITY REALITY CHECK

You can easily find an opportunity to put these principles into practice. Consider the top two or three expectations for which someone up-line in your Expectations Chain currently holds you accountable. Use the LOOK Model to analyze how you would change the way you inspect those expectations. Remember the purpose of effective inspections: to assess the condition of how closely key expectations are being fulfilled, to ensure continued alignment, to provide needed support, to reinforce progress, and to promote learning, all in order to bring about the delivery of expected results. Be sure to prepare the people you will be working with for a different way of inspecting. Track how much more effectively you conduct inspections after taking this important step in the Outer Ring.

INSPECTING WITH STYLE

As usual, applying the LOOK Model will vary for each of the Accountability Styles. Think about the ways in which your own style influences your inspections. The Coerce & Compel style may overdo the inspection by asking too many questions, checking in too frequently, or beating people to the punch by asking for a report before they have time to prepare it. People who prefer this style will deem their approach entirely reasonable and will not readily understand why people do not proactively report or why they take so long to get back to them to let them know what is going on. With their predisposition for speed and results, those with this style will always feel a sense of urgency, sometimes more than the situation warrants. If that applies to you, we suggest you carefully consider when you really need to know, clearly communicate that expectation, and then patiently give people the agreed-upon time to get back to you.

Someone with the Wait & See style may tend to skip some of the steps in the LOOK Model, relying too heavily on trusting people to do the right thing at the right time. Again, those with Wait & See tendencies will benefit from formalizing their approach by carefully looking more frequently and formally, asking more questions, taking more time to observe, paying more attention to traditional reports, and staying more informed. People with this style will tend to approach their inspections more informally and will need to incorporate more structure before they can make any real changes. They are good at engaging people, but not so good at inspecting for results. Using the LOOK Model to structure their follow-up will help them capitalize on their strengths and more effectively inspect what they expect.

MANAGING UNMET EXPECTATIONS

This last, critical step in the Outer Ring can make or break all the good work you've done in the previous three steps of the Accountability Sequence:

Form, Communicate, and Align expectations. If you fail to Inspect, you will fail more often than not to get what you expect. Learning how to do this more effectively will help you eliminate surprises, see more of your expectations fulfilled, and help you to develop your ability to empower the people you work with to deliver results on a daily basis. If they succeed, you succeed.

Even when you follow every step in the Outer Ring perfectly, there are times when people will fail to meet your expectations. How you respond and the manner in which you hold them accountable can make the difference between salvaging a bad situation and ensuring that success ultimately happens. We will explore this crucial aspect of holding people accountable as we travel the Inner Ring of the Accountability Sequence—managing unmet expectations the positive, principled way.

Chapter Five

THE POSITIVE, PRINCIPLED WAY

Chapter Five provides the crowning principle of the steps in the Outer Ring: Inspecting Expectations. This recap highlights the main ideas you should keep in mind when it comes to inspecting so that you make sure you do it the positive, principled way.

Getting People Ready to Be Inspected
Use the steps in the Outer Ring to create the Inspection Expectation by Forming, Communicating, and Aligning around your inspection process.

Inspection Purpose Statement
"To assess the condition of how closely key expectations are being fulfilled, to ensure continued alignment, to provide needed support, to reinforce progress, and to promote learning, all in order to bring about the delivery of expected results."

- **Assess the Condition:** Periodically check in to assess the condition (either positive or negative) of progress toward fulfilling the expectation.
- **Ensure Continued Alignment:** Create joint accountability for the inspection and avoid becoming a "Chaser." Keep "the main thing the main thing" so that people stay aligned.
- **Provide Needed Support:** Avoid "testing" people and focus instead on "checking in" with the intent of helping people succeed by facilitating solutions.
- **Reinforce Progress:** Don't just address shortcomings but emphasize the progress people are making. Be sure to hold people accountable for what they do right.
- **Promote Learning:** Foster real-time learning to enhance capability and capture best practices for future success.

The LOOK Model

The memorable acronym LOOK captures the best practices that will assist you in designing the most effective inspection (**Listen, Observe, Objectify, Know**).

Trust but Verify

Use the inspection process to build trust.

Chapter Six

THE INNER RING

THE REALITY OF UNMET EXPECTATIONS

I f you do a good job using the steps in the Outer Ring to establish expectations, you will minimize the number of key expectations that go unmet. However, sometimes even the most painstaking efforts to Form, Communicate, Align, and Inspect your expectations cannot prevent disappointment. That's when you move into the Inner Ring of the Accountability Sequence and implement its strategies for dealing with any surprises and disappointments that come your way.

One of our clients, "Nigel," a highly successful CEO, related to us an episode in his career when he was caught totally off guard by someone on whom he greatly depended. Nigel had conducted a careful review of the references and background of "Fabian," a strong candidate whom Nigel was considering for a key position in the company. Fabian looked great on paper. He was an ex-Marine with executive experience in several major corporations, and he presented impeccable references. During Nigel's investigation into Fabian's background, he heard repeatedly that this candidate was "the best guy for the job in the industry." To top it all off, Nigel discovered that Fabian had worked previously with one of Nigel's own direct reports. When that person corroborated all the positive references, Nigel confidently offered Fabian the job.

As one of Nigel's direct reports in a staff position, Fabian traveled extensively with his new boss, who seized the opportunity to give Fabian advice and coaching on his personal development and future opportunities. Fabian respectfully listened to his mentor and took careful notes on everything Nigel said. Not surprisingly, Fabian quickly settled into his groove and began producing excellent results. As his success mounted, the time came for Fabian to take on more responsibility as a direct-line manager. Given this continued success, Nigel became even more outspoken in support of his protégé. Given Fabian's reputation for getting things done, everyone naturally expected him to set a new standard of performance in his expanded role.

Fabian did indeed establish a new standard of performance, though not the one anyone expected. When one of Fabian's own direct reports suddenly quit and lodged a complaint about his overbearing management style, a thorough investigation revealed similar complaints throughout the system. After reviewing the case, Nigel could only conclude that Fabian was, in actuality, a big-time bully with a highly parochial and confrontational management style. He frequently berated people in public, sometimes even screaming at them—behavior Fabian never exhibited around his superiors. While almost everyone seemed aware of the problem, it took Nigel by complete surprise.

Of course, Nigel wanted to know how this had happened. As he looked into it, he learned that one of Fabian's best friends worked in the human resources department, and because of that relationship, people elsewhere in the organization hesitated to approach HR with complaints, fearing it would get back to Fabian. Even worse, people believed that they couldn't go to Nigel himself, due to his apparently close relationship with Fabian. This fearful silence took a huge toll on the organization, as talented people, fed up with Fabian's bullying tactics, began leaving for greener pastures. The more Nigel learned about Fabian's behavior, the more he worried that people in the organization would think Nigel supported such tough and disrespectful management practices. For Nigel, nothing could be further from the truth.

Despite all of Nigel's careful coaching, Fabian ultimately failed to deliver on the CEO's expectations. What, Nigel wondered, could he have done to avoid wasting such a huge investment of time, energy, and effort? And what should he do about it now? That's precisely the sort of questions we will answer as we travel along the Inner Ring of the Accountability

Sequence. In each of the next four chapters, we will address the four primary reasons why people fail to meet expectations and the four solutions
you can implement to solve the problems related to those unfulfilled expectations. When you understand these potential solutions, you will also find
it easier to prevent these same problems from recurring. First, however, we
will address some foundational issues that, correctly understood and effectively applied, will accelerate your journey within the Inner Ring.

   Problems like Nigel's can be fixed, but there are times when unmet
expectations lead to catastrophic consequences. One of the deadliest commuter train crashes in the history of rail transportation injured 135 people
and left 25 dead. A careful investigation by the National Transportation and
Safety Board (NTSB) pinpointed human error as the likely cause of this
tragic case of unmet expectations. A teenager, who knew the engineer of
the train, eventually told a local television reporter that he had been texting with the engineer at the time of the crash. On camera during an interview, the teenager held up his phone with a text from the engineer dated and
timed just prior to the crash, thus proving that the engineer had not been
paying attention even while he had the lives of his passengers, literally, in his
hands. The continuing NTSB study revealed that there were fifty-seven text
messages sent that day by the engineer while he was driving the train—one
sent only twenty-two seconds before the crash. It was further revealed that,
in the past, this engineer had allowed teenagers to sit at the train's controls
and texted one that very day to make those arrangements. The company
spokesman for the offending commuter railroad company, Metrolink, said
that they would find it "unbelievable" that any engineer would distract himself with texting during the operation of a train. How could the engineer
disregard his training and not follow through with the primary aspect of his
job, keeping the passengers safe? How did that happen? That's the question
most of us ask when people fail to meet expectations.

   Sometimes people fall short of expectations despite their own best efforts.
Rau'Shee Warren, an Olympic contender and world champion flyweight
fighter, believed that he held the lead with only thirty-five seconds left in the
gold medal round. He was so close to achieving his dream, it was as though
he could already feel the medal around his neck. That's when he heard someone yell, "Move! Move!" These words echoed over and over in his ears. The
message was clear: since he held the lead, he would become the champion
if he simply avoided receiving any further blows. While the strategy made
sense for someone in the lead, Rau'Shee was, in reality, trailing his opponent

9–8, and his coaches were screaming from the sidelines to "Attack!" Rau'Shee spent the final moments of the fight following a voice in the crowd, dancing around the South Korean former world champion with his gloves at his waist, avoiding any contact. Ultimately, Rau'Shee, the two-time American boxing Olympian who had trained four years for this moment, lost the fight. It was a stunning defeat. One of his coaches lamented, "I was confused about why he stopped [punching]. He said he heard somebody saying to him to move [and avoid his opponent]. He was looking up in the stands. I don't know what he thought they were saying." After all of that grueling training and effort, how could some down-to-the-last-second confusion obliterate any chance of success? Would anyone question Rau'Shee's tremendous heart and effort? No, but the stunning loss left everyone bewildered and wondering, "How did that happen?" Whatever the answer, Rau'Shee's experience shows that even the most talented performers can fail to meet expectations, sometimes in the most surprising way.

IS TALENT THE ANSWER?

Most organizations devote a lot of time and effort these days to talent management, and rightfully so. Acquiring, retaining, and managing the talent in the organization has become job one for enlightened leaders who have come to realize that their people, above technology, above strategy, above anything else, can make the greatest strategic difference. Jim Collins, in his book *Good to Great*, emphasizes the importance of getting the right people "on the bus." His research leads him to assert, "The right people will do the right things and deliver the best results of which they are capable, regardless of the incentive system. . . . The right people don't need to be tightly managed or fired up; they will be self-motivated by an inner drive to produce the best results and to be part of creating something great." To accomplish this, he suggests, "first get the right people on the bus, the wrong people off the bus, and the right people in the right seats." By so doing, you fill the organization with "disciplined" people who need less motivation and less management, and ultimately produce better results.

Who can argue with these conclusions? But with Collins's claim that only eleven companies out of the entire Fortune 500 meet his "great" criteria, you might well wonder about the 489 "good" or "average" companies that aspire to greatness but seemingly lack a sufficient number of the right people in the right seats on the bus. Where does that leave them? And is the accompanying transition from learning organization to talent organization realistic, achievable, and right? A great company may recruit a lot of highly talented people, but even then it can at times fall short of expectations.

While our own experience convinces us to endorse many of Collins's conclusions, we would argue that no organization is able to acquire all the talent it needs all the time and must therefore find ways to develop their existing people. In our opinion, skillfully managing unmet expectations is a characteristic of any organization that enjoys or aspires to greatness. For most of us, we must do that almost daily, and the way we do it can often make all the difference between success and failure. Getting "the wrong people off the bus" may sound simple, but we all know that's easier said than done. Clearly, the prevailing theories on management reinforce the strategic value, or rather the imperative, to do something about the people who don't meet expectations. *Newsweek* magazine first referred to Jack Welch, much to his chagrin, as "Neutron Jack, the guy who removed the people, but left the buildings standing." Under his direction, GE fired nearly one hundred thousand people due to reasons associated with poor productivity. That's a lot of seats to change on the bus!

Welch promoted the concept of the "Vitality Curve," a performance evaluation process where, among other things, managers routinely identify their bottom 10 percent performers, their middle 70 percent ("the vital 70"), and their top 20 percent achievers. They do this every year, and every year there is a bottom 10 percent. When you grade on a curve, you will always identify a bottom 10 percent, and every year at General Electric these underperformers, who "generally had to go," were counseled out of the organization. Of course, that becomes difficult for managers to do year after year as they develop their teams. Under this system, even when people improve, some team members end up among the bottom 10 percent and must be let go. Imagine the mental gymnastics managers went through as they evaluated reliable team members they had come to depend upon and appreciate, knowing that they had no choice but to rank someone in the bottom 10 percent. The exercise grew so difficult, according to *Newsweek*, that "one business even went to the extreme of putting into the bottom 10 category the name of a man who had died two months before the review." While letting people go is sometimes the only solution, it's not always the easiest, or the best.

Taking the concept a step further, we smiled when we read that Sprint had "fired" their most troublesome thousand cell-phone customers because they complained too much. The *Wall Street Journal* reported that Sprint Nextel sent out letters to their most needy customers stating:

> *"Our records indicate that over the past year, we have received frequent calls from you regarding your billing or other general account information. While we have worked to resolve your issues and questions to the best of our ability, the number of inquiries you have made to us during this time has led us to determine that we are unable to meet your current wireless needs. Therefore, after careful consideration, the decision has been made to terminate your wireless service agreement . . ."*

The company then gave the now ex-customer one month to find a new carrier. Amazing! Your customers don't conform to your expectations? Fire them! The idea that a business can improve performance, and even achieve greatness, by eliminating the nonperformers who may require too much effort to turn around may tempt frustrated and busy managers, but it does not always make sense. Yes, letting people go is sometimes necessary, but doing it properly and lawfully can take a great deal of time and effort. Sometimes it makes much more sense to invest a similar amount of time and energy in helping people become successful and thus render it unnecessary to let them go.

Even the best performers can occasionally underdeliver. Carl Hubbel, Major League Baseball Hall of Fame pitcher, said something about professional sports that eloquently describes the never-ending expectation of performance that exists in business: "A fellow doesn't last long on what he has done. He has to keep on delivering." Since every new quarter brings a heightened expectation, you are only as good as your last game. At some point, even the very best of us will suffer an off day, an off month, or an off quarter.

When expectations go unmet and people fail to deliver, getting a better result will greatly depend on how you go about holding others accountable. At such defining moments, you often feel taken advantage of, let down, surprised, and disappointed. In many cases, the disappointment can carry far-reaching consequences, as it did for Rau'Shee. Hopefully, you have avoided the sort of "train wreck" event where unmet expectations result in catastrophe. Whatever the case, if you find yourself surprised or let down from time to time, take some comfort from the fact that you are not alone.

THE REALITY WINDOW

Before you can effectively tackle the problem of unmet expectations, you need to help people see what the real problem really is, something that is not always easy to do. In *The Oz Principle*, we show that the first step to taking accountability is to "See It." "Seeing It" happens when you muster enough courage "to acknowledge the reality of your own situation, no matter how unpleasant or unfair that reality may seem." When it comes to holding people accountable and managing unmet expectations, accurately diagnosing the problem so that you can do something about it requires a clear sense of reality; it requires you to *see things as they really are*.

But what is reality? Having watched businesspeople wrestle with all sorts of problems over the years, we have boiled it all down to three separate realities: the "Phantom Reality," the "Reality," and the "Desired Reality." Each of these realities plays a role as you seek to gain a correct understanding of the problem behind unmet expectations. Each of these realities offers a different view of the circumstances in which you find yourself. Each one always exists, and you must acknowledge and understand each if you want to see things as they *really* are. We don't think anyone can effectively resolve unmet expectations and apply the Inner Ring without grasping each of these realities.

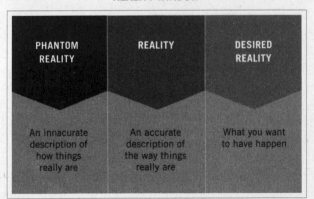

REALITY WINDOW

PHANTOM REALITY	REALITY	DESIRED REALITY
An innacurate description of how things really are	An accurate description of the way things really are	What you want to have happen

Phantom Reality

A Phantom Reality is *an inaccurate description of how things really are*. When you operate under the assumptions of a Phantom Reality, your inaccurate view of "how things really are" can cause you to make the wrong decision, solve the wrong problem, and move in the wrong direction. Phantom Realities frequently lead to wasted time and effort and almost always impede people from achieving the intended result.

Take, for example, the University of Memphis Tigers basketball team. After the Tigers lost the 2008 NCAA Championship game by a score of 75–68, the Associated Press headline read, "Too bad for the Tigers, they lived up to their reputation at the end—a wonderful team that simply couldn't make free throws." This came as no surprise to the fans or the opposing team, but it did seem to have eluded the attention of the Tigers coach, John Calipari. All season long the team had struggled with the fifteen-foot free-throw shot, completing only 59 percent of their attempts, third worst in their division. The AP article reported, "Calipari always laughed at that notion, saying the Tigers would nail them when it counted. Sometimes he got downright mad, as if anyone who would suggest such a thing didn't know much about basketball. Asked again Sunday, Calipari brushed it aside. 'We spend no time thinking about free-throw shooting.'"

Unfortunately, the opposing team, and the eventual NCAA champ, the University of Kansas Jayhawks, did. They intentionally fouled Memphis players during the last minutes of the game because, as one of the top Jayhawks players stated, "All along, people have been talking about how bad a free-throw shooting team they are . . . We just took that and ran with it." One of the top Tigers players expressed disbelief after the game when he said, "I really can't explain why (we missed so many free throws) . . . I mean, when you play basketball, you can't describe things like that. You really can't. I missed them."

Operating under the Phantom Reality that "my team will nail them when they count," the coach saw the NCAA Championship slip through his hands. When you fail to see things as they really are and rely instead on a Phantom Reality, you cannot possibly solve the problems that really do exist. As Mark Twain so aptly put it, "It ain't what you don't know that gets you into trouble. It's what you know for sure that just ain't so."

Everyone operates under the assumptions of Phantom Realities from time to time, even medical doctors, who, most of us assume, always base their conclusions on scientific studies and clinical tests. Illustrating that point, the *British Medical Journal* reported seven medical myths held by many in the medical profession that have gained widespread acceptance among the general public.

1. **Myth:** Reading in dim light ruins your eyesight. **Fact:** Poor lighting makes you squint, but does not negatively affect your ability to see well.
2. **Myth:** You use only 10 percent of your brain. **Fact:** Scientific scans of the brain have never revealed unused areas.
3. **Myth:** You should drink eight glasses of water each day. **Fact:** While you do need a minimum amount of water each day, the food you eat fulfills most of this requirement.
4. **Myth:** Fingernails and hair grow after death. **Fact:** They do not, although the soft tissues shrink after death, giving the impression that they do.
5. **Myth:** Shaved hair grows back faster, darker, and coarser. **Fact:** Shaving does not affect hair growth at all.
6. **Myth:** Eating turkey makes you drowsy. **Fact:** Actually, science proves no such thing, but any large meal (the rule rather than the exception at Thanksgiving) can make you sleepy.
7. **Myth:** Mobile phones pose great danger in hospitals. **Fact:** Recent studies show no interference with medical devices and their use even helps doctors make fewer mistakes.

Small Phantom Realities creep into our lives every day, causing all sorts of problems, but not always major or dangerous ones. However, truly serious ones can and do create big problems in the business world.

Consider the challenges Boeing encountered with their new plane, the 787 Dreamliner, an aircraft built with a carbon-composite substance and titanium materials and designed to carry two hundred to three hundred passengers using 20 percent less fuel than its predecessors on long-range flights. As the sole developer of this $10 billion new design, Boeing faced a six-month or more delay in getting it into operation, a delay that could severely damage the company's bottom line. The *Wall Street Journal* reported that "a look inside the project reveals that the mess stems from one of its main selling points to investors—global outsourcing." Apparently, Boeing outsourced almost 80 percent of the critical parts to suppliers all over the world, mostly to Asia and Europe, hoping that it could eventually "snap" it all together at its Seattle-area factory. "But outsourcing so much responsibility has turned out to be far more difficult than anticipated," the *Journal* went on to say. "The supplier problems ranged from language barriers to snafus that erupted when some contractors themselves outsourced chunks of work. An Italian company struggled for months to gain approval to build a fuselage factory on the site of an ancient olive grove. Boeing overestimated the ability of suppliers to handle tasks that its own designers and engineers know how to do almost intuitively after decades of building jets. Program managers thought they had adequate oversight of suppliers but learned later that the company was in the dark when it came to many under-the-radar details."

Boeing itself reported that, when it came to their suppliers, "We tended to say, 'They know how to run their businesses.'" Maybe so, but clearly that notion helped cause an epidemic of Phantom Realities all the way down to the assembly line. Again, according to the *Journal*, "When mechanics later opened boxes and crates accompanying the fuselage sections, they found them filled with thousands of brackets, clips, wires and other items that already should have been installed. In some cases, officials say, components came with no paperwork at all, or assembly instructions written in Italian, requiring translation."

In Boeing's case, the assumption that it could rely on "business as usual" to complete this massive project was a Phantom Reality that would ultimately result in an extremely long and expensive delay. According to Reuters, due to "underperforming suppliers and parts shortages," airlines would have to wait up to two years or possibly longer for the more than nine hundred 787s they had ordered. On top of that, the outsourcing has led to what may turn into the longest labor strike in the United States since 1948, resulting in a staggering cost of about $100 million a day. Had Boeing recognized a potentially ruinous Phantom Reality early on, the company might have figured out a way to revise its strategy for bringing the Dreamliner to market. At the very least, they would have asked themselves what else they needed to do to ensure crucial supplier deliveries, and, without a doubt, they would have determined what else they could do to maintain essential cash flow for their business.

Despite the frequency with which Phantom Realties occur in your life and your work, they can easily elude detection. Almost a decade ago one of our clients received the Malcolm Baldrige National Quality Award. They still proudly speak of that achievement, and they do so as if it represents their current reality—but that was then, and this is now. If you asked people who work there whether the organization would win the award today, most would say no. Surprisingly, however, they have allowed themselves to buy into a very deceptive Phantom Reality with potentially alarming costs to their business. Clearly, this client would benefit greatly from stepping back and taking a long, hard look at their present reality. From time to time, everyone benefits from asking themselves whether they, their team, or their company are clinging to inaccurate views that may get them in trouble. To help you do that, we recommend a periodic review of the following five clues for spotting a Phantom Reality and for discovering whether you are "under the influence" of one right now.

FIVE CLUES FOR KNOWING WHEN YOU ARE UNDER THE INFLUENCE OF A "PHANTOM REALITY"

Clue No. 1: People repeatedly suggest, imply, or tell you outright that you don't really "get it."

Clue No. 2: You keep getting small glimpses of evidence, which you explain away, that suggest you are not seeing the situation quite right.

Clue No. 3: You make statements about the way things are today based solely on old information and perceptions.

Clue No. 4: You catch yourself checking out mentally when people appear to disagree with you and begin to tell you what they really think.

Clue No. 5: You find yourself looking in vain for someone who will validate your perception of "how things are."

Discovering that you have let yourself fall victim to a Phantom Reality can really surprise you, but that discovery can suspend all of the negative consequences of remaining unaware.

Reality

Unlike the Phantom Reality, Reality accurately describes *the way things really are*. Science fiction writer Philip K. Dick, whose books were made into such popular movies as *Blade Runner* and *Total Recall*, once said, "Reality is that which, when you stop believing in it, doesn't go away." Abraham Lincoln made a similar point when he asked, "How many legs does a dog have if you call the tail a leg?" He responded in classic Lincoln form, "Four. Calling a tail a leg doesn't make it a leg." And so it goes with reality. *Reality is what reality is*. Obviously, knowing the reality of things dramatically increases our ability to solve real problems and get real results. Had Boeing

acknowledged the real difficulties associated with global supplier outsourcing to suppliers, and their likely impact on factory workers at home, they
would have greatly improved their chances of designing the systems and
processes needed to deliver the Dreamliner on time.

Breaking through a Phantom Reality to get to "Reality" requires getting the right information. Everyone, at one time or another, has received
credible information that greatly influenced the perception of how things
really are. But none of us can be sure that we are seeing things as they really
are if we rely solely on our good fortune to receive such information. For
this reason, we suggest you perform a Reality Check by asking yourself
some simple questions aimed at determining whether you are seeing reality or laboring under the influence of a Phantom Reality. These questions
might include: "What am I pretending not to know?" or "Am I ignoring or
discounting the obvious?" or "Have I made a false assumption that may
come back to hurt us later on?"

If appropriate, you can replace "I" with "we," but in either case you
should carefully consider the answers. If you discover a view that suggests
you may have fallen under the influence of a Phantom Reality, but don't
know for sure, then you should continually check your assumptions over
time. Make a list of "Possible Phantom Realities," and use the Reality Check
to keep tabs on any signs that suggest you should alter your view of the situation.

Customizing a Reality Check for your particular business and
unique situation can provide you with a very helpful list of questions to
ask yourself. Invite the people you depend on to help you develop this list.
Make sure you include all the appropriate key links in the Expectations
Chain to help you refine a list of questions everyone can ask each other
about targeted issues you know may arise. Getting everyone in the chain
to remain on the "lookout" for times when a view of the Reality is no longer real can make a crucial difference in the successful fulfillment of key
expectations.

By conducting frequent Reality Checks, you can better evaluate your
current assumptions and head off many problems before they ever happen. Asking these questions from time to time to test the validity of your
assumptions, and getting everyone else to do it as well, will help you recal-
ibrate your activities in order to keep from wasting valuable time, energy,
and resources. As you work with others on the Inner Ring, you may find it
useful for them to conduct their own Reality Checks as they work to fulfill
the expectations you have of them.

Desired Reality

The third view in the Reality Window, Desired Reality, is quite simple. Your Desired Reality embodies *what you want to have happen.* Realizing your Desired Reality depends, of course, on effectively establishing key expectations in the Outer Ring. When any of those expectations go unmet, that's when you move into the Inner Ring. Borrowing from Mark Twain again, "When you don't know where you are going, any road will get you there." Once you know your destination, your Desired Reality, you are better prepared to chart a clear path toward the future and employ the Inner Ring when things go off course.

Looking through the Reality Window is essential when working in the Inner Ring and managing unmet expectations. The Reality Window speeds up the process of identifying problems and then fixing them in order to achieve results.

SOLVING UNMET EXPECTATIONS

We recall a human behavior class we took many years ago, where the professor confidently suggested that you can attribute people's failure to deliver to two simple facts: they were "unwilling" and/or "unable" to do what they were asked to do. This concept has attracted the attention of a number of practitioners in the field of leadership and human performance management, who rely on it extensively, particularly Paul Hersey and Ken Blanchard in their dynamic work with Situational Leadership. The concept suggests a two-part problem with a twofold solution: to manage unmet expectations and get people back on the right track, you must provide more training and/or more motivation.

TRADITIONAL VIEW OF HOW TO SOLVE UNMET EXPECTATIONS	
Able	Willing

Over the past two decades, as we have learned more and more about human performance and the failure to deliver results, we have seen individuals, teams, and whole organizations effectively deal with unmet expectations, turn things around, and obtain record-setting results. As we have worked with our clients to help facilitate these shifts in performance, we have come to see this traditional view of the world (Able/Willing) as incomplete and even harmful, in the sense that it can actually slow down the process of finding solutions.

Our experience while working with thousands of people in the laboratories of hundreds of companies, including some of the largest in the world, has convinced us that you need to consider two additional variables before you can fully understand why people have failed to deliver results. These are the variables of "Accountability" and "Culture." Those two factors have been the focus of our consulting and training practice over the past twenty years. Adding them to the traditional model provides a more complete view of what stands in the way of success: one that enables faster diagnosis of problems and quicker delivery of results.

THE POSITIVE, PRINCIPLED VIEW OF SOLVING UNMET EXPECTATIONS	
Able	Willing
Accountability	Culture

Even the most able and willing people can still fall short of expectations. We have seen this time and again in organizations populated by talented people who are anxious to succeed and want to be a part of an enterprise that makes a difference in the world, but who, for some unknown reason, just do not deliver the results. They were willing and they were able, but they either lacked accountability or were operating in a culture ("the way we do things around here") that hurt their chances of succeeding. Weighing these two additional causes of a shortfall allows you to solve the right problem with the right solution, thus more effectively applying your leadership, accelerating change, and improving performance.

An interesting example of this occurred while we were working on a cabin we own in the mountains. We expected the contractor to finish a certain room with pine tongue-and-groove wall panels, just like all the other rooms in the cabin. It seemed so simple, yet when we stopped by to inspect the work, we discovered that the installers were installing the right material *rough side out*.

Not only would the wall's rough texture expose splinters to the unwary hand, it also did not match the cabin's other interior walls. When we asked the carpenter why he was putting the rough side out, he told us he did it this way on most of the jobs he does. It did not occur to him to make it consistent with every other wall in the house. When the general contractor learned about the problem, he seemed quite surprised and wondered how the carpenter could have made such a mistake. The carpenter was a real pro (Able), he was working long days to get the job done (Willing), and he had done a good job making the joints tight and the surface well-patterned, but it was all wrong!

Closer inspection revealed that the contractor was not following up as much as he should have (accountability) and that the carpenter was making decisions without checking in because he could not reach the contractor (culture). Why did the carpenter feel free to make the decision to put the rough side out? Apparently the subcontractors had learned to cope with lack of access to the contractor by assuming that if they couldn't contact the general contractor, they should just make the decisions themselves and do what they thought would look best. When they routinely passed on that bit of wisdom to any new person on the job, they passed on the working culture of the project and the potential for obvious mistakes, like rough side out. Here, accountability and culture factors explained why expectations were unmet. The cost? Three additional days of the carpenter's time to sand the walls to match the rest of the cabin, along with the time and hassle on our part to deal with the mess the additional sanding created in the rest of the cabin. Understanding the problem led to a better accountability process on the part of the contractor and a change in the culture on the job that got the result we wanted.

THE INNER RING: THE FOUR SOLUTIONS

Adding Accountability and Culture as variables to the equation provides a more complete model for managing unmet expectations. By doing so, you get a complete positive, principled model that identifies all four variables that contribute to someone's failure to deliver on expectations.

These same four variables also provide direction and clarification to those who hold others accountable. These four variables make up the Inner Ring Solutions and are fundamental to the Accountability Conversation. The Accountability Conversation allows you to deal effectively with people who are falling short on expectations, whether they report to you or not.

THE ACCOUNTABILITY CONVERSATION

Unmet expectations. Whether they surprise you because you failed to investigate a situation thoroughly enough, shock you because someone made an unbelievable mistake, or ruin your chances of success despite everyone's best efforts to do a great job, unmet expectations are a fact of life.

The Inner Ring and the Accountability Conversation that lies at its heart provide an effective approach to managing unmet expectations and creating the kind of accountability that produces results.

**THE INNER RING:
MANAGING UNMET EXPECTATIONS**

When you deal with unmet expectations, you can choose one of three courses of action: (1) you can *lower* the expectation to accommodate people who are not delivering; (2) you can replace those people; or (3) you can engage them in the Accountability Conversation with an eye toward helping them produce the results you want throughout the Expectations Chain.

No one happily lowers their expectations, but it happens all the time, usually by default, when you don't know what else to do to improve performance. Lowered expectations may seem like the right decision at the time, at least in the short term and in light of some constraint on resources, but when you lower your sights, everyone usually loses in the long term. That argues for seeking a better course of action.

Does that mean replacing people? It's a hard choice, because doing that bears a significant cost, not just the turnover cost of bringing on new people (estimated by some to be 300 percent of the salary of the replaced person), but the cost of time lost as you bring a new person up to speed. Realistically, there are times when this is the only thing you can do.

The third option involves the Accountability Conversation, which aims to improve the performance of those in the Expectations Chain. It involves three simple steps:

THE ACCOUNTABILITY CONVERSATION

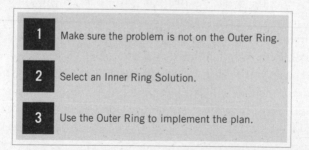

1   Make sure the problem is not on the Outer Ring.

2   Select an Inner Ring Solution.

3   Use the Outer Ring to implement the plan.

Step One: Make sure the problem is not on the Outer Ring. To do this you need to examine your own accountability and determine how well you established the expectation in the first place. You need to determine whether you effectively followed each of the four steps in the Outer Ring: Form, Communicate, Align, and Inspect. Validating your own perceptions by checking in with other people to make sure that you have implemented each of the steps of the Outer Ring correctly will make you feel more confident that you are seeing the reality of the situation. More often than not, you will emerge with a better understanding of what else you can do to improve your skill using the Outer Ring. Simply traveling the Outer Ring with them one more time, just more effectively, may solve the problem. In the case of the contractor and the carpenter, it became clear to the contractor that he had been negligent in effectively implementing each of the steps of the Outer Ring.

Step Two: Select an Inner Ring Solution. This begins by identifying where the problem is on the Inner Ring. Here, you look closely at the person or team to diagnose the exact nature of the problem. You will need to assess whether the difficulty stems from the culture itself or from a lack of training, motivation, or accountability. Then, select and implement the appropriate solution: provide training, inspire motivation, create accountability, or change the culture.

The remaining chapters of this book deal with learning how to determine the true nature of the problem and what to do about it. In the cabin-remodeling example, the culture of the job site and the contractor's lack of accountability for follow-up led to the missed expectations. Pinpointing that problem opened an effective avenue for implementing solutions that got things back on track.

Step Three: Use the Outer Ring to implement the plan. Finally, you use each of the steps of the Outer Ring to establish your expectations around improvement in the most effective way possible. Following through on the plan built with the Accountability Sequence will help you enjoy success, even in circumstances where you had all but given up hope. Knowing how to conduct the conversation that transforms failed effort into renewed success will enable you to deal more completely and effectively with unmet expectations. And that will save you time and money in the long run.

As you engage in the Accountability Conversation, avoid these "conversation killers."

CONVERSATION KILLERS

- Immediately blame the other person for not getting the result you want.
- Put them on the defensive by asking questions intended solely to magnify the mistakes they made.
- Allow your tone to reveal your frustration over what has happened and your current unwillingness to move forward and solve the problem.

- Resist the suggestion that you did not effectively establish the expectation in the first place.
- Threaten them with reminders that you can easily replace them.
- Communicate to them, verbally or nonverbally, that you have lost all faith in their ability to get the result.

Conducting the conversation with the intent of solving the problem and lending your sincere support in helping them succeed will do a lot to energize people, move them forward, and encourage them to make the necessary changes to deliver the result.

ACCOUNTABILITY REALITY CHECK

Revisiting the Reality Window, take a current situation where someone is failing to deliver on a key expectation and use the Reality Window to help you analyze what's going wrong. Identify any Phantom Realities influencing your current actions. Consider whether you could have recognized those Phantom Realities sooner. Think about what you have learned, share your insights with others involved in the situation, and invite their input. Conducting this postmortem will help you more clearly see reality and better solve problems.

WORKING THE INNER RING WITH STYLE

As with all the other steps in the Accountability Sequence, your style will undoubtedly influence how you go about working in the Inner Ring. Those with an inclination toward Coerce & Compel may let their frustration show to make sure people really "get it" and know beyond a shadow of a doubt that you feel disappointed with their results. They are never completely satisfied until they convince themselves that the other person fully appreciates the inconvenience and trouble they caused by not delivering on the expectation. Without a "mutual" understanding of both the problem and the consequences that stem from the other person's failure to deliver, someone with this style is unwilling to move forward. In that case, we advise them to set aside their emotion, relinquish their need to make someone "feel their pain," and focus, instead, on getting to a better place.

On the other hand, those with a Wait & See style often delay dealing directly with unmet expectations. They value maintaining rapport to such an extent that they often avoid confrontation. They tend to do everything they can to minimize the discomfort that might come from holding others accountable. They often find it difficult to achieve a high level of honesty in the conversation and resist telling people what they really think. They need to bear in mind that the level of candor needed in the conversation will not necessarily kill rapport. It may, in fact, strengthen it. In addition, telling people what they really need to hear and doing it in a timely way will help eliminate repeated conversations that make it all the more difficult in the end. We advise people with this style to take a more constructive approach and proactively schedule the Accountability Conversation before things go too far astray.

THE INNER RING

Managing unmet expectations in the Inner Ring can be every bit as important to achieving results as working effectively through the Outer Ring. Everyone deals with unmet expectations on a regular basis. The Accountability Conversation, conducted the positive, principled way, provides a powerful approach to working with difficult circumstances and turning failure into success. Effectively working the Inner Ring means speeding up the process of diagnosing what is wrong and managing the four variables that lead to unmet expectations, the focus of the following chapters.

Chapter Six

THE POSITIVE, PRINCIPLED WAY

As we transition to the Inner Ring, take a moment to review the foundational principles and ideas associated with managing unmet expectations. Keeping them in mind will help you benefit fully from the solutions offered in the following chapters.

The Inner Ring
The second part of the Accountability Sequence Model that helps you diagnose and solve the problem of unmet expectations.

Reacting to Unmet Expectations
Managing your frustration with unmet expectations is critical to the effective application of the Inner Ring Solutions. Avoid the Five Mistakes You Never Want to Make.

The Reality Window
There are three views of reality: Phantom Reality (an inaccurate description of how things really are), Reality (an accurate description of the way things really are), and Desired Reality (what you want to have happen).

Solving Unmet Expectations
Unmet expectations can usually be traced back to one of four variables, which lead to the Four Inner Ring Solutions: Training, Motivation, Accountability, and/or Culture.

The Accountability Conversation
Key to solving unmet expectations in the Inner Ring are the three steps of the conversation: (1) make sure the problem is not on the Outer Ring; (2) select an Inner Ring Solution; and (3) use the Outer Ring to implement the plan.

Chapter Seven

EXAMINE MOTIVATION

WHEN MOTIVATION IS THE SOLUTION

After concluding that unmet expectations have not resulted from your failing to implement all the methods of the Outer Ring effectively, the first step of the Accountability Conversation we presented in the previous chapter, you can turn your attention to finding the right solution on the Inner Ring: Motivation, Training, Accountability, or Culture. While there are times when it may prove difficult to isolate the one variable that has led to the disappointment, in certain cases you may quickly spot lack of motivation as the primary culprit. Take the case of Edith Rodriguez, a patient at Martin Luther King Jr. Harbor Hospital in Los Angeles. For several years, the hospital had been plagued by serious health and safety violations and a continued lack of compliance with federal standards, resulting in the loss of $200 million in federal funds and the eventual closure of the hospital itself. Ms. Rodriguez had been in and out of the emergency room several times in the days preceding her death and each time she received prescriptions for pain-relieving drugs before being released. Then, on her final visit, something went terribly wrong.

On her last visit, county police officers escorted her into the emergency room after they found her lying in pain on a bench in front of the main gates of the hospital. Later, a video surveillance camera showed a nurse, two nursing assistants, and three other hospital workers walking past the clearly visible Edith lying on the floor; she was writhing in pain for forty-five minutes before she died. The video even shows a janitor mopping the floor around the dying woman, who was conspicuously lying on the ground. Apparently, many who saw her (and who had perhaps been present during her earlier visits) assumed she was putting on a desperate act in order to obtain more pain medication to feed a drug addiction. Edith's husband and one other person waiting in the lobby even called 911 to get emergency aid to come and rescue Edith from just outside the hospital's emergency room. That day, Edith died of a perforated bowel, a condition most experts believed to be treatable. How could hospital employees let such a horrible thing happen? Did they lack the motivation to help someone in pain? Had they not received the proper training to deal with the situation? Or did the tragedy result from either too little accountability or a flaw in the hospital's organizational culture? Good question. You might argue that some combination of all four of these factors contributed to this sad case of unmet expectations turned deadly, and you could be right. However, we have learned a good rule of thumb: if you suspect your organization's problem stems from a lack of motivation among workers, that's the first issue you should tackle.

When we talk about a lack of motivation as the driving force behind unmet expectations, we are not suggesting that people are just too lazy to do the job well. Assume for a moment that the people in your Expectations Chain are, in fact, quite industrious. They can and do work hard. So, why don't they do what you expect them to do? The dictionary defines motivation as "the reason or reasons one has for acting or behaving in a particular way." That's what we mean by motivation: giving people a compelling reason to work hard on the cause at hand. When that cause matches their own personal goal they become motivated to do what you need them to do. James Cash Penney, the founder of JCPenney stores (named one of Fortune's "Most Admired" general merchandisers), once said, "Give me a stock clerk with a goal and I'll give you a man who will make history. Give me a man with no goals and I'll give you a stock clerk." When people see a compelling reason to do something, they will work much harder to achieve desired results.

In today's complex work environments, it takes more effort than ever to capture people's hearts and minds, but that effort always pays huge dividends. One of our clients, ranked among the top ten hospitals in the country according to U.S. News and World Report's list of "America's Best Hospitals," was struggling to achieve a seemingly simple goal: obtaining complete next-of-kin information when patients first arrived in the emergency room. "Why," the emergency room doctors wondered, "do we get that information only 42 percent of the time?" "Liz," the manager responsible for that area, told us she felt extremely frustrated with the lack of progress and that it so completely absorbed her attention, she found herself talking about it with her staff all the time.

Even after Liz took everyone through specific training over several months on when and how to collect the right information, she was shocked when the number only rose to 47 percent of the time. She was inspecting what she expected, but that seemed to do very little to solve the problem. Would she need to follow people around, nagging them to do what she asked? She had always thought that they should just do it because it was part of their job. During one of our workshops at the hospital it dawned on Liz that if she were going to see any real progress in collecting next-of-kin information, she needed to get her people to understand the "why" behind the policy. Appreciating the "why" would, she hoped, motivate them to do the job well.

Changing tactics, Liz brought the team together and spoke convincingly about the importance of collecting next-of-kin information. She shared two recent stories, one of which involved a college student who was rushed into the emergency room of another hospital in the system. The ER staff at that hospital failed to obtain her next-of-kin data before she grew unresponsive to treatment and died. After identifying the family and talking with them, they discovered that the student had been taking medication, a fact they could have obtained from a family member had they been able to access next-of-kin information when the patient became unresponsive. That information most likely would have enabled the treating physician to take the necessary steps to save the patient's life. In the second story, the staff of the same hospital did obtain next-of-kin data from an elderly gentleman admitted to the same ER. He also became unresponsive. In this case, however, the doctors were able to speak with his family, learn more about his condition, and take measures that ultimately saved his life.

These life-or-death examples struck a nerve with Liz's team. They always knew that collecting next-of-kin data was important, but these close-to-home experiences captured their attention in a different way. Making it even more personal, Liz asked her team to consider how they would feel if the person who died was their sister or their father. After hearing these two stories and understanding more deeply the "why" behind collecting next-of-kin information, each member of the team committed to get the information, no matter what. In two short weeks, Liz's department went from 47 percent to 92 percent efficiency in collecting the next-of-kin information. More important, they did it without Liz micromanaging and continually harping on them to get it done. The people on her team now connected more personally with the reason behind the expectation: they were motivated. And that motivation provided the solution to lifting her team's commitment to deliver the desired result.

WHEN IT'S ONLY THE HANDS AND FEET

When people lack sufficient motivation and put nothing more than their hands and feet into their work, expectations go unfulfilled, morale dwindles, and results disappear. Take, for example, one of our clients, "TechPro," a product development company with a long history of profitable performance. When we got involved with TechPro, the company had reached a point where its customers needed a more interactive, next-generation product with more user-friendly interfaces. This new platform would require sophisticated programming, a massive overhaul of the manufacturing process, and the very best efforts of the product development team.

A swift transition to the new product was sorely needed to ensure TechPro's competitive position, and this would require a huge initial investment of capital, most of which the company expected to come from customer commitments the sales department would deliver. However, because the sales organization doubted that the product development people could deliver the new platform in a timely fashion, they hesitated selling the existing product to new accounts. They knew that if, by some miracle, the new product did come online soon, any new customers who had bought the old one would feel betrayed. It was a classic Catch-22 and not an easily resolved one, due to long-standing distrust between product development and sales.

While everyone in the organization, including sales itself, knew that sales was only halfheartedly striving to hit their numbers, everything looked okay on the surface. Sales people were going through all the motions, making their daily calls and promoting TechPro products, yet the results suggested that they had not only taken their foot off the accelerator but were gripping the hand brake at the same time. Although they believed in the strategic value of the new product, they had not committed their hearts and minds to making it a reality. Because product development liked to hold its cards close to the vest, most of the information on the progress of the new product came to the sales group by way of the rumor mill. The resultant lack of investment, and the attendant hands-and-feet effort, all but sabotaged the launch of the new product. Once executives recognized the motivation problem, they worked to get everyone in the sales department to understand the importance of their role in driving the new sales needed to fund the product development effort. They also assured sales that the company would work with any customers who wanted to upgrade to the new technology so that customers felt that the company was treating them fairly. That's all the sales organization needed to hear. It didn't take long for results to improve.

Spotting a motivation problem early can help you avoid the potential chain of events that can derail your ability to deliver the results that people expect you to produce. Consider these telltale signs that might indicate a lack of hearts-and-minds commitment in your own organization and throughout your own Expectations Chain.

Telltale Measures of Motivation

"HANDS AND FEET"	"HEARTS AND MINDS"
People are more tactical in the way they work.	People are both strategic and tactical in their approach to the job.
People make sure they complete the task at hand, sometimes even when it does not make sense to do so.	People make sure they get the result, increasing the amount of personal effort to meet the need.
People easily fall into the "tell me what to do" mode.	People don't solely wait for instructions, but show a lot of initiative.
People demonstrate less creativity in solving problems.	People get energized by solving problems creatively.
People typically don't speak up because it's just not worth the effort to them.	People push back if something does not make sense to them.
People define success by the amount of time and effort they expend on the job.	People define success by the results they get.
People are not "into" their jobs and lack fulfillment.	People are engaged in their work and find their jobs highly satisfying.

While you don't need a "hearts and minds" effort from everyone on everything you do, you do need to engender a high level of commitment and investment from everyone in the Expectations Chain when you need people to follow through and deliver on key expectations. Unfortunately, employees in many organizations today often lack the level of motivation necessary to deliver. A *Harvard Business Review* article by John Fleming, Curt Coffman, and James Harter reported a Gallup survey indicating that just 29 percent of employees are energized and committed at work, and that 54 percent are effectively neutral—they show up and do what is expected, but little more. The remaining employees, almost two out of ten, are disengaged. Another job satisfaction survey conducted by TNS, a leading market information company, shows that 25 percent of the American workforce is just "showing up to collect a paycheck," while two of every three workers "do not identify with or feel motivated to drive their employer's business goals and objectives." And a worldwide study by Towers Perrin, a well-known HR consulting firm, found that "just 3 percent of Japanese workers say they're putting their full effort into their jobs," thus proving that accountability is a global issue. Amazingly, many younger workers turn down promotions in order to keep jobs with less responsibility. At the Tokyo Metropolitan Government, where many career-minded professionals gather, "only 14 percent of eligible employees took higher-level exams for management positions in 2007—down from 40 percent three decades ago." Judging from these statistics, which support our own experience, when motivation declines, so do results.

So, just how do you engage people's hearts and minds in a way that motivates them to get great results? The old-fashioned way relied on threats and coercion. In sixteenth-century England, officials applied a doctrine of law called Livery of Seisin (pronounced "season") as the primary method for transferring land from one party to another. This "transfer of possession" occurred as a formal ceremony, during which the parties would gather in public and, as a symbol of the change of ownership, pass a twig, clod of dirt, or key from one party to the other. At a time when most of England could neither read nor write, these public ceremonies helped memorialize this important event. But how would you motivate people to remember it? Officials would take young men, usually potential heirs to the land in question, and dunk them in cold water or whip them so that the experience stayed fresh in their minds. That's not the way we recommend you do it today. When you motivate people to do what you want through compulsion and negative consequences, you may gain their compliance but you will never capture their hearts and minds.

Fred Roberts, who played small forward in the NBA for thirteen seasons, tells a story about one of his teammates who was ordered to run some extra laps by the coaching staff in order to make up for poor performance during practice. The coaches, intent on making the player work hard, shouted, "Run hard," as he circled the gym. The player, who had developed a reputation as something of a "free spirit," responded to the coach, "You can make me run as long as you want, but you can't make me run as hard as you want!" He then began his laps, only to jog around the court at a leisurely pace. Think about it. "You can make me run as long as you want (hands and feet), but you can't make me run as hard as you want (hearts and minds)." This player captured the truth about motivation. When we compel people to do what we want, we just get their hands and feet. When we engage their hearts and minds, we get real motivation that produces real results. Everyone up and down the Expectations Chain has a job to do, but it takes more than stern orders, shouted commands, a whip, or a bucket of cold water to inspire them to do it well, a fact that applies especially to the new, younger workforce.

One effective executive-level leader we know, "Sharon," told us of her experience with a senior analyst with whom she was working on a project. The analyst, "Jane," was young and bright with seemingly great potential. For some reason, however, Jane could not hit deadlines on a project Sharon had assigned to her, one that involved researching and organizing information on the potential of an emerging market for the senior management team. When Sharon asked Jane to make the report a high priority, Jane simply responded, "No, I'm not going to do that report." Astonished at that response, Sharon asked, "Why not?" Jane was adamant. "I know we will not go into that market, so why would I spend my time on that?" Eventually, after Sharon managed to convince Jane about the report's value to senior management, Jane went on to do a good job on it. Recounting the episode, Sharon pointed out that her interaction with Jane typifies, to some extent, what many experienced managers discover when trying to motivate the new generation workforce: "Coerce & Compel" does not work as well as "Persuade & Convince."

Another executive-level client in the retail-grocery business adds this thought about working with the younger generation. Many years ago, when he was still working his way up in the business, everyone took it for granted that an ambitious employee would put in a full day and then would keep working, even on weekends, to get the job done. Nowadays, he told us, younger workers can and do work quite hard, but not in the "old school" way. One of his district managers, whom he was helping solve some work-life balance issues affecting people in a particular store, told him, "We have given them two days off—something we never had coming up—and they tell us they are not too excited about what we've done because we should have been doing it all along. These new, younger generations enter the workforce with different expectations than we had when we were coming up, and we need to learn how to manage them differently, because the new generation will not put up with it. . . . If you tried to manage somebody today with the behavior I put up with coming up in our industry, two things would happen: (1) they'd quit, and (2) they'd file a lawsuit against you."

Since you can't normally *command* high performance, it's important to understand how you can motivate people to *want* to meet your expectations. Baby boomers may have been willing to do it because a boss demanded they do it, but the "Y" Generation wants to know *why* you want them to do it. In a *Fortune* magazine article on the subject of training this generation, Nadira A. Hira states, "The young people they're (i.e., UPS) trying to train aren't just Generation Y, they're Generation Why?—a tribe of disbelievers who've learned to question absolutely everything." Confirming this view, Jordan Kaplan, an associate professor at Long Island University–Brooklyn, New York, said in a *USA Today* article, "Generation Y is much less likely to respond to the traditional Command & Control type of management still popular in much of today's workforce. They've grown up questioning their parents, and now they're questioning their employers. They don't know how to shut up, which is great, but that's aggravating to the fifty-year-old manager who says, 'Do it and do it now.'"

Hira shares the story of Mark Meussner, a former Ford manager who recalled an occasion when he needed to solve a serious, long-standing manufacturing problem and two eager young engineers wanted a crack at it. When Meussner agreed to give them the opportunity, they, along with an experienced mentor, solved the problem so well that the company gained a $25 million increase in revenue. Given their success, management adopted a policy of using junior staff members to attack other issues throughout the company. Meussner concludes, "We need to use 100 percent of an employee—not just their backs and minds, but their innovation, enthusiasm, energy, and fresh perspective." Key expectations often require 100 percent of everyone in the Expectations Chain and you can't expect that level of effort without the right level of motivation. Today, we believe, getting that 100 percent effort depends on showing people how fulfilling key expectations will make a big difference, not just for the organization, but for them personally.

IN SEARCH OF A CAUSE

Our experience over the years has taught us that successfully motivating people hinges on getting them engaged in the cause. When people fully engage in a cause, they make an all-out hearts-and-minds commitment to it. Perhaps you remember Jack LaLanne, the founder of the country's first comprehensive health club and the star of the first televised all-exercise program, *The Jack LaLanne Show*. A review of his life shows that he was all about his "cause." After a failed attempt to find sponsors, Jack created his own line of now-famous instant breakfast nutrition drinks to fund his goal to fashion a health and exercise franchise. Overcoming the initial financial hurdles, Jack eventually developed his business into an empire of more than two hundred health clubs, which he ultimately sold to Bally. Now in his nineties, he continues his efforts with a radio show and commercials for various products, which air all over the globe. Clearly, the motivating power of his cause spread to important stakeholders in his enterprise, such as employees, investors, and customers. When people have a compelling reason to do something, then their ability to overcome difficult obstacles and fulfill expectations can be quite impressive. When that reason becomes a cause, then the resulting motivation almost guarantees achievement of key expectations.

The cause need not involve life-or-death situations. It can be as simple as providing secure and lucrative employment for people. But it's always meaningful. Connecting people with the "cause," whatever it may be, can provide the missing motivation to fulfill unmet expectations. Do you recall the story of the passerby who stopped and asked the two bricklayers, "What are you fellows doing?" One worker muttered in response, "Laying bricks." The other glanced up toward the sky and proudly proclaimed, "Building a cathedral." Which one would you expect to do the better job? We believe that you can get everyone in the Expectations Chain more motivated to do great things, no matter how basic their job, if you can get them to see the "Cathedral" in what they are doing.

The motivating power of such commitment works in all fields of endeavor. In a National Press Club address, Professor Barry Marshall, winner of the Nobel Prize in Physiology or Medicine in 2005, recounted how other scientists dismissed his work and that of co-winner J. Robin Warren. They were, he told the audience, "decried as scientific heretics" and "branded as fakes and frauds by members of our own profession." They won the prize for their breakthrough work on peptic ulcers, which, until they overturned the theory, had been attributed to stress. In fact, many businesspeople still boast of their ulcers as a "badge of success," remedied, as doctors once advised, by avoiding spicy foods, reducing stress and anxiety, gulping lots of antacids, and, in extreme cases, undergoing surgery. Dashing those conventional beliefs, Warren and Marshall discovered evidence as early as 1979 that ulcers arose due to the presence of a strain of bacteria in the stomach. Their colleagues, clinging to the prevailing wisdom that bacteria could not survive in the stomach's "sterile acid bath," dismissed the new theory as hogwash.

Undeterred, the two mavericks worked for years to prove their theory and establish a revolutionary treatment for the condition. Despite the publication of numerous scientific papers marshaling their evidence, they found it almost impossible to secure the funding needed to take their research to the next level. Consumed with what had now become a driving passion, Warren did the unthinkable. One cold winter morning he consumed a dose of the bacteria, a concoction he described as a "vile-tasting brew with an aftertaste not dissimilar to swamp water." A week later, he confirmed that his stomach was "swarming with spiral bacteria." When he treated himself with antibiotics, the infection disappeared within days. Even with those results, the two researchers continued to encounter resistance as most doctors clung fast to prevailing dogmas. Marshall concluded that "it was not until 1994—twelve years after Robin and I first made the connection between *H. pylori* and ulcers—that the powerful National Institutes of Health accepted the bacterial causation of ulcers and stipulated that infected ulcer sufferers should be treated with antibiotics." Motivation, dedication, passion, and commitment eventually triumphed over all odds. As Marshall told his audience, "Although I admit to being frustrated during the more than a decade it took the medical community to finally accept our work, I was never really dispirited in my heart because I knew that what I was doing was right and that our work would ultimately be accepted." Once again, one man's belief in a cause propelled him forward, and, despite initial opposition, eventually spread throughout the medical community.

When you can get the people you depend on enrolled in achieving a cause, just like LaLanne and the Nobel Prize winners, then you will see the same type of motivation, energy, and effort throughout the entire Expectations Chain solving their problems and achieving results.

Never underestimate the power of such a deep-seated belief in the value of your work. While working in Singapore with 150 senior leaders from six different Asian countries with Baxter Health Care's Asia Pacific division, one of the workshop attendees rightly observed, "People will work for money. They will work harder for good leaders. But ultimately they will work hardest for a cause. We have been robbing our team of the cause." In the most frequently requested article from the *Harvard Business Review*, "One More Time, How Do You Motivate Employees?" Frederick Hertzberg talks about motivating factors that lead to satisfaction, such as the work itself and a sense of achievement, as well as the factors that lead to dissatisfaction, such as pay and benefits. While Hertzberg concludes that money alone does not serve as a strong motivator, he acknowledges that money does play a role. What does Hertzberg say to people who say money doesn't motivate them? "When they tell me that money doesn't motivate, I double my fees." Proving his point that money plays a role, Hertzberg states an important truth: "money alone cannot truly capture people's hearts and minds. Rob people of satisfaction and meaning in their work and no amount of money will motivate them to do a great job."

What produces meaningful motivation in others? Our work on hundreds of successful client projects has convinced us that nothing you do will truly inspire people if they do not enroll in a cause—a cause that they can wholeheartedly embrace. Ultimately, the great motivator is a cause that makes people feel as though they can make a difference if they accomplish it.

One of our clients, "GBD Diagnostics," produced a product that required the use of extremely expensive small Pyrex glass beads. Unfortunately, during the manufacturing process close to 30 percent of the glass beads ended up as scrap. "Sandy," a lead-manufacturing technician involved with the manufacturing process, began to question why GBD could not reprocess and use the rejected beads. Each time she raised the subject, however, she met with the same resistance. While working to contain an unrelated problem with the product, the tech team had determined that the beads should not be reused, an opinion management had sanctioned as a final decision. Had Sandy been working with only her hands and feet, she would have accepted that fact and moved on to other issues.

After a brief promotion away from that part of the manufacturing facility, Sandy soon won yet another promotion that brought her back to the area as the operations manager. In that role, she quickly set her sights on figuring out a way to reuse the rejected beads and thereby save the company what she expected to be a good deal of money. She immediately established a team and created a project charter. Again she encountered strong resistance, this time from her group's cross-functional team partners—quality engineering, compliance, and product support—who vehemently opposed reusing the beads. The opposition based its position, not on direct empirical evidence of product performance, but on a historical belief that had been well tested and handed down over the years.

Without the support of the cross-functional team members, Sandy's new project would go nowhere. Meetings convened to study the matter were candid and even grew heated at times, but Sandy could not persuade the group to approve moving forward on the project. She learned that you can never underestimate the power of a belief in the status quo, even when facts no longer support that belief. However, that lesson only motivated Sandy and her group to press forward. After running the glass beads through their own testing process, they determined that the reprocessed beads could not only be used in the manufacturing process but that those beads actually produced better results than the original beads. Not only would recycling the beads save the company money, it would improve product quality.

Then something unexpected happened. In an unrelated development, GBD's customers began to complain about major problems with the existing product. If GBD did not resolve the issues quickly, they stood to lose several large customers. An emergency deployment of the higher-quality reprocessed beads not only helped fix the problem, it also improved the overall diagnostic ability of the product. GBD immediately informed its worried customers about this development, which put an end to a possible calamity. Ultimately, the inspired work of Sandy's team reduced product costs by at least $1.1 million a year, helped GBD retain many key customers, and improved the overall quality of the product. Once again, hearts and minds won the day.

Consciously and deliberately enrolling people in the cause can greatly influence people's motivation to rise up and meet expectations. To determine if you should take some extra steps to help everyone in your Expectations Chain enroll in the cause, answer True or False to the following questions. Base your answers on one of your current key expectations and the people in the Expectations Chain associated with that expectation.

HOW STRONG IS YOUR CAUSE?

Answer True or False to each statement below.

_____ 1. I hear people describing the cause to others and repeating it frequently.

_____ 2. I find myself regularly talking about the cause in compelling ways.

_____ 3. I feel personally committed to the cause and feel that my own heart and mind are fully invested.

_____ 4. I can see evidence that people are aligned with our direction and are actively engaged in making it a reality.

_____ 5. I find that people are so passionate about our cause that they express their opinions openly and frequently if they think we are getting off course.

_____ 6. From time to time, I am amazed at the effort people make and the resourcefulness they demonstrate in making sure we are on track to get the result.

_____ 7. I see a number of the positive signs of the Telltale Measures of Motivation (see page 148) in people throughout the Expectations Chain.

If you answered True to most or all of these statements, then it's likely that most of your people are highly invested in your cause. If you answered False to a few of them, you should probably do more to capture the hearts and minds of people in your Expectations Chain.

CAPTURING THE HEART AND MIND

What more can you do? First, you can master these four simple steps: Define It, Sell It, Advocate It, and Celebrate It.

By "Define It," we mean crafting a compelling story that captures people's imaginations and inspires them to achieve the objective. When you express the cause in the form of a story, you make it real and tangible. People can see it in their mind's eye and more easily remember *why* it deserves an all-out effort on their part. A good story will be retold over

ENROLLING OTHERS IN THE "CAUSE"

DEFINE IT	State the cause in the form of a story with a plot, the setting and the characters.
SELL IT	Become a good storyteller who persuades and convinces people in the Expectations Chain to buy in to the cause. Always address the pertinent Why Questions.
RE-SELL IT	Continue to support the cause publicly by reinforcing the story with additional supporting evidence and telling and re-telling the story over time.
CELEBRATE IT	Acknowledge progress and success in a public way, not only the ultimate success of achieving the goal, but important milestones along the way.

and over because people find it compelling. Ed and Steve Sobel, creators of NFL films, said it beautifully: "Tell me a fact, and I'll remember. Tell me the truth, and I'll believe. But tell me a story, and I'll hold it in my heart forever." A compelling story creates context and gives people a vehicle they can use to readily pass the information on to others in a powerful and persuasive way. Everyone loves a good story. If you want people to pay attention to your cause, tell them a story they won't soon forget.

Every good story contains certain essential elements: the plot, the setting, and the characters. The plot lays out a sequence of events, from beginning to end, during which the characters deal with a pressing issue or conflict. At some critical point, the climax, they confront the issue head-on and resolve it, one way or another. The setting establishes the context for the story by placing it in time (the future, the past, or the present) and in a place. The characters involve all the people, major and minor, who get swept into the unfolding events and always include a protagonist and an antagonist. In the story of *The Wizard of Oz,* the plot entails a journey of self-discovery by the protagonists (Dorothy and her companions) to a realization that through their own resourcefulness, and with some benevolent help along the way, they can solve their own problems. The issue for Dorothy revolves around getting home, for the others, obtaining a heart, a brain, and courage. The Wicked Witch is the antagonist and the climax arrives the moment the protagonists realize that they always possessed the power within themselves to solve their problems. This story has become so deeply ingrained in the cultural consciousness throughout the world that we employed it in our first book, *The Oz Principle,* to capture our readers' hearts and minds.

In our second book, *Journey to the Emerald City,* we described how one of our client organizations, ALARIS Medical Systems, led by Dave Schlotterbeck and his former executive team, crafted a compelling story that helped their people achieve incredible success. It went something like this: We, as an organization (the characters), have a unique opportunity to save lives and make our company more profitable by shifting our strategy over the next twelve months. Our strategy (the plot) will shift from making pump infusion equipment to partnering with hospitals to ensure the safety of their patients by adapting our current technology in a way that will give hospitals an integrated system for monitoring patient status and administering the correct dosage of medications. If we don't make this shift and simply continue to focus on our current product offering, current market conditions and our two largest competitors (the antagonist) could ensure that we become obsolete as a company and fall prey to a hostile takeover, threatening jobs and our own company mission (the setting). On the other hand, if we act now and successfully make the necessary short-term sacrifices (the climax), we will advance patient safety and all but eliminate fatal human mistakes, save thousands of lives every year, create a huge competitive advantage in the marketplace, provide even more job opportunities, and amass unprecedented profits.

The story began with a weak status quo and ended in a strong future, it required the efforts of a large cast of characters, and it made the undertaking a matter of more than merely making money. By embracing it, ALARIS's people made a difference, not just in their company and their own lives, but also in the lives of every patient lying in a hospital bed. Schlotterbeck's story became "the" story when the organization actually made it come true, winning big by almost every measure and eventually scoring one of the largest equity investment gains in their sector in Wall Street history.

Remember those "connect the dots" activity books you enjoyed as a child? As you connected all the numbered dots on a page, you would see a picture slowly emerge, until what initially looked like nothing but a random arrangement of specks magically became something you easily recognized. A well-crafted story works the same way. You "connect the dots" for people (all of the facts, points, evidences, and positions) in a way that allows a clear and compelling picture to appear, one that motivates people to enroll in the cause.

By "Sell It," we mean becoming a storyteller with the objective of persuading people to buy into the cause. To succeed at that you must harness the power of ideas, and not employ the power of position, to captivate people's imaginations. You cannot motivate by "edict" to enlist people in the cause, but you can persuade and convince people to move in the right direction. Dave Schlotterbeck and his team at ALARIS did it by engaging in an ongoing conversation with the organization through a series of "town hall" meetings with everyone involved in the Expectations Chain. They connected the dots and repeated that effort on a regular basis. The story emerged. People bought into it. By creating a compelling picture with all the elements of a good story, they managed to create a Culture of Accountability that made everyone feel like they were the main characters in a gripping story. Could they thwart the antagonist (aggressive competition) breathing down their necks and save the day? Yes, they could! As the Culture of Accountability took hold, everyone in the company, from the assembly line on up, told and retold the story, not only within ALARIS but also to family and friends outside of the organization. In fact, it was not uncommon to run into someone at a soccer game or other community event and hear them talking about what was happening at ALARIS.

Selling it means answering the "why" questions. Whatever your own cause, you need to address the "whys" behind the task in a way that speaks to your particular audience. In our business we have a saying: "No need, no sale!" If you cannot convince people that what you are asking them to do satisfies their own personal or business needs, then don't expect them to do it. It's that simple. As you craft your story, be sure to address the "need" with questions like these:

THE WHY QUESTIONS

1. Why is it important?
2. Why me (and not someone else)?
3. Why now?
4. Why do it this way?
5. Why would I want to do this?

One executive we worked with answered these sorts of questions in a way that brought about an amazing transformation in his organization. Faced with the prospect of closing a hundred-year-old plant because of production problems, union conflicts, and changing consumer preferences in the market-place, "Jeff" knew he must quickly make some dramatic changes. To engage the hearts and minds of his leadership team and enroll them in the cause he expected them to undertake, he gathered his key people for a meeting in a quiet getaway in the Smoky Mountains, where he spent a couple of days lay-ing out the rationale behind the new strategy. While they had discussed all the pieces of the new direction beforehand, Jeff was now ready to tell the story in a way that would enroll his team.

He addressed each of the "why" questions by making sure each team member knew why their role was critical to the mission's success, and why all of the company's stakeholders would win if everyone executed their roles well. As all the dots began to connect, a clear case for change emerged. Then, "eyeball to eyeball," as the team now recalls, Jeff went around the room, ask-ing each individual, one by one, if he or she was "in." He gave all the people on his team an option to step aside if they did not feel they could sign up, but he made it clear that he hoped they would join the cause. It was a dramatic moment, one that his people still recount. The climax? Jeff's leadership, the way he crafted his story and sold it to his people, and the amazing results the team obtained by eventually resolving the union conflicts transformed the organization into one of the most productive plants in the company.

By "Advocate It" we mean continuing to support the cause publicly, reinforcing the story with additional supporting evidence, and telling and retelling the story over time. Your continued efforts to keep the cause in front of people so that they don't forget it figures critically into your ongo-ing hearts-and-minds effort, particularly when the going gets tough or the fulfillment of the expectation seems in jeopardy.

The president of a state college we had taken on as a client was wrestling with the challenge of years of declining enrollment. Since the school's bud-get depended on enrollment, she faced the unpleasant prospect of discon-tinuing some offerings to students and reducing staff and faculty. Worse, if the declines dropped to a certain point, the state might close the school altogether. With all of this in mind, the president presented her story to the school's governing board and called the cabinet. She announced that they would increase enrollment by 2 percent for the year and proceeded to tell the cabinet why that would happen. At first, the skeptical cabinet greeted her remarks with audible laughter, but the more they listened to her persuasive argument, the more they believed that it not only could, but *must*, happen.

Everywhere the crusading president went, she would tell the story. The cabinet followed suit. The enthusiasm for achieving this expectation began to spread throughout the entire organization. Members of the college community, all the people "down-line" in the Expectations Chain, began to see how utilizing new programs, re-invigorating traditional programs, and considering new avenues of recruitment could boost the enrollment figures. With the continued advocacy, more and more people who could make a difference in one way or another enrolled in the cause. With the college staff and faculty motivated by the new ideas, student enrollment increased for the year by an astounding 4.2 percent.

The next step to enrolling people in your cause is to "Celebrate It." By this, we mean publicly acknowledging success. You should not only praise people for achieving the ultimate goal, but you should also reinforce all the progress made along the way. One job satisfaction survey in the military put jet fighter pilots at the bottom of the list and cooks at the top. That may strike you as upside-down, but, apparently, the fighter pilots received positive reinforcement rarely, only on those few occasions when they got a chance to do what they were trained to do, while the cooks heard immediate positive feedback on their performance three times a day. Nothing energizes people and keeps them enrolled in the cause more than a celebration of their accomplishments.

The U.S. Army knows how to do it. While we were writing this book, we received a letter from Daniel Thompson, of the U.S. Army's 325th Combat Support Hospital. In his letter, Daniel recounted his experience using ideas we had taught him to enlist his unit in a "life or death" cause. With a deployment in Tikrit, Iraq, Daniel was the officer in charge of the emergency department, which consisted of fourteen combat medics and six registered nurses. When his team arrived in theater, Daniel recognized that they needed to change the team process for taking care of trauma patients. As he wrote in his letter, "This went over like a lead balloon initially, because it gave the appearance of taking care away from the medics and giving it to some of the nurses. The previous unit had a medic dominant system that, in my opinion, set my relatively inexperienced medics up for failure." To address this, Daniel assigned the nurses to perform the primary and secondary assessments, with the physician serving as team leader. "This was uncomfortable for some of my Registered Nurses because it put a lot more responsibility in their hands. Historically, physicians would perform this function; however, in this environment the physicians were often less experienced in trauma care than were the nurses."

As Daniel thoroughly trained his staff in the new system, telling and retelling his story about providing better care for wounded soldiers, he decided to lead by example and take the first few patients himself. He knew he was taking a big personal risk with the as yet unproven approach. However, that simple act clearly demonstrated to everyone his belief in this new approach and his story about better care. As the new approach proved its value, one case at a time, Daniel made sure they celebrated each success. In due course, he wrote, "The doubters started to come around." Celebrating the little successes while modeling the new process helped others see that it really was the way to go. The light came on for the whole team, and, from that point on, they all embraced and advocated the new approach, often with stories of their own.

The results were gratifying. Daniel's unit won recognition throughout the theater as a polished "pit crew" that saved lives. Team members invested their hearts and minds and passionately looked for other ways to improve the process. They brought ideas to Daniel, 90 percent of which were implemented. In recognition of his work to make his unit the highest-performing team at the hospital, Daniel was awarded the Bronze Star. More important than that honor, Daniel notes, "Many lives were saved because of our ability to adapt to change and maintain a focus on constant improvement." And the celebrations did not stop there. When the army ultimately introduced many of the processes developed by his team throughout the theater, hundreds of wounded soldiers received the best care the army could provide.

KEEPING THE CAUSE ALIVE

You will need to work continually at keeping the cause alive by Selling It to newcomers, Advocating It with those already enrolled, and Celebrating It with everyone involved. Be sure to take advantage of all the genuine opportunities to celebrate progress and achievement. We don't suggest that you turn every little step forward into an excuse for a lavish party, but we do recommend that you frequently deliver praise when people take important steps forward. Failing to do so can dampen almost anyone's motivation and morale. Silence is a Cause Killer.

In your effort to harness the motivational power of your cause, you should beware of all the potential Cause Killers lurking out there. Any of them can put a dead stop to your efforts to engage the hearts and minds of people throughout the Expectations Chain.

CAUSE KILLERS

1. You stop promoting the cause and telling the story as you question your own level of support.
2. You act out of sync or in contradiction to the cause you are promoting.
3. You don't celebrate the successes along the way, sending the message that the focus is not really as important as you said it was.
4. You enroll people in the cause, but you expect them to just do what you tell them to do, without encouraging their input, involvement, or creativity in moving forward.
5. You let other causes dilute their effort around what is most important.
6. You don't give people the opportunity to dialogue with you and ask the questions and receive the answers that would help them become fully engaged.
7. You ignore a growing perception that people are concerned that they are not hearing the whole truth and are feeling manipulated in some way.

Any of these Cause Killers will reverse your efforts to engage the hearts and minds of people throughout the Expectations Chain in accomplishing your key expectations.

Please keep in mind that when it comes to engaging people, there is a huge difference between motivation and manipulation. No one likes to feel manipulated, but everyone loves the energy and exhilaration that comes with true motivation. Manipulators try to get people on board through deception or force, and while that may initially get people moving in the right direction, it will not retain their enthusiastic support over the long run. Motivators, on the other hand, rely on persuasion to convince others to dedicate their hearts and minds to the undertaking. They speak from their own hearts in a sincere, genuine, and honest way; their stories always ring true. Every effort to enroll people in the cause and to motivate them to fulfill unmet expectations requires a sincere, genuine, and truthful effort without the hint of manipulation in any form. People pick up on the subtle facial expressions and body language that signal someone's attempt to manipulate them. A false smile or overly emphatic fist pumping can reveal insincerity or a lack of complete honesty.

ACCOUNTABILITY REALITY CHECK

To put these concepts into practice, consider someone in the Expectations Chain on whom you are counting to do a great job but who, at the moment, seems to be letting you down because of an apparent lack of motivation. Create on paper the story you think will capture that person's heart and mind. Consult the guidelines for enrolling people in the cause by defining the cause, selling it, advocating it, and celebrating progress toward achieving it. Remember that you need to craft the story with the necessary plot, characters, setting, and climax. It need not involve something as dramatic as saving lives, but every business, even the most mundane, needs a compelling cause for its people to do great things. Remember to continue to advocate the cause as you work to develop the necessary motivation for people to invest themselves in getting the job done. You may even consider telling the story all the way through the Expectations Chain.

MOTIVATING WITH STYLE

As with all the steps in the Accountability Sequence, your style will affect how you approach enrolling people in the cause. For those with Coerce & Compel tendencies, exercise caution to avoid actual or perceived manipulation. Check your penchant for using position power as a tool for getting people to do what you expect them to do. Remember, whenever people feel forced, they will also feel manipulated. Take the time to put together a persuasive argument and story that will convince people to sign up and invest in the cause. Avoid any words and actions they might interpret as an insincere attempt to get them on board.

If you tend to practice the Wait & See style, you should also avoid creating a perception of manipulation, but for quite different reasons. You may make the mistake of selling too hard, trying to convince someone with an avalanche of facts, some not entirely valid, and conclusions strongly skewed to match your own point of view. This lack of objectivity and the propensity to persuade may cause people to feel later on that you have taken advantage of them by promoting an exaggerated or not fully accurate story. You don't want people thinking that you merely talked them into doing it. Rather than employing the power of your personality, make a sincere effort to help others understand the ramifications of moving forward, letting the sheer force of the correctness of the idea do the convincing.

MOTIVATION DRIVES TRAINING

When you discover that the solution is motivation, you can set about conveying a compelling cause that people can get behind, one they can embrace, one they believe will make a real difference. Again, it's not about people being lazy, although that may occur from time to time. Rather, it's about people needing something they can believe in, something worthy of an investment of their hearts and minds. Learning how to tell the story that connects the dots for people enrolls them in the cause and helps to secure the kind of commitment that will motivate people to overcome obstacles and find creative solutions. That's the level of skill that comes with a well-trained and knowledgeable group of people throughout the Expectations Chain, the objective of the next solution on the Inner Ring.

Chapter Seven

THE POSITIVE, PRINCIPLED WAY

A review of this chapter's highlights will help you engage the people in your Expectations Chain and capture their hearts and minds to resolve unmet expectations.

Hands and Feet versus Hearts and Minds
You can easily get people moving (hands and feet), but it's not so easy to get them fully invested in a cause (hearts and minds). Key expectations usually require both hands and feet and the hearts and minds to get the result.

Enroll People in a Cause
Take four simple steps to enroll people in your cause. First, "Define It" by crafting the story; second, "Sell It" by becoming a storyteller and addressing the "why" questions; third, "Advocate It" by continuing your public support of the cause; and fourth, "Celebrate It" by acknowledging success in a public way.

• Define It
State the cause in the form of a story with a plot (including the issue or conflict and the climax), the setting (with time and place), and the characters (the protagonist and antagonist).

• Sell It
Become a storyteller with the objective of persuading and convincing people in the Expectations Chain to "buy in" to the cause. Be sure to address the "why" questions.

• Advocate It
Continue to publicly support the cause by reinforcing the story with additional supporting evidence, and telling and retelling the story over time.

• *Celebrate It*
Acknowledge success in a public way, not only the ultimate success of achieving the goal, but also milestones along the way.

The Why Questions
When telling the story, make sure you address each of the critical "why" questions tailored to your specific audience.

Chapter Eight

EVALUATE TRAINING

WHEN TRAINING IS THE SOLUTION

Having explored motivation as a way to solve unmet expectations, we will now examine the second of the Inner Ring's four solutions: targeted training. If you suspect that people are failing to meet expectations because of a deficiency in training, then, ideally, you will want to provide training that not only addresses the current problem, but also increases the capability of everyone in the Expectations Chain to deliver over the long term. In our work with Valassis, we encountered a great example of the impact targeted training can have on people's ability to deliver on expectations.

Valassis, upon acquiring ADVO Inc., the nation's largest direct-mail marketing company, went from $1.1 billion to $2.3 billion in total revenue, making them one of the nation's leading media and marketing services companies. The operating approaches of the two companies differed greatly. Valassis practiced a quick get-it-done approach, while ADVO took a more deliberate approach, operating "by the book," thoroughly planning and seeking full consensus before taking action. ADVO had built a reputation as a first-class outfit and ranked number one in its industry. John Lieblang, Valassis's chief information officer, ended up wrestling with the challenge not only of combining two disparate IT departments, but of solving some serious cultural, organizational, and technological challenges facing his group. Every department in the company needed to combine with its sister department to form one smoothly functioning unit as quickly as possible. Since the success of the company depended on the combined IT departments running smoothly, Al Schultz, the CEO, insisted that the integration happen with speed. John understood the CEO's expectation.

As John contemplated the challenge, he took solace from the fact that he had assembled a highly motivated IT team that could solve exactly this sort of problem. They took getting results seriously and shouldered accountability for on-time, on-budget delivery, doing every job well and for pleasing their customers. Far from intimidating them, the merger had pumped new life into everyone and had ignited a sense of urgency and purpose for every project. John just had to figure out what he needed to do to cascade accountability to all IT associates throughout the organization and combine the two departments quickly and efficiently. We will never forget what John said to us as he reflected back on this whole experience. "I knew when I was hired that I had three options. Option one was to do nothing and eventually get fired. Option two was to do something bold and dramatic to change things, have that fail, and then get fired. Option three was to do something bold and dramatic to change things, have that succeed, and prove the IT group were leaders."

John preferred option three, but he recognized that to make that happen his team needed common skills and methods for quickly aligning and integrating these departments. That's when he brought us to Valassis to train the IT team in the use of specific models and tools that would help the team take ownership for creating a newly integrated department in line with CEO Al Schultz's expectations. As the training commenced, John introduced the desired results, completely avoiding the subject of "merging the departments." Instead, he defined and communicated four key business results that the united IT department needed to achieve: (1) reduce IT spending (which would free up cash and improve profit); (2) improve investment return (by making sure that every investment had a clearly defined detailed financial return); (3) enhance associate careers (foster retention and advancement opportunities); and (4) reduce cycle time (implement solutions faster).

He then quantified the expected results for each of these four categories and insisted that every leader of each group attend the planned training. As the training progressed, John led the team through an alignment discussion that united the team around the key results. The training then focused on helping the team create ownership and accountability for each of the key results throughout the IT organization. Again, they did not focus on merging the organizations, but on what actions they could take to achieve the four business results.

The outcome: by the end of the fiscal year, IT was the first department in the entire company that had successfully integrated two departments into one. While taking the best practices from the markedly different worlds of Valassis and ADVO, the associates in IT were able to combine their operations in a staggering short four months, improve service levels, and deliver high-quality new development projects on-time and on-budget. Most important, John had used the right training at the right time to energize his team and deliver the key results the CEO expected, making IT the top-performing group in the company.

The Valassis example shows how training and, in this case, training that focuses on defining and communicating the key results you expect people to deliver, can dramatically improve the ability of people to meet expectations. When another client, Coffee Bean and Tea Leaf (the specialty coffee and tea industry's second-largest company in the United States), assembled their senior team for training on this very topic, only two of the top twenty senior managers could write down the top three key results the company needed to achieve in the coming year. Just ninety days after the initial training, however, this time with the company's top 275 general managers assembled, a follow-up exercise revealed that every one of these general managers could accurately state those top results. Even more impressive, but not at all surprisingly, over the next year all of their key leading performance indicators improved, turnover dropped dramatically, and the level of quality soared by almost 100 percent.

While all organizations should make it a priority to help their people increase their capability to fulfill expectations, few do it as well as they should. A study by the global management consulting company, Accenture, revealed that the leaders of two-thirds of the companies surveyed felt that the vast majority of their employees do not "have the skills necessary to execute their jobs at an industry-leading level." Another study of U.S. and European workers reported by the American Society for Training & Development (ASTD) found that "74 percent of workers, on average, have been asked to do tasks for which they feel they are insufficiently trained." So what does this all mean? It means expectations often go unmet as a result of too little training. What can you do about it? Implement the right training at the right time throughout the Expectations Chain.

As we pointed out in the last chapter, simply relying on finding the right talent as the solution to developing organization capability, while clearly a desirable goal, is at best unrealistic. Resource constraints, changes in technology, evolving organizational cultures, and finite and limited talent in the job candidate pool all make assembling the right "talent" and the right *amount* of talent not only challenging but virtually impossible, as evidenced by the skill deficiencies cited in the studies by Accenture and ASTD. We agree with Marcus Buckingham and Curt Coffman, who argue in *First Break All the Rules: What the World's Greatest Managers Do Differently*, that "the right talents, more than experience, more than brainpower and more than willpower alone, are the prerequisites for excellence in all roles." Buckingham and Coffman also proclaim that unlike knowledge and skills, you cannot teach talent. We agree. Most organizations struggle to recruit and retain the right amount of talent. Even if they succeed in doing so, they still must equip that talent with the direction and development required for focusing their efforts in a way that produces desired results. Whether you have recruited the right talent or not, you should make developing capability and skill throughout your Expectations Chain a top priority.

Our experience in the training and consulting industry over the last two decades has convinced us that providing people with the right training at the right time can quickly improve results and mark the difference between success and failure. We have witnessed this time and again for ourselves, and we have watched as countless organizations have infused their own Expectations Chains with targeted training that has turned around performance and reversed downward trends. Once you identify training as a primary cause of unmet expectations, you can focus the Accountability Conversation to provide the right solution for the right problem.

GETTING CONSCIOUS, STAYING CONSCIOUS

It's not always easy to pinpoint training as the solution to the problem, because it requires a high level of awareness about what you really need to improve. For good and bad, people tend to fall into comfortable habits and routines of which they are barely conscious. To address that issue, we use the Phases of Competency Model, which we based on sound behavioral science. We use this model to shed light on the various levels of awareness and ability people experience as they move from "Novice" to "Master" when involved in learning something new. The model also offers important insights for teachers into the level of awareness they personally need as they play the role of coach and trainer.

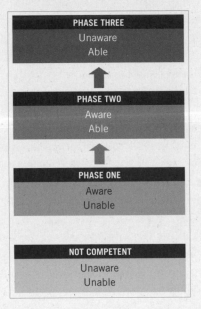

PHASES OF COMPETENCY

Let's see how this works by applying the model to a child learning to ride a bicycle, something almost all of us have experienced. At her first lesson, she stands there propping up the shiny new bike. She's excited to learn how to do it, but she also feels a little bewildered and confused. She's seen others ride a bike but feels a bit uneasy as she contemplates how to coordinate all the skills (balancing, pedaling, steering, and braking) required to glide smoothly down the street. At this point, she is *unaware* of all she needs to know to do this on her own, and she's *unable* to put it all together at one time. Frankly, she is just not competent enough to complete the task.

Given some training in the form of explanation and demonstration, the would-be bike rider advances to a new level of understanding. She becomes aware of everything she has yet to learn; at least she knows what she can't yet do. She reaches the first stage of competence, *aware*, but still *unable*. With a little practice (okay, a *lot* of practice) she eventually puts it all together and makes it work. Balancing herself on her bike, though wobbly, and steering around road hazards, though not smoothly, she gets the job done. With practice, she gets pretty good at it. However, putting it all together still requires great concentration, with any distractions usually resulting, at least early on, in a loss of balance and a skinned knee or elbow. In time, she grows *aware and able*, the second stage in the competency model.

With more time and practice, she becomes something of an expert rider. In fact, she can now pedal safely around the neighborhood and even perform little tricks, such as gliding slowly without holding on to the handlebars. "Wow," exclaims her riding coach, "you're a real pro now!" At this stage she rides the bike without thinking about balancing, steering, and pedaling. Distractions no longer confuse her or cause her to lose her balance. Finally, she is once again *unaware*, though in a different way, not needing to think about what she is doing, and she is certainly *able*, the final stage of competency.

Phases Two and Three reflect high levels of competency because people at those stages can do what they need to do. Interestingly, Phases One and Two both offer great opportunities to train others. While the *aware and able* phase might strike you as the ideal platform for coaching, you don't want to dismiss Phase One. When it comes to training others, *aware* sometimes matters more than *able*. There's some truth to the old maxim, "Those who can, do; those who can't, teach." Just consider all the great coaches in sports who did not excel on the field themselves. Notable in this regard is John Madden, who gained a place in the Pro Football Hall of Fame for his coaching accomplishments with the Oakland Raiders, not for his performance as a player. Drafted in the 21st round to the NFL (244th overall), Madden found himself permanently sidelined with a knee injury suffered during training camp. Vince Lombardi played football in college but never played in the NFL. Yet he went on to become a coaching legend.

In Phase Three, you achieve such a high level of proficiency that the behavior becomes so ingrained you do what you need to do without giving it much thought. You operate on "autopilot" (ability without conscious thought). When was the last time you consciously thought about tying your shoelaces or peeling an orange or even driving your car? However, when conditions change suddenly, an immediate drop all the way back down to *not competent* commonly occurs. Imagine, for example, that you are cruising down the highway at sixty-five miles per hour, engaged fully in the highest stage of competency, the *unaware and able* mode, when the brake lights of the

car in front of you suddenly flash. Most of us, at least those who do not compete in NASCAR races, will fall back down to *unaware and unable,* momen-
tarily paralyzed, not knowing whether to speed up and pass the braking car
or slam on the brakes, hoping the person in the car behind you will more
consciously and quickly react to the situation.

When it comes to performance, the final phase represents the greatest
level of competency, but people at this phase do not necessarily make the best
teachers or coaches. The fact that performing the task has become so uncon-
scious and "second nature" to you can actually make it harder for you to teach
someone else how to do it because you have forgotten all the little steps it took
for you to become masterful at the task. Consider the challenge of teaching
someone else how to serve a tennis ball, drive a golf ball 250 yards without a
slice, or roll a bowling ball straight down the middle of the lane, and you come
face-to-face with the difficulties associated with becoming more "aware."

During a recent trip to England, we stepped onto a busy street in Tra-
falgar Square. Looking left, rather than right, for oncoming cars was such
an ingrained habit for an American that we had to remind ourselves that
in England we needed to look in the opposite direction for danger. Sounds
easy? It wasn't. It took a lot of concentration and constant reminding
for us to make the new behavior automatic. We easily fell back into our
old pattern of thinking. However, we realized we were not the only ones
struggling to remain conscious when we noticed that city officials had
painted "LOOK RIGHT" with an arrow pointing in the right direction on
the road by the curb at each crosswalk. Clearly, this was not just a courtesy
for all of us accustomed to looking left before we step out into the street
but also an acknowledgment of the difficulty to remain conscious, even
with the absolute knowledge that a misstep could result in an unpleasant
confrontation with the front end of a speeding taxicab.

Becoming more conscious can pay big dividends. During one of our recent
senior team trainings, we were facilitating what we call the "Solve It" competition. "Solve It" follows the crucial "See It" and "Own It" steps of the Steps to
Accountability, which we describe in our book *The Oz Principle.* When we
asked the CEO to identify the problem the organization most urgently needed
to solve, she quickly replied, "Top-line sales." Given tremendous pressure in the
international marketplace, the company needed, more than anything else, to
hit an ambitious new number. During the "Solve It" competition, the senior
team focused solely on what else the company could do to achieve that result.
In other words, they spent time increasing their awareness and consciousness
about opportunities they could exploit. As a result of this exercise, they even-

tually identified opportunities worth over $1 billion. The CEO challenged the team to refine the list during the next ninety days and pinpoint "the lowest-hanging fruit" among those opportunities. Just three months later the team reported back, having targeted $40 million of immediate opportunity. The company went after the $40 million and quickly realized the additional revenue. This highly effective team found great value working in the second phase of the Competency Model as they became more aware and asked themselves what else they could do to create top-line growth.

Of course, the opposite can hold true. A lack of awareness, even when it results from having achieved a high level of proficiency, can cause you to miss big opportunities. You may recall the story of Tim Paterson, a programmer at Seattle Computer Products, who, back in 1980, wrote the 86-DOS operating system, which Bill Gates, former head of Microsoft, purchased for only $50,000. Gates needed the system to fulfill a license agreement he had signed with IBM to provide software for their computers. Once Seattle Computer learned what Gates had done, they accused Microsoft of swindling them by not disclosing the customer's name. Microsoft settled by paying an additional $1 million. We all know the rest of the story. This essential deal provided the foundation for Microsoft's dominance in the $253 *billion* software business. We can pay a big price for our inability to become "aware."

Moving into the awareness phase of the Competency Model allows us to see things as they really are, thus enabling us, and those around us, to capitalize more effectively on the opportunities that exist. Rather than just sitting back and letting people figure things out and flounder with insufficient skills, you should try to increase your own awareness about the needed training in your own Expectations Chain. The How Conscious Am I? Self-Test will help you see where you stand in that regard.

HOW CONSCIOUS AM I? SELF-TEST

Answer True or False for each of the following statements.

_____ 1. I can easily identify the top area in which I need training and can see how that training would allow me to deliver more fully on the expectations others have of me.

_____ 2. I have participated in some kind of training during the last year to enhance my ability to fulfill the expectations others have of me.

_____ 3. I have encouraged the people I am counting on to get the training they need to ensure their ability to deliver.

_____ 4. I have supported (both directly and indirectly) the training of others in my Expectations Chain during the last six months.

_____ 5. I often suggest additional training for others as a remedy for unmet expectations.

If you answered "False" to any of these statements, you may be leaving unmet expectations unresolved simply because you have not applied additional training that could get things more surely on track. If so, then you may not be as aware as you should be of the role that training can play in helping people solve unmet expectations. Getting more conscious, and staying conscious, in using training as a solution could potentially pay large dividends on the time, energy, and resources you invest in this Inner Ring Solution.

TRAINING TRIGGERS

If you decide that you can best solve unmet expectations with a training solution, you will first want to identify the level of intervention needed to help others succeed. The Training Triggers Model helps you do that.

TRAINING TRIGGERS

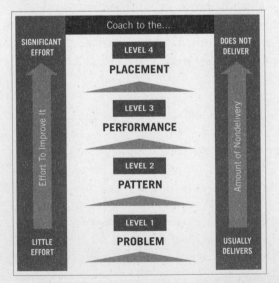

There are four levels of training intervention, each dependent upon two factors: how much effort it will take to improve the performance of those who need training, and how often they fail to deliver results. Once you identify the level of unmet expectations, you can then select the appropriate training solution: coaching to the Problem, the Pattern, the Performance, or the Placement.

At Level One, the person generally performs well and only occasionally fails to deliver. Such a situation triggers a training intervention you can implement quickly. For example, we recently visited a major retail clothing store to buy a couple of casual shirts. After making our selection, we went to the counter where a sales associate greeted us with a big smile and a friendly "May I help you? Please follow me to this other register." Apparently, we had gone to the wrong counter on the other side of the store. We followed her to the other counter, where we noticed this sign: BUY TWO SHIRTS AND GET $5.00 OFF. When we pointed that out to the clerk, she said, "Sorry, that doesn't count. The sale's over." We questioned that. "Oh," she said, "we can ask the manager." As it happened, her manager was standing right next to the cash register, chatting on the phone. Since the clerk was obviously eager to solve the problem, we waited. However, the manager, even though she could see us waiting, seemed in no particular hurry to get off the phone. Finally, she finished her conversation and addressed our question. Visibly annoyed, she turned to the clerk and said, "Oh yeah, it's five dollars, just take it off." The clerk protested, "I don't know how to do it!" The frustrated manager, without even looking at the clerk, rattled off some fairly technical instructions. Our clerk, clearly new on the job, got completely flustered, a look of utter dejection replacing her friendly and eager smile. The manager had given her a clear set of instructions, but she had rattled off so much information so quickly, she had defeated the purpose of this little "training session." Now, both the teacher and the student were frustrated. Fortunately, however, the manager overcame her annoyance and said, "Let me show you." She then walked the clerk through it, step by simple step, and finished the transaction.

The only thing our clerk needed was for someone to take the time to show her what to do. A typical Level One performer, she usually did a good job and required little effort by her manager to do an even better job. While she had been shown how to do it before, she needed to see it more than once to get the hang of it.

This also holds true for medical students, who for many years were supposed to learn important skills according to the standard of "see one,

do one, teach one." Eileen Rattigan, once the chief medical resident responsible for student education at New York University School of Medicine,
decried the ineffectiveness of that tradition. She thought that the notion
that it should take only seeing it once and doing it once to master a potentially lifesaving medical procedure was not only unrealistic but potentially
dangerous. She offers a more effective alternative: "See many, do many, and
teach one."

At Level Two, where you detect a more consistent pattern of missed
deliveries, you need to invest more time and effort in the training. Solving these unmet expectations involves more than just the demonstrating
and practicing we saw with the retail clerk and her manager. Rather, you
must employ significant coaching and feedback to make it work. One of our
clients, "Tim," assigned a very capable person on his team, "Jay," to act as
team leader on an important project for the senior management team. This
was Jay's first opportunity to lead a team on such an important and time-
sensitive project. To his chagrin, Tim found Jay annoyingly reluctant to give
him project updates. Jay seemed almost secretive. When he did provide an
update, it came only at Tim's request and with barely enough information
to make Tim feel okay about progress, and not enough to make him feel
comfortable about whether the team would actually complete the project
on time. Tim tried several times to coach to the problem of too little information and insufficient collaboration, but Jay did not respond to those
efforts.

Ultimately, the time came for the presentation, and, to everyone's relief,
especially Tim's, it turned out well. Notwithstanding the communication
problems, Jay ended up doing an excellent job on the project. Despite the
successful outcome, however, everyone on the project team bitterly complained about Jay's project management skills. Throughout the project Tim
had tried Level One training strategies by coaching and modeling some of
the needed skills, all to no avail. He needed to move on to Level Two.

Tim decided to utilize Jay's talent on a new project immediately after
his first success, but only if Jay responded to a serious training intervention. To make that happen, Tim brought in an external project manager
to coach Jay and sit side by side with him as the project unfolded. In fact,
Tim hired two external coaches: one to help Jay with his project management skills and the other to help him understand why executives want to
see a two-page executive summary, not a fifty-page detailed report. Jay not
only took it well, he felt flattered by the investment in his development and

by the fact that he would once again oversee a highly visible and crucial company project. This time, the work went much more smoothly from a project management perspective: reports were clear, concise, and informative, deadlines were met, and the management team not only praised the end result, they praised the way Jay did the work and achieved the result.

At Level Three, a serious pattern of problems persists, making it clear that the person will never succeed without developing much greater capability. While you might feel tempted to skip and move directly to Level Four by counseling people with big performance problems out of your organization, applying training at this interim level can produce a payoff, albeit not always an immediate one. This level of unmet expectations triggers coaching, not just to the problem or the pattern, but to the overall performance as well. Since on-the-job training and coaching has not solved the problem, a person at this level may need off-site formal schooling, training courses offered by professional groups, and a lot of after-hours studying.

"Joan," manager of the marketing department of a fast-growing company, knew almost nothing about state-of-the-art Internet marketing practices, because she had never received any training in this rapidly evolving area. The shift from print to virtual marketing happened quickly and had passed her by. She knew she could not possibly learn all that the company was asking her to do on the job. It would, instead, require outside help for her to get comfortable with such Internet marketing solutions as Web site development, search engine optimization, e-mail campaigns, and online Webinars.

With a clear Level Three training need, Joan's company made the investment in outside help. She received coaching and schooling by experts in the field and advice about best practices from vendors who knew the Internet marketing game inside and out. Equally important, she made a personal investment of after-hours time, both before and after work, to bring her skills and understanding up to speed. As she gained knowledge, she experimented and applied the learning in the real-time laboratory of her daily job. The result: she now knows more than most of the vendors who advised her. At this point, her managers believe they could not hire an Internet marketing guru who could bring more to the party than the newly trained Joan. The company saw two big payoffs: a desperately needed new capability for the company and a new skill for Joan.

Level Four includes those who have not responded at all to your attempts to develop and train them. Their continued missed delivery triggers the only solution left: coaching to placement. You can place them in another job better suited to their abilities, or, if that does not seem viable for either the person or the organization, you can counsel them out of the organization using your organization's accepted procedures and policies for doing so. Mike Snell, our literary agent, who once worked as a publishing executive, related to us a time where he used coaching to placement in another job to his employer's advantage. He was working with a newly promoted editor, Jack, who lacked the patience to deal with all the painstaking details of manuscript development, a key capability for an editor. However, Jack was very good at defining a new book's mission, its features, and its benefits to readers. Rather than counseling Jack to seek employment with a firm where he could better apply his talents, Mike convinced the publisher's marketing department to give him a chance to work on promotional campaigns. Within a few months, Jack won the new position and went from a problem child in editing to a star performer in marketing.

Once you have identified a willing, accountable, and capable person who just needs the right training to deliver the results you want, you can consult the Training Triggers to make the appropriate investment to develop that person's skill. The Training Triggers enable you to think through what it will take to help others succeed, and they stimulate others to identify their own developmental needs.

So, why the review when it comes to training others, particularly if you are an executive and that is no longer a part of your job description? No matter how high you ascend in your work environment, your ability to discern training as a performance improvement solution for managing unmet expectations, and to provide it to those with whom you work directly, can greatly enhance your organization's ability to achieve results. When it comes to managing unmet expectations, the Training Triggers can help you determine what needs to be done, either by yourself or someone else, to assist anyone in your Expectations Chain in developing the greater capability they need to deliver the results you want.

TRAINING ACCELERATORS

Knowing how to speed up the training process and make it most effective can return large dividends. We recommend four training accelerators that will help you do that: solicit a commitment to adopt the training, streamline your communication, help people apply the feedback, and show them what you want.

Solicit a Commitment to Adopt the Training

No one wants to invest in training for either an individual or an entire organization if it won't produce a return. It always alarms us that much of the training people receive never gets put into practice. As Dr. Mark Allen of Pepperdine's Graziadio School of Business and Management has observed, "Research shows that 60 to 90 percent of job-related skills and knowledge acquired in (training and education) programs are not being implemented on the job. If 75 percent of the $60 billion U.S. training investment is being wasted, we're wasting $45 billion a year!" A study on the same subject by Accenture revealed that 87 percent of the executives surveyed were less than "very satisfied" with the results of training efforts. Clearly, while most executives believe in the value of training, they often question its implementation and follow-through.

To get the most out of training as a solution to unmet expectations, you must first make sure people are ready for it. Too often, we assume a commitment to learning that doesn't actually exist. Getting the up-front commitment from others to put the training into actual practice will speed up their ability to get the result. When training, it is important that you concentrate on optimizing learning, which is your ultimate objective. The old farmer had it right when he said, "We'll have to learn you to milk the cows!" It's one thing to teach others what we know, quite another to get people to learn.

On a personal level, soliciting a commitment from people to adopt the training means creating accountability for implementation and follow-through. You can gain this commitment by using the steps in the Outer Ring of the Accountability Sequence. FORM the right expectation concerning the desired outcomes of the training, then deliberately communicate, align, and inspect that expectation. That will go a long way toward ensuring the necessary commitment for people to follow though and apply what they are learning.

Streamline Your Communication

Nothing hampers training efforts more than ineffective communication. By the same token, clear two-way communication can do a lot to accelerate the impact of all your training efforts. To streamline your communication, make sure that both the trainer and the learner consider how they deliver and receive messages: listening is as important as speaking. Effective communication will accelerate the training process and more quickly improve the capability of those struggling to reverse unmet expectations.

Your own experiences probably underscore the fact that most people do not listen very well. That's quite common because everyone tends to filter what they hear through their beliefs and past experiences. And we all bring certain idiosyncrasies to our interactions with others, such as multitasking, finishing other people's sentences, or rehearsing what we are going to say while others are talking. In almost all training situations, we have noticed a clear and direct correlation between how effectively people listen and how quickly they adopt what you want them to learn.

Although no two people are exactly alike in terms of their listening habits, we've come to believe that most people fall into one of two categories: Literal Listener or Figurative Listener. The Literal Listener listens to what someone says and focuses primarily on the exact meaning of the words. That's fine, but when people take everything too literally, they may not fully comprehend the speaker's true intent. For example, Jane says to Robert, "That memo is so poorly written you might as well throw it away." Robert shreds the letter, not realizing that Jane really meant that he should revise it. The Figurative Listener listens more conceptually to what someone says and not so much to the specifics. That's okay, too, but if people only pay attention to the "spirit" of the message and not the "letter," they can miss the point of Jane's message to Robert: "You could make that memo much clearer if you added some facts to support your conclusions." Robert might change the memo by adding some additional opinions, but never actually add the factual data Jane really wants.

People also tend to practice a literal or figurative communication style. Literal Communicators attempt to say exactly what they mean, choosing their words carefully and precisely. They want their listener to take what they say word for word. By contrast, Figurative Communicators do not express themselves so precisely and worry less about the details and more about communicating the general idea they want to convey. Consider these characteristics as you determine your own listening and communication styles.

Listening Styles	
LITERAL LISTENER	**FIGURATIVE LISTENER**
• Listens with exactness to what someone says	• Listens for the general idea behind what someone says
• Tends to ask questions to clarify exactly what others mean	• Tends not to ask questions, as long as the general idea is clear
• Pays attention to the meaning of words	• Pays attention to the feelings and emotions behind the message
• Takes the communication at face value	• Looks for hidden meanings
• Passes the communication through fewer filters	• Passes the communication through many filters

Communication Styles	
LITERAL COMMUNICATOR	**FIGURATIVE COMMUNICATOR**
• Carefully selects words to reflect precise meaning	• Uses words to express what they feel about the topic
• Tends to emphasize details in their instructions, leaving nothing to chance	• Covers the topic in a conceptual way, providing a "big picture" perspective
• Prefers short and pointed communication	• Enjoys lengthier and more engaging conversations
• Expects people will do exactly what they are told	• Expects people to figure out what to do
• Views communication as a tactical experience for getting information across	• Sees communication as a rapport-building experience for connecting with people

When it comes to training, understanding both your styles and those of the people you train will help you streamline your communication, eliminate a lot of frustration, and speed up the improvement process. As you can imagine, the greatest challenge comes when a Literal Communicator encounters a Figurative Listener and vice versa. We all tend to project our own style onto others, assuming they communicate and listen the same way we do, when in fact, they may do just the opposite. Take that into account whenever you find yourself on either the giving or the receiving end of training.

Help People Apply the Feedback

In our consulting and training work, we stress the value of feedback when it comes to getting the results you want. Proper feedback can also greatly accelerate the improvement you hope to see from additional training and ensure its effective adoption throughout your Expectations Chain. Over the last twenty years, we have implemented the feedback process in hundreds of organizations with tens of thousands of people at every job level and industry in countries all over the world. That experience has taught us several valuable lessons.

TEN FEEDBACK LESSONS

1. Feedback doesn't happen unless you make it happen.
2. People tend to stop giving feedback over time, even if they once did it frequently.
3. It is easier to give appreciative feedback than it is to deliver constructive feedback.
4. People often do not act on feedback without some sort of follow-up.
5. It is easier to filter feedback than to accept it.
6. People more fully appreciate the feedback they receive after they have applied it and seen its impact on their results.
7. Feedback declines after people improve because they assume it's no longer necessary.
8. People struggle to know how to respond to the feedback they receive.

9. People typically fear receiving constructive feedback because they see it as criticism rather than helpful input.
10. Organizations always underestimate the difficulty of getting people to give and receive feedback.

One successful executive whom we worked with told us that, in his way of thinking, you can show no greater respect for other people in the business world than by offering them direct, honest feedback, particularly constructive feedback intended to help them improve their performance. We liked the way he put it. "Do you think not giving feedback to somebody is respectful? Is going around them to their boss respectful? Is going to a peer in the hopes that they will mention something respectful? I often remind myself that delivering a tough message is the ultimate way in which I demonstrate respect to another human being. When I do this I put my fears aside and instead put their needs first, telling them what they need to hear. I have learned to deal with my discomfort while giving a difficult message and to not procrastinate in its delivery. That is one way I show respect for people."

Show Them What You Want

You can also accelerate training by demonstrating exactly what you want your people to do. As with most learning experiences, people learn best when someone *shows* them, rather than merely tells them, how to do something. The 5 D's Fast Training Model offers a few simple "show, don't tell" steps anyone can use to train someone and raise their level of competence.

Suppose you want to teach someone in your Expectations Chain how to coach others more candidly when they are not delivering needed results. First you describe how to do it, using an actual situation in their work. Then you demonstrate how to do it yourself by involving them in a similar situation in your own work, or by role-playing the conversation they might conduct with the person they need to coach. Next, you would encourage them to try their hand at it by actually engaging in the conversation you have recommended. Ideally, you would watch it firsthand. If not, you would at least hear about how it went and, in either case, provide feedback, both appreciative and constructive, to help them do it better the next time. Finally, they continue to practice applying what they have learned, while you continue

THE 5 D's FAST TRAINING MODEL

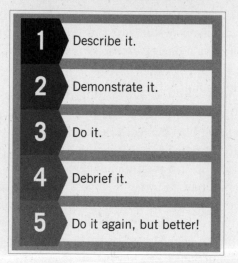

1   Describe it.

2   Demonstrate it.

3   Do it.

4   Debrief it.

5   Do it again, but better!

to monitor their progress. You may need to repeat this cycle a few times, but in the long run, you will see that it greatly speeds up the learning process.

In many cases, this sort of modeling provides training you cannot easily deliver any other way. We are constantly amazed that people do not rely more often on modeling the behavior and skills they want the people in their Expectations Chain to learn. It works in everyday life, and it can work just as well in even the most complex and technical work environments.

ACCOUNTABILITY REALITY CHECK

To heighten your level of awareness when it comes to using training to manage unmet expectations, take a moment to identify a situation in which others in your Expectations Chain are letting you down and not delivering on your expectations. This need not involve a huge or disastrous mistake, but it should represent a circumstance where performance and delivery have disappointed you. Would training improve the situation? If not, think of another instance where it would. What level of training would you select to bring about a remedy, Level One, Two, or Three? Once you have determined the level, sit down with the person or persons you have identified and engage in an Accountability Conversation. Work toward an agreement that training will help solve the problem, and discuss exactly what sort of training will work best. The steps of the Outer Ring will help you Form, Communicate, Align, and Inspect the best expectation. Once training has commenced, look for progress and ask for feedback on the value of the training and your role in helping to make it work. We would be very surprised if the right training at the right time did not greatly enhance the performance and results you desire.

TRAINING WITH STYLE

As with everything else, your Accountability Style influences how you approach the training solution. For those who tend toward the Coerce & Compel style, taking the time to train people may seem like a questionable investment. Slowing down to train someone and, possibly, to model the desired behavior or skill, may seem like an annoying distraction. This may hold particularly true with a Level Three intervention where you usually incur a greater personal investment of time and effort. However, patience with the process of developing both individual and organizational capability can pay off in a big way. If your approach generally reflects more of a Coerce & Compel style, you will probably benefit from a little more patience and a heightened awareness that training can ultimately help achieve desired results. Those prone to the Coerce & Compel style will want to communicate that they welcome feedback. They quite often do not realize that people find their style intimidating and therefore hesitate to offer input and direct feedback. Whenever you express the fact that you really appreciate candid feedback, you make people feel much more comfortable telling you what you need to know, even if it's not good news.

Those with a preference for the Wait & See style fully appreciate the opportunity to train others and see them develop, but they may not follow up thoroughly enough to make sure people apply what they have learned. Wait & See people are usually strong on supportiveness but weak on the follow-through that ensures people are putting their training to work. By taking a more structured approach and using the Outer Ring's steps to implement training solutions, those with a Wait & See style will get more traction in the training process and more return on the time and money invested.

Wait & See people may also hesitate to give direct, honest, and timely feedback. They may not be as candid as they should be when they do provide it and they may not provide it in as timely a manner as would be useful. They don't want to risk hurting people's feelings. They want to maintain rapport with people because they think that's the best way to get people to perform to the best of their ability. However, the Wait & See style should understand that they do people a big favor and actually demonstrate their deep respect by saying what needs to be said, when it needs to be said. Doing so will help them use feedback to accelerate performance improvement through training.

TRAINING BUILDS ACCOUNTABILITY

When you provide the right training at the right time, people usually improve, and so do the results they achieve. Knowing what kind of intervention it will take to get the job done and then providing the right amount will greatly assist you in managing unmet expectations. You might even consider what additional training could do for you personally as you continue to fulfill the expectations others have of you. Anyone who has experienced the value of training in reversing the effects of unmet expectations recognizes that training builds accountability. When people know how to make it happen, they look forward to making it happen again and again. Ensuring a high degree of personal accountability, the third of the four Accountability Conversation solutions, is the subject of the next chapter.

Chapter Eight

THE POSITIVE, PRINCIPLED WAY

A quick review of the principles and ideas associated with the training solution for managing unmet expectations will remind you how to use training to help people deliver on results.

Stages of Competency
For your training of others to work, you and they must move from "unaware/able" to "aware," the highest stage of competency.

Training Triggers
Four levels of training needs trigger four different interventions: "Level One" requires coaching to the Problem, "Level Two" coaching to the Pattern, "Level Three" coaching to the Performance, and "Level Four" coaching to the Placement.

Training Accelerators
Four training accelerators can speed the process: (1) solicit a commitment to adopt the training; (2) streamline your communication; (3) help people apply the feedback; and (4) show them what you want.

Listening Styles
There are two listening styles: the "Literal Listener" and the "Figurative Listener." Knowing the style of the person you are training will help you modify your approach in a way that speeds up the learning process.

Communication Styles
There are also two complementary communication styles: the "Literal Communicator" and the "Figurative Communicator." Adapting your communication style to the person you are training will also accelerate learning.

5 D's Fast Training
Five simple steps enable you to model skills you wish to teach others: (1) Describe it; (2) Demonstrate it; (3) Do it; (4) Debrief it; and (5) Do it again, but better.

Chapter Nine

ASSESS ACCOUNTABILITY

WHEN PERSONAL ACCOUNTABILITY IS THE SOLUTION

Sometimes people fail to deliver on expectations because they do not take sufficient personal accountability to overcome obstacles and determine what else they can do to achieve a desired result. Even highly motivated and well-trained people sometimes suffer from a lack of accountability. In fact, we have devoted much of our careers over the last twenty years to helping individuals and organizations learn how to step forward and take personal, positive, empowering, and productive accountability for achieving results. It is one of the solutions to unmet expectations in the Inner Ring, and, as we stressed in *The Oz Principle*, it can also prevent a lot of problems from happening in the first place.

Thousands of individuals and teams around the world have used *The Oz Principle* to create greater personal accountability in their work and their lives. The book demonstrates that accountability is not something that happens to you when things go wrong, but something that you should continually embrace with every new task. The truly accountable person doesn't ask "Who can I *blame* for this problem?" but "What else can *I do* to achieve the result?" The principle of positive accountability enables people to rise above their circumstances and overcome the obstacles they face. The Steps to Accountability Chart featured in *The Oz Principle* captures the essence of this kind of personal accountability.

STEPS TO ACCOUNTABILITY

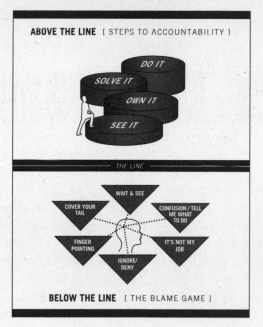

The top half of the chart, "Above the Line," is where people take the Steps to Accountability to See It, Own It, Solve It, and Do It. They "See It" by obtaining the perspectives of others and hearing those perspectives, whether they agree with them or not, which allows them to acknowledge reality more readily. They "Own It" by making the connection between the circumstances they face and the actions they have taken. "Solve It" consists of personally and constantly asking "What else can I do?" and "Do It" requires people to follow through on their commitments, without blaming others for failure, and take the necessary action to change the situation, make progress, and ultimately achieve the result.

The bottom half of the chart, "Below the Line," is where people participate in the Blame Game and make excuses for missed delivery and unmet expectations, justifying their inaction and lack of progress by chalking it all up to things that lie beyond their control. Here, they languish in a feeling of powerlessness, unable to change their circumstances or move forward and make a difference. When people get stuck Below the Line, they fail to take accountability for their circumstances and blame others for their lack of progress. Instead of delivering on expectations, they deliver excuses and explanations about what went wrong. Note, however, that it is not *wrong* to slip Below the Line from time to time; in fact, it's human nature to do so. All of us fall Below the Line on a regular basis. The trick is to recognize when you do so and to get back Above the Line as quickly as you can. Since you can only get results when you're working Above the Line, the less time you spend Below the Line, the better.

Most of us bump into Below the Line attitudes and behavior every day. Recently, one of our clients, frustrated by what he referred to as "their daily dose of this results-stopping attitude," recounted an experience that illustrates the point: "I'm down in the cafeteria at about seven A.M., getting my cup of coffee and bagel, and there is a guy in front of me in the line to check out who's also got a bagel, and he says to the worker at the counter, 'There isn't any peanut butter. Do you have any in the back?' The counter worker says, 'Ah, the lady who scoops out the peanut butter isn't here today, so we won't have any.' I almost dropped my plate when I heard her say that. I soon learned that this is the way the cafeteria works, which means that when the guy who makes the pizza is on vacation, they shut the pizza station down!"

This example reveals an incredible lack of resourcefulness, characteristic of what happens when people blindly choose to live Below the Line.

In another example, a CFO, "Terri," got a big surprise when she investigated a sharp decline in the quality and productivity numbers turned in by a recently reengineered assembly line. Despite a huge investment in buying new equipment, repositioning old equipment, rearranging seating for the workers, and implementing new training, the numbers had gone south. "How did that happen?" asked Terri. "Blame the management!" insisted the frontline workers. Frustrated with people wasting time playing the Blame Game, Terri resolved to get to the bottom of the problem.

Somewhat uncharacteristic for a CFO, Terri went directly to the plant floor to speak with an outspoken senior assembler, a woman who had worked for the company for a long time and who was intimately familiar with the problem. "Why the decline in productivity?" Terri asked. Pointing down the line, the assembler answered with a question, "What do you see?" Terri said she saw women working to put things together. The assembler shook her head. "Look again, particularly at the bins of parts and the height of the women." Terri couldn't believe what she now saw. She quickly surmised that when maintenance workers, mostly men, set up the new line, they placed the bins higher than the women—who made up a majority of the line workers—could easily reach. Terri watched as assemblers climbed stepladders to reach into the bins for the parts they needed. Within twenty-four hours, Terri, working with operations, saw to it that the maintenance crew lowered the bins to the assemblers' height, eliminating the need for a stepladder. Productivity improved immediately.

We see it in organizations all the time. While the assemblers were frustrated that no one approached them directly about the problem, management was frustrated that they were not seeing the expected return on their investment. Everyone was languishing Below the Line. It wasn't until the CFO herself moved Above the Line and asked the question, "What else can I do?" that the real problem got solved. Whether you're dealing with peanut butter in a cafeteria or parts bins on an assembly line, when you help people take accountability, you help them overcome the hesitancy and inaction that characterize Below the Line behavior, replacing it with results-producing Above the Line attitudes and action.

That's exactly what "Jennifer," a district manager at "The Women's Boutique" did. Every year The Women's Boutique, a nationally branded chain, conducted a women's "Suit Contest," a sales event that lasted for several weeks and consisted of a competition to see who could sell the most women's suits. Jennifer's district, which was comprised of ten retail stores, had always come in dead last in the contest. Worse, her district consistently turned in only average overall sales results. When we talked to her about her experience with the contest, she told us that when she questioned people in her stores about the poor results, they would usually blame the economy (too bad), the weather (too hot), and the customers (too picky). She admitted that she always found their explanations convincing. In a rather emotional argument for why the company should not hold her accountable for meeting corporate expectations, she exclaimed, "I can't sell suits here in Nevada!"

She then explained that her new regional manager had informed her that corporate was evaluating and ranking all district managers. He said that all of the company's managers fell into one of two groups: "owners" and "renters." Then he looked her straight in the eye and told her, "Sadly, Jennifer, you are a renter!" Jennifer was taken totally by surprise. She had worked for The Women's Boutique for many years and had always considered herself a competent manager. "Why," she wondered, "have they singled me out as one who does not own our business?" Only later would she realize that this was the best "wake-up call" she had ever received and precisely what she needed to hear, when she needed to hear it.

Taking accountability, Jennifer began to recognize that her failure to fulfill the expectations that others had of her stemmed from her inability to get the people in her region to take accountability for achieving the desired results. Armed with a determination to move Above the Line, Jennifer set to work. She began with the area in which her team most consistently failed to deliver on expectations: the annual Suit Contest. She took care to help her store managers understand what could happen when they took accountability and moved Above the Line. After persuading her managers to agree that the excuses they, and she, had habitually made were preventing them from achieving better results, she secured their commitment to lift each other up when they fell Below the Line and get back to Seeing It, Owning It, Solving It, and Doing It.

She identified the "VIP Sale"—an event for which they closed the store and invited select customers to shop in comfort and enjoy enticing discounts—as a key to improving their standing in the Suit Contest. This event, she told her managers, could make or break the Suit Contest for their district. "Let's go out and make it happen!" In the past, Jennifer had relied on her store managers to host the VIP parties each week during the contest, but she had not sufficiently helped them take accountability and own the success of the event.

Jennifer did not exclude herself from asking "What else can I do to get the result?" She began visiting each store to provide coaching and assistance to the managers who were hosting the parties, focusing her input around what everyone could do to get preferred customers excited about the contest. She was delighted to discover that her managers, far from resenting her visits as unwelcome intrusions, welcomed her presence and admired her obvious commitment to making the "VIP Sale" the sales event of the year. A job they previously viewed as something that "just needed to get done" became, in their minds, an essential part of their plan to win the Suit Contest. Jennifer noted a marked improvement in her team. Even those who once bad-mouthed the contest got on board and demonstrated ownership for the district's standing in the contest.

The VIP Sales turned into a huge success, and this success fueled a new sense of innovation throughout the district. Following an employee's creative suggestion, Jennifer installed a "Think Box" in each store where people would place their ideas about what more could be done to drive sales throughout the district. People became totally engaged in thinking up ways to draw more customers into the excitement, such as offering them the opportunity to win a Fossil Watch or a new suit for a penny. As Jennifer continued to meet one-on-one with her store managers, their descents Below the Line became occasional events rather than the norm. Above the Line thinking became infectious and everyone in the stores got on board, committed to making a difference.

Jennifer told us this story after having just returned from the Women's Boutique annual Leadership Conference where her district was recognized for finishing first in the four-week Suit Contest. This delighted her, but something else that happened at the meeting delighted her even more. Her regional manager congratulated her on making the move from an entrenched "renter" to a solid "owner" of the business. She went on to tell us that the top brass even invited her to speak to the other district and regional managers at the conference about the transformation she had engineered in her district. When she rose to speak she made a point of saying, "A lot of you know me. I've been with the company for twelve years and I have never been the number one district in anything before. But I will tell you what changed for me this year: I applied what I learned about how to help people take accountability, and it totally changed my life."

We have seen this time and again throughout the last two decades. Good organizations, many of whom have made significant contributions in their industry but who find themselves no longer making desired progress toward hitting their numbers, have gotten impressive results from helping people take accountability. Sometimes, getting people Above the Line where they take personal accountability for their circumstances and overcome obstacles by asking the question "What else can I do?" is the best solution to the problem of unmet expectations. Personal accountability arms people with the right mind-set and attitude for solving problems and helps them become more resourceful and imaginative when looking for ways to move forward and get the result.

The Oz Principle defines accountability as "a personal choice to rise above one's circumstances and demonstrate the ownership necessary for achieving desired results—to See It, Own It, Solve It, and Do It." Just like the characters in *The Wizard of Oz*, people can find solutions to the problems they face and often overcome the circumstances that seem beyond their control. Our experience has shown that helping people take accountability for their circumstances, and for what else they need to do to achieve the result, can work wonders.

While working with "BGC," a large fast-food chain, we heard the CEO, "Nelson," tell his management team something that we will never forget. Prior to addressing his team, he played a video clip from a popular cable news show to which he had granted an earlier interview. In the clip, the reporter describes the interview with Nelson, saying, "You know I had a conversation recently with the CEO of BGC Corporation, and the entire conversation revolved around how the company is being pounded by the economy. Their CEO spent our entire conversation complaining and crying about their challenging environment." The news anchor then went on to describe a conversation that he had with the CEO of BGC's top competitor. "My conversations with their biggest competitor were dramatically different. As I spoke with their CEO, he did not see any problem with the environment in which they are operating. Their entire organizational focus centers around what else they can do to create growth opportunities. That's why their business is thriving." The anchor ended the segment with an observation. "The shareholders of these companies don't care how the food tastes. They care about how the leaders are leading their companies to achieve results in spite of the current economy."

Now, Nelson knew that he was taking a big risk in showing the clip to his entire leadership team, but when the screen went dark, he stood up and said, "This cable news anchor is right. I've been Below the Line as our CEO, and I owe all of you an apology for that. I've got to get Above the Line and, going forward, I need our entire organization standing with me, asking the question 'What else can I do?'" It was a powerful moment, and it marked a major turning point for the company.

MANAGING THE ACCOUNTABILITY CURRENT

An Accountability Current flows in every organization, and through every Expectations Chain. The current is the directional flow of accountability and identifies where the accountability originates and the direction it moves. That flow can be either top-down or bottom-up; that is, accountability may either flow from you or toward you. You know you have really harnessed the power of accountability when the current flows toward you. That means people in the Expectations Chain (which, for an organizational leader, includes the entire organization) *take* accountability for fulfilling key expectations and take action on their own initiative and with their own energy and effort, to report back, report in, raise issues, resolve problems, and, in general, make things happen.

Top-down accountability keeps everyone at the top of the Expectations Chain busy trying to regulate all the important activity in the organization. Every process needs a process control, and in the top-down model those at the top become the process control for ensuring that everyone is accountable. Those who control the process work so hard to keep tabs on people and projects that they often end up feeling as if they are the only ones taking accountability for the result. When they take their hands off the controls, the current ceases to flow and the accountability process breaks down. Only when they return and resume their oversight does accountability once again take effect.

What's the problem with a top-down flow? Everyone below the top can feel as if they must obey orders or suffer the consequences. When people responsible for fulfilling expectations feel that way, they can easily draw the conclusion that accountability is something that happens to them when something goes wrong. People tend to resist and avoid that sort of accountability, and they dodge taking responsibility because it feels coercive to them. They often sense that they have lost some amount of personal freedom and choice in what has deteriorated into a potentially paralyzing "tell-me-what-to-do" mode of operation. You can see the obvious risk: people abdicate their personal accountability to those at the top of the chain who visibly (and often solely) work so hard to create it.

In our opinion, top-down accountability, which has become the way of life in far too many organizational cultures, has led to the crisis of accountability we see throughout the world today. The old Command & Control approach, as we described at the beginning of this book, may have worked well enough in the past, but it does not engender the ownership and personal investment necessary to get things done in today's complicated and ever-changing world. While the bottom-up approach requires a greater investment of time up front, it pays off handsomely in the long run, because when people invest themselves in accountability, those at the top of the chain will expend far less energy and effort sustaining a results-producing effort throughout the organization.

When an Accountability Current flows in a bottom-up direction, people take accountability and proactively report to their boss, their teammates, and their peers. Follow-up becomes a natural, ingrained habit. They don't just sit around and wait for someone else to do something, but instead take charge of tasks at the outset. This powerful form of accountability does not originate at the top of the Expectations Chain; it begins with the individual. With a bottom-up flow, people at all levels in the Expectations Chain hold everyone upon whom they depend accountable. This includes the people to whom they report, the people who report to them, peers, customers, vendors, suppliers, and all other stakeholders. We call this 360° Accountability.

360° ACCOUNTABILITY

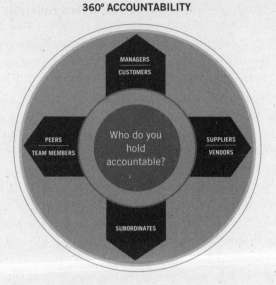

The 360° view illustrates the full range of people you hold accountable. Notice its inclusiveness. Unleashing the potential of the organization with a bottom-up flow creates a more participative environment that allows people to embrace accountability and ownership for achieving results. Does accountability in your Expectations Chain flow in a top-down or bottom-up direction? Answer "True" or "False" to the statements below to find out. Of course, you may need to generalize because not everyone in your chain operates the same way.

WHICH WAY DOES ACCOUNTABILITY FLOW IN YOUR ORGANIZATION?

Answer True or False to the following statements:

_____ 1. People generally do not report on their progress unless you ask them to do so.

_____ 2. You focus on "holding people accountable," as opposed to getting them to "take accountability."

_____ 3. When problems arise, people do not move forward without your involvement.

_____ 4. You often feel as if only you are fully accountable to do whatever it takes to make things happen.

_____ 5. You must constantly follow up on everyone to make sure the
right things happen.

Determine the direction of the Accountability Current in your organization by awarding yourself three points for every True statement and one
point for every False statement. Use the table below to interpret your score.

9–15 points	A top-down Accountability Current most likely flows through your Expectations Chain. This means that you are probably working harder than you should to get the benefits of accountability and will get "more for less" by changing the flow's direction.
5–8 points	A bottom-up Accountability Current probably flows through your Expectations Chain. You have effectively created a culture where people take accountability. Your long-term success will depend on sustaining this culture.

Establishing a 360° bottom-up Accountability Current will help the
people in your Expectations Chain do a far better job in the future.

PPL Montana, a company that runs thirteen power plants statewide,
did just that. When the company, based in Billings, Montana, found itself
with a below-standard work safety record and workers' compensation losses
running into the millions of dollars, its leadership set to work creating a
bottom-up Accountability Flow to deal with the issue of worker safety. In
the end, that effort resulted in a much better safety record and the reduction of workers' compensation losses from the "millions" to the "tens of
thousands." All it took was a sharp increase in personal accountability on
the part of every employee throughout the Expectations Chain. Now, before
their work shift begins, employees conduct safety checks and search for problems that could potentially lead to safety incidents. Before, few people took
any accountability to follow through on safety checks. A task that once "fell
through the cracks" now occupies a front-and-center position in the minds
of workers at every level in the plant. Employees attend safety meetings for
their teams and work areas and feel empowered to voice their concerns and
implement creative suggestions that often impact everyone in the plant. The
reversal of the accountability flow from top-down to bottom-up has helped

employees take accountability for addressing an extremely important unmet expectation: their own safety and well-being. Approximately 150 of 350 union workers are now rewarded for serving as safety audit officers, working on safety committees and leading safety meetings.

That's the sort of approach described by Louise Esola in the trade magazine *Business Insurance*, when she wrote in the October 2008 issue about a problem-solving project at Toyota. "Change used to go top-down and now we are seeing that it needs to be both top-down and bottom-up." When executives at the Toyota manufacturing plant in Princeton, Indiana, asked the people working in its body welding shop to figure out how to reduce "upper extremity injuries," everyone involved took accountability and fully engaged their hearts and minds in the project. "The task force of managers and production floor workers created an innovative delivery system that helped reduce injuries by 87%," reported Esola. These changes were later implemented in Toyota plants throughout the country. Nothing gets the Accountability Current flowing in the right direction more surely than the sort of complete employee involvement and engagement that propels people to throw themselves, body and soul, into solving problems and delivering on expectations. It all starts with the right attitude toward accountability.

ACCOUNTABILITY ATTITUDES

People respond in many different ways to the idea of embracing accountability, and their attitudes about it greatly affect your Accountability Connection with them. The quality of your connection affects your ability to hold others accountable for results in both the Outer Ring and the Inner Ring of the Accountability Sequence. Nowhere does attitude become more important than when you are attempting to implement accountability as the Inner Ring Solution to unmet expectations. In our work helping organizations create greater accountability, we have identified the three most common Accountability Attitudes present in most organizations today: Deflecting, Calculating, and Embracing. Understanding these general attitudes will help you more effectively apply accountability as an Inner Ring Solution.

These attitudes describe people's general views and reactions to taking accountability. Of course, specific views and reactions can and do vary from person to person and situation to situation. The same person may demonstrate an Embracing Attitude in one circumstance and then a Deflecting Attitude in another. That is, someone might display one attitude at work, another at home, and yet another when it comes to his or her involvement in a favorite hobby. While you should be careful placing people in any one category, we think you will find our approach to Accountability Attitudes quite useful when it comes to accelerating a change in the way people think and act within your organization.

People with a Deflecting Attitude generally do not want to take any accountability. Instead, they almost always deflect ownership. They react defensively when things go wrong, almost incessantly claiming, "It wasn't me!" or "It's not my fault." They tend to spend a lot of time Below the Line and frequently feel like victims of their circumstances. Rather than taking personal ownership for moving things forward, they tend to respond in a "tell-me-what-to-do" mode, only completing the project or assignment with minimal effort, producing "just good enough," but never spectacular results. They're quite content to "just get by." Remember the cafeteria worker who shook his head and said, "The peanut butter lady is out, so we won't be having any peanut butter today?" That's deflection.

In the extreme, someone with a Deflecting Attitude reminds us of the main character in the movie *Rocket Man*. In the film, actor Fred Randall plays Harland Williams, an obnoxious spacecraft designer whose dreams come true when he gets a chance to travel to Mars in the first manned mission to the planet. During the course of mission preparations, Harland bungles his way through one mishap after another, all clearly his own fault. Yet each time something goes wrong, he cries, "It wasn't me!" even though he may be standing red-handed in the midst of the chaos. Someone with a Deflecting Attitude will always find a way to deny reality and explain why he or she was not responsible for any failure or lack of progress.

People who think and act with a Calculating Attitude practice "selective accountability," carefully choosing the situations in which they will or will not become personally invested. At times they give the impression that they are deflecting; other times they seem to be embracing. Their decisions to invest themselves depend on a number of variables, such as their current circumstances, the specific teammates involved, their personal interest level, or their perceived workload. Before determining to what extent they will take accountability, they carefully consider the risk of failure and balance that with their own interests and desires. They always do what they are asked to do, but you can tell the difference in the quality and impact of their work when they are not fully engaged.

The Calculating Attitude brings to mind the character Han Solo from the *Star Wars* movies. Harrison Ford played a rebellious pilot who would carefully pick and choose which battles he would fight and which causes he would join as the Alliance worked to defeat the Empire. Every mission would ignite the personal debate over whether or not he would participate and to what extent he would get involved. When he chose to take accountability for the task, he performed heroically; when he chose not to invest himself, he invited our scorn. People with a Calculating Attitude spend time both Above and Below the Line, moving between the two quite frequently and experiencing the frustration associated with straddling the "line." People who work with someone who has a Calculating Attitude find them somewhat unpredictable and unreliable. Can you count on them when the going gets rough? Maybe. Maybe not.

Finally, people who generally display the Embracing Attitude neither deflect nor calculate but eagerly take accountability for the task and quickly become personally invested in doing their best to get it done. When things go wrong due to their own mistakes, they tend to acknowledge their role immediately. As a result, they willingly take risks, even if doing so may result in failure. When they encounter difficult obstacles and pesky problems, they move relentlessly forward. People with this attitude spend a lot of their time Above the Line. While not immune from dropping Below the Line occasionally, they quickly recognize that fact and ask themselves "What else can I do?" to move back up Above the Line. These folks stand out in any organization and in any setting because they are the proactive, results-oriented people who almost always make good things happen.

When we think about the Embracing Attitude, we recall the movie *Rudy*, which tells the true story of Daniel "Rudy" Ruettiger who, despite extraordinary obstacles, achieved his dream of playing football for the University of Notre Dame. Facing challenge after challenge, he did whatever it took to press forward. He constantly asked, "What else can I do?" to solve a problem. Rudy could have easily languished Below the Line and felt justified in doing so, but rather than harboring feelings of self-pity, Rudy rose above his circumstances and overcame the great odds stacked against him. He represents the accountable person who maintains a strong See It, Own It, Solve It, and Do It Attitude and holds himself accountable for the results he gets, good or bad.

As you consider the Accountability Attitudes of those in your Expectations Chain, consult the table below. How do your people's attitudes toward accountability affect the way they fulfill expectations and get results?

Characteristics of the Accountability Attitudes

DEFLECTING	CALCULATING	EMBRACING
Avoids taking any risk that might result in failure	Carefully determines what risks to take	Willingly takes risk because he/she does not fear failing
Usually feels like a victim	Can drop Below the Line quickly, depending upon the situation	Takes responsibility for circumstances and spends little time externalizing the reasons for a lack of progress
Often operates in a "tell-me-what-to-do" mode	Can appear inconsistent in his/her work ethic, sometimes giving an extraordinary effort, other times a halfhearted one	Usually takes the initiative and demonstrates great resourcefulness
Runs for cover and denies any responsibility for what happened when things go wrong	Often tells a carefully crafted story about why it was not his/her fault when things go wrong	Admits his/her own mistakes when things go wrong
Sees any obstacle as a reason to stop working	Views obstacles either as roadblocks to progress or as exciting challenges, depending on his/her interest in the task	Greets obstacles as challenges that he/she can creatively attack

You might suggest to those who are failing to deliver on expectations that they apply this assessment to themselves. Doing so can help them see how a shift in attitude might improve their ability to fulfill your expectations. It may surprise you how quickly most people can alter their attitudes once they examine them within the context of accountability's impact on results. In our experience, when people see how a Below the Line attitude can hurt them personally and undermine the effectiveness of the organization overall, they usually choose to get Above the Line and adopt an Embracing Attitude as fast as they can.

THE PARADOX OF ACCOUNTABILITY

Over the years, as we have worked with a multitude of organizations, teams, leaders, individual performers, and senior executives, we have seen people wrestle with three paradoxes that typically arise as they work to implement accountability: the paradox of success, the paradox of consequences, and the paradox of shared accountability. The reality of these paradoxes helps explain why creating accountability is so hard to get right.

First, consider the paradox of success. Many high performers we have worked with feel tremendously frustrated when it seems that the harder they try to get people to take accountability, the less accountability people actually embrace. That usually happens because they have gotten others to take accountability (or, at least, something that resembles it) using methods that ultimately cause people to shrink from truly embracing it. Those methods include the old Command & Control approach that never obtains the buy-in you get when you persuade and convince people to do something of their own volition. Of course, you can create a certain level of accountability with "force," but when you leave the scene, a person's sense of accountability leaves with you. When people use any form of coercion, they do not really get people to take accountability, they just get people to *act* accountable. There can be a great difference between the two. When people assume true accountability, they invest their hearts and minds and show a level of ownership that transcends any behavior that could be motivated by other tactics. More important, they continue that behavior in your absence.

One highly trained and successful leader, "Jeff," experienced an epiphany with the paradox of success late in his career. He had always considered himself highly respectful of others, even though he loved to gather information about his organization through an informal internal network and then spring it on his direct reports who had not obtained that information themselves. Even he admitted that he would "bushwhack" the people who reported to him by asking questions he knew they could not answer correctly. This tactic, he thought, cemented his authority and credibility and motivated all of his reports to prepare themselves more thoroughly before they met with him. The results he generated seemed to validate his approach.

His success as a manager won a series of promotions to positions with an increasingly larger span of control and greater complexity. However, as he worked in these different assignments, he began to realize that this particular management style was not sustainable over time. He had built a system that demanded accountability from the people he worked with (he got them to *act* accountably), but he did not create in people a sense of personal ownership for achieving results (he did not get them to take personal accountability). Yes, people would readily respond to his demands, but when he went away, things began to break down. He eventually noticed an unsettling pattern: every time he received a promotion to a new area, his prior area of responsibility would immediately show a decline in performance. Of course, to his chagrin, even though he had moved on to a new job, he was still responsible for results in the previous area, but now that he occupied a more senior position, he could not make as direct an impact on that area as he once could.

While Jeff knew how to get people to take accountability when he was watching, he did not know how to get them to embrace their accountability in his absence. Finally, the light dawned on him. In his own words, he acknowledged, "The coercive style is *not* sustainable in the absence of the coercionist." That was an important insight for Jeff, learning that an approach that seems to yield success in the short run actually undermines the very fabric of accountability in the long run.

The second paradox is the paradox of consequences. To most people, accountability requires that someone suffer consequences for unmet expectations. After all, without consequences, what difference does accountability make? If you think that accountability is something that you're forced to take as punishment when things go wrong, you will come to fear those negative consequences, and, as a result, shy away from taking greater personal accountability. This way of thinking comes easily to people who accept the conventional Oxford dictionary definition of accountability: "Liable to be called to account." As a rule, our society only calls for an accounting when something has gone wrong. That accounting leads to punishment, and no one submits willingly to punishment. Fearing retribution, people run for cover when they hear that management wants to hold people more accountable. Here again, people mistakenly believe that accountability is something that the organization's leadership imposes on everyone, rather than something everyone in the organization embraces to get results.

This is a mistake people have been making for centuries. In the fifteenth and sixteenth centuries, the Tudor and Stuart monarchies practiced the time-honored tradition of the "whipping boy." Whipping boys were young men born to families of high status, educated with the prince of the realm, who also enjoyed many of the same privileges. However, because people believed that kings received their authority from God and were answerable to him alone, no one could improperly touch a monarch or his heir. Thus, if the prince did something that warranted punishment, another boy would take his place at the whipping post. Too often, people in organizations feel just like those whipping boys. To them, accountability is all about management dispensing punishment for negative consequences and denying their own responsibility by using others as scapegoats when something goes wrong.

Unfortunately, most people in corporations throughout the world do view accountability as a negative activity. True, accountability implies consequences, but those consequences are both positive and negative. While the fear of consequences may discourage people from taking accountability, the anticipation of positive consequences should encourage personal ownership. Unfortunately, not many organizations practice the latter.

The third paradox is the paradox of shared accountability. While the task of taking accountability lies with the individual, the end result depends on many people throughout the Expectations Chain sharing ownership for obtaining the result. Teams, departments, divisions, and organizations are rarely held accountable, at least not as accountable as their respective leaders. Individuals, including leaders, are called to account for the success or failure to fulfill the stewardship entrusted to them by those who put them in charge of fulfilling expectations. In reality, the ability of others to do the things they say they will do greatly affects your ability to fulfill the expectations for which others will hold *you* accountable.

Increasing the likelihood that the people in your Expectations Chain will come through for you is what this book is all about. When it comes to managing unmet expectations, you must resolve the paradox of shared accountability by helping people take the personal accountability necessary to get the result, even when they share that accountability with others. The notions of individual and shared accountability can compete with each other to establish who, at the end of the day, is truly accountable for what happened. Keep this paradox in mind as you help people better understand that their personal accountability transcends that of the group and that they should *own it* as if everything depended upon them. When you establish that level of personal ownership, then the tension inherent in the notion of shared accountability disappears.

Take, for example, the experience one of our own senior management team members had when he and a group of chaperones took their Little League baseball team to Walt Disney World. They had expected to receive discounted entrance tickets to the park, and when they checked into their hotel, they learned that they could pick up those discounted tickets at the park's ticket counter. Upon arriving at the ticket counter, however, the Disney employee behind the counter said no, the person at the hotel's front desk had misspoken. All discount tickets were available through the hotel, *not* at the park's ticket counter.

One of the chaperones told the Disney employee that a round-trip to retrieve the tickets from the hotel, with twenty disappointed boys in tow, would take ninety minutes, meaning the group would not get back to the park until 7 P.M. with only three hours left before closing time. On her own initiative, the Disney employee called the hotel and worked out a creative solution: the company would charge one parent's room for all tickets to enable the discount (no small saving, considering the four-figure price for all the tickets combined); the parents and chaperones could settle among themselves later. Not only did the Disney employee solve the problem, she also gave the group "fast-pass" tickets to make up for the delay at the ticket counter. This Disney employee demonstrated the kind of personal accountability that helps the entire Expectations Chain succeed. She *owned it* completely and refused to pass off the responsibility for solving this problem to the other Disney Hotel employees who comprised the rest of the Expectations Chain.

Recognize that these paradoxes do exist and can affect anyone in your Expectations Chain. Understanding and resolving them yourself and helping others to do likewise will promote the sort of personal accountability that allows people not only to meet, but also to *exceed*, expectations.

ACCOUNTABILITY REALITY CHECK

You can begin to put the power of positive accountability to work for people throughout your Expectations Chain by explaining to them exactly what it means to be both Above and Below the Line. Then, identify someone in your Expectations Chain who is not delivering what you need and for whom greater personal accountability could solve the problem. Help that individual identify why and how they may have fallen Below the Line and what steps he or she might take to move Above the Line. Encourage them to ask, "What else can I do to make progress?" Make sure you provide supportive coaching. Sharing your own experience with moving from Below to Above the Line will model for them what you are asking them to do. Your example will play an important role in making them feel comfortable acknowledging exactly where they need to improve. Albert Schweitzer once said, "Example is not the main thing in influencing others. It is the only thing." Remember the one key question that moves people Above the Line and inspires them to greater resourcefulness and tenacity: "What else can I do?"

ASSESS ACCOUNTABILITY WITH STYLE

Of course, your style will influence your ability to enroll others in taking greater personal accountability as a solution to unmet expectations. If you tend toward a Coerce & Compel style, you may find it difficult to understand why someone would not eagerly take accountability. If so, reflect for a moment on your experiences during the past week and count the number of times you went Below the Line yourself. Keep this in mind while you work on helping others move Above the Line. You cannot force someone Above the Line. Making the shift from Below to Above the Line requires a personal choice to do so, a commitment that is empowering and enabling and comes from within. Taking accountability means just that: people must *choose* to accept and embrace their accountability. Someone with a tendency toward Coerce & Compel will need to exercise a good deal of patience with this process, understanding that the payoff will be better results in the short run and increased capability in the long run.

For someone with a Wait & See orientation, it may take some effort to tell people that moving Above the Line is a requirement for continued opportunity and involvement on the team. While the transition does depend on a personal choice, people make better decisions when they clearly understand their options. Persuading people about the advantages of Above the Line behavior should also include stating the expectation that nothing less will suffice. When the people you work with understand that taking personal accountability is a key expectation that you have of them, they will make a greater effort to look at their own personal accountability as they work to meet expectations. Those with a Wait & See style run the risk of people not taking their request to become more accountable seriously because they do not see it as any more or less important than anything else they are being asked to do. You will want to communicate your message clearly and in a way that stresses the importance of making this transition to Above the Line.

A CULTURE OF ACCOUNTABILITY

When you begin to see the signs of Below the Line behavior and attitudes, then you can rest assured that the solution to unmet expectations will involve greater personal accountability. Once you draw that conclusion, you can then begin to coach people in your Expectations Chain to move Above the Line by taking greater personal accountability for better results.

How you go about coaching others to do so will become a story that travels through the Expectations Chain, one that people tell over and over again. Will they tell one that convinces people to embrace greater personal accountability, or will they tell one that causes people to run away from it as fast as their legs will carry them? Good or bad, such stories weave the very fabric of the culture in which you, and those you depend upon, work; and that culture will either facilitate people achieving the results you need, or it will create an obstacle to getting things done. Creating the former, a Culture of Accountability, is the focus of the next chapter and the final solution to unmet expectations.

Chapter Nine

THE POSITIVE, PRINCIPLED WAY

The following recap summarizes the keys for using accountability as a solution to unmet expectations. Applying these principles will accelerate your ability to help others take greater personal accountability for achieving results.

Steps to Accountability
The accountability model describes what it means to take personal accountability by moving Above the Line to See It, Own It, Solve It, and Do It. When people deflect their accountability, they can get trapped Below the Line in the Blame Game. Asking the question, "What else can I do?" propels people Above the Line to greater accountability.

The Accountability Current
The directional flow of accountability identifies where the accountability originates and the direction in which it moves. Traditionally, many organizations have relied on a top-down flow where those in authority positions assume responsibility for generating accountability. A bottom-up flow places the focus of accountability on the individual, at every level, and their proactive efforts to embrace and create accountability in their own Expectations Chain.

360° Accountability
People you depend upon and hold accountable to fulfill your expectation surround you: your boss, subordinates, peers, other team members, and even people outside your organization, such as vendors and suppliers.

Accountability Attitudes
People display three general attitudes when it comes to taking greater personal accountability: Deflecting, Calculating, and Embracing. You may

demonstrate different attitudes in different settings, and you may from time to time shift from one to another in any given setting.

The Paradox of Accountability

Three accountability paradoxes make creating greater personal account-ability even more difficult: the paradoxes of success, consequences, and shared accountability.

Chapter Ten

CONSIDER CULTURE

WHEN CULTURE IS THE SOLUTION

S ometimes you can attribute unmet expectations to problems with
an organization's culture. Even highly motivated, well-trained people
who take personal accountability to get a job done can find a particular
organizational culture so daunting that it undermines their ability to deliver
results. Of the four Inner Ring Solutions, culture can be the most elusive
and difficult to address. Despite that, however, accelerating cultural change
so that people think and act in the manner necessary to achieve results can
greatly increase the chances of success. The change we recommend creates a
Culture of Accountability, which we discuss at length in *Journey to the Emerald City*, and it provides a powerful tool for managing unmet expectations.

Have you ever brought new team members on board, hoping their
enthusiasm would light a fire with their uninspired fellow workers, only
to see them become part of the problem? A person can enter the organization all fired up about their prospects for success, excited about the company's bright future, and eager to get started on their first project, but then,
a few short weeks later, they become deflated, dispirited, guarded, and less
optimistic about their work. To your great disappointment, the person you
hired to help make needed changes and take things to the next level has
quickly adopted the moribund culture you were hoping to transform. We

call this the "Bell-Shaped Head" syndrome, a name invented within the Bell Telephone system prior to the breakup of the old phone service monopoly that existed in the United States. When new employees showed up at Bell Telephone, their managers handed them the "Green Book," which outlined all the tried-and-true policies and procedures employees should follow for almost every possible situation. New hires were not asked to think, just to follow the "Green Book." Eager new employees who came up with an innovative idea were told to keep it to themselves for a few years until they had learned "how things are done around here." They were told that they really could not make creative contributions until they developed what everyone called a "Bell-shaped head." Imagine that—a company that actually *dissuades* its employees from thinking creatively and innovatively.

We often see the Bell-Shaped Head syndrome, along with other maladies, operating in today's organizational cultures. These cultural weaknesses invariably impede progress and make the culture itself an obstacle to getting things done. Since an organization's culture can either help or hinder people as they work to fulfill expectations, learning to recognize the symptoms of a cultural malady will set you on a path toward curing it. A few pointed questions can guide you in that direction.

CULTURE QUESTIONS

1. Do people who are otherwise very resourceful seem unable to overcome obstacles and make progress?
2. Do people complain about a lack of cooperation within the organization?
3. Do people frequently ask for support to move things along in the organization?
4. Do people often warn others with statements like, "That's not how we do things here"?
5. Do people seem personally willing to get the job done, but express doubt when it comes to getting others on board?
6. Do people hesitate to commit to timelines when meeting those timelines requires involvement with the rest of the organization?
7. Do people cite different aspects of the culture, such as people not saying what they really think, as a roadblock to getting work done?

If you find yourself answering yes to any of these questions, then you probably need to make some changes to your culture. That's the bad news. The good news is you can take immediate steps to turn things around.

The first step toward strengthening your company's culture requires an accurate appraisal of just how and why people have come to think and act in unproductive ways. To help organizational leaders do this, we developed the Results Pyramid. In short, the model identifies how and why people draw conclusions about what to do, and what not to do, in their daily work.

THE RESULTS PYRAMID

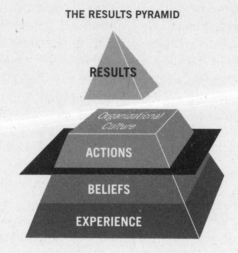

We have used this model for the past twenty years with companies around the world and everywhere we go leaders praise its simplicity. Results, Actions, Beliefs, and Experiences: just four words, yet they capture the essence of why people do what they do, as well as what they will need to do, to achieve results.

At the top of the pyramid, we find "Results." As we said before, accountability begins by clearly defining the results you want. Similarly, a Culture of Accountability begins in the same place. With specific results in mind, you can ask yourself, "What are the actions people must take to produce those results?" The "Actions" list might include considerations like taking more initiative, searching for innovation, cutting costs, reducing cycle time, hiring and training the needed sales staff, thoughtfully planning the product launch, or learning how to work in a dedicated team environment filled with highly skilled and trained colleagues.

Next, the pyramid prompts you to ask: "What are the beliefs people must hold to drive those actions?" In other words, how do people need to think differently in order to take the initiative and do the things that need to be done to achieve desired results? What beliefs will propel people to embrace the new team approach to development, how will the ground rules change so that decision-making occurs at the appropriate level, and how will the organization create the level of openness and trust required to create and maintain alignment over time?

Finally, there's the foundation of the pyramid and the key question, "What are the experiences people must have to form those new beliefs?" While it's often hard to do it well, nothing helps shift a culture more swiftly than providing new experiences that reinforce new beliefs. The consistency with which these new experiences occur helps anchor the desired beliefs in the hearts and minds of any work group, team, department, division, or entire organization. In addition, these experiences work their way into the stories people tell and retell throughout the organization. We have observed that people do not necessarily need firsthand experiences to change their beliefs. Good stories are "experiences by proxy" and can, in and of themselves, both create and sustain new beliefs. In one of our training workshops, a client told a story about someone who had been fired for a specific reason. Everyone in the room had heard the story before. When we asked the firm's leader to do some research and find out when that event had taken place, we learned that it occurred in 1972—thirty-five years earlier! Yet, people retold this story as though it had happened yesterday. That "experience by proxy" continued to influence this company's beliefs long after the original cast had disappeared from the scene.

We often remind leaders that the act of holding an individual accountable is really the act of holding an entire organization accountable. Everyone can, and will, tell and retell the story about what you did, how you did it, and whether or not you did it appropriately and fairly. People will share the story throughout the Expectations Chain as if it had happened to them directly. If the right stories about the right experiences travel throughout your organization, they will contribute greatly to a positive environment of accountability and trust. Unfortunately, people like to tell and hear negative stories even more than they do positive ones. Remaining conscious of the fact that your actions will become the source of stories that drive Cultural Beliefs will help you to more carefully craft your experiences and ultimately speed up cultural change.

The Results Pyramid illustrates how a culture comes about, how it actually develops, and what you can do to change it quickly. Because the model works at both the individual level and the organizational level, it applies to the entire Expectations Chain. In one unionized plant, management asked our advice about dealing with the fact that no one wanted to accept ownership for solving problems. If something went wrong, people generally kept to themselves, not wanting to share any information that might get a fellow worker in trouble. The culture embodied two unwritten rules: "Do your job and keep your nose down" and "Mind your own business and do what you are told to do." Management wanted to change that environment. Using the Results Pyramid, they began creating a Culture of Accountability, beginning with management itself and working all the way down to the unionized plant floor.

Management began engaging people throughout the plant, including the union leaders, by defining the cultural shifts needed to eliminate the problems that were blocking the road to results. With the shifts well defined, we helped them shape a set of Cultural Beliefs that would guide the way people thought about how to do their jobs differently. Applying the Results Pyramid, they created new experiences for one another that reinforced and supported the Cultural Beliefs and the associated actions needed to produce results.

The new culture faced its first real test when an explosion destroyed a key manufacturing system, causing $39 million in damages to the plant and nearly shutting down production all together. While they did get the system back up and running, they could not achieve the system's former throughput in the mill, a number they sorely needed to hit. The plant manager, "Fred," did something he would never have dreamed of doing in the old culture; he went straight to the union laborers closest to the work to get their input. One of the hourly operators piped up: "The first thing I want to ask you is this; is there a rule against laptops in the plant?" The question surprised Fred, who asked why the operator wanted to know that. In response, he pulled out the drawer of the desk at his workstation and displayed several Excel spreadsheets full of figures on downtime, utilization, and other technical aspects of the system. He said that he had been doing some calculations at home and would like to bring his laptop into the plant to continue his analysis. He said that he could prove his theory that the vibration sensor was causing the machine to shut off prematurely, thus producing the lower throughput number. "I know what it feels like when the mill vibrates," he said, "and I don't think it is vibrating. I think the vibration sensor is bad."

Fred told us that before the culture change, this operator would have "sat in a chair, waiting for the machine to reset once it tripped." The operator would never have considered himself the least bit responsible for figuring out what was going wrong. However, in the new culture, the operator had taken the initiative to tell the maintenance people about his analysis. Unfortunately, maintenance had dismissed the theory because they never encountered bad sensors before. Now, having alerted Fred to the situation, the operator won approval to confirm his theory. He brought in his laptop, continued running the numbers, and was vindicated when the plant's engineers verified his numbers and his conclusion that overly sensitive sensors were unnecessarily shutting down the machine.

The old culture kept laborers on the shop floor—a motivated, trained, and accountable workforce—from taking initiative. The new culture inspired ownership and personal investment in finding solutions. Amazingly, after fixing the sensors, this mill hit a higher throughput number than *all seven* of the company's mills combined had ever reached prior to the explosion. In this case, removing the culture as an obstacle was just the right solution to overcome unmet expectations.

We define a Culture of Accountability as "a place where people think and act, on a daily basis, in the manner necessary to develop successful solutions, find answers, overcome obstacles, triumph over any trouble that might come along, and deliver results." In such a culture everyone continually asks, "What else can I do to achieve results, attain objectives, and accomplish goals?" In short, it is a place where people think and act in the manner necessary to achieve organizational results. Not all accountability-based cultures accomplish that.

ACCOUNTABILITY CULTURES

As we have examined organizations around the world, we have come to the conclusion that there are five primary types of accountability-based cultures: a Culture of Complacency, a Culture of Confusion, a Culture of Intimidation, a Culture of Abdication, and a Culture of Accountability. Each represents a different way of understanding, creating, and sustaining accountability.

In a Culture of Complacency, jobs are typically well defined and people feel accountable to do what is expected of them, but only within strictly narrow parameters. People practice selective compliance, carefully picking and choosing what they will and will not take accountability for. When a problem pops up, you'll often hear people saying some form of "It's not my job." In such an environment, people tend to resist change and, clinging to the status quo, lack any spontaneous drive for continuous improvement. While everyone probably works quite hard to do their job, they focus solely on what their job description says they *have* to do, and not on what they *can* do to improve results. One frustrated client described her experience with this kind of culture. She had requested that the physical facilities department install on her office wall a metal strip with hooks attached, which would allow her to hang up and display the flip charts she liked to use. The total cost would run somewhere between $40 and $60. The facilities folks shook their heads and told her, "You can't have that . . . someone with your title has to have a cabinet." They proceeded to describe a very expensive ornate wooden cabinet that opens up to reveal a whiteboard. "Too big," she objected. "And it's *not* what I need." The facilities folks huffed away and never contacted her again.

After several weeks, she asked her administrative assistant to call and find out the status of her little metal strip. Informed that the budget had been cut for people at her level, it now seemed she would have to buy it herself. No big deal, she thought. But when she shared this experience with a friend, who was one level above her but had only recently joined the organization, she got quite a surprise. Her friend looked at her, blushed, and said, "You know I'm getting all new furniture . . . and a flat-screen TV. I told them that I did not want it, but they said everyone at my level is getting it." They both burst out laughing. It was, our client told us, a "culture moment." Imagine, one person can't get a $60 strip to hang up flip charts while another must accept a flat-screen TV she will never use. The facilities department was "just doing their job," never bothering to ask themselves whether what they are doing makes any sense or not.

A Culture of Confusion poses a different problem. In this environment, accountability is not clearly defined; thus people find it difficult to predict when they will or will not be held accountable. It is accountability by surprise. People make their best guess about which task deserves follow-up, at least in the near term, and then they hope and pray they made the right guess. The "surprise" may come from a lack of clarity around objectives, often caused by a lack of communication, frequent changes in priorities, or an overabundance of objectives. One health care industry client kept an organizational scorecard with sixteen objectives on it. When we asked a member of the senior management team to enumerate the objectives, he fished out his card and said, "Let me read them to you." Read them to us? He didn't know them by heart? If he couldn't tick them off from memory, how could they expect anyone else in his organization to know them? "Oh," he insisted, "the objectives are *well* understood, we discuss them in our quarterly leadership town hall meetings, and we have them on a dashboard on our internal Web site." Not surprisingly, everyone on the senior team responded to our query the same way that he did, rifling through some papers or opening an e-mail attachment and saying, "Let me read them to you."

In reality, they were falling quite short of meeting the objectives listed on the scorecard. When we observed the team discussing their progress, we heard these explanations: "My key objectives on this list of sixteen conflict with the objectives of two other departments," or "I was focused on the two of the sixteen that I could really accomplish, so I didn't really spend any time on the others" or even, "I didn't realize that we were really working on all sixteen objectives on the list." The leader could not comprehend the flood of confusion that had engulfed the team. He knew that this kind of confusion would seep throughout the entire organization and erode everyone's ability to take accountability for achieving any of those sixteen objectives. Clearly, people were not following up on a regular basis. That alone would have brought the confusion to light much earlier.

To remedy the situation, the team edited their scorecard down to the top four objectives (the numbers have been adjusted to maintain anonymity): Increase Patient Volume by 10 percent, Improve Patient Safety (reduce infections), Improve Patient Satisfaction (improve to the "A" level as measured by a consumer watch group), and Reduce Costs by $5 Million. With this tighter focus came a regular effort to follow up and call attention to progress in each of these areas. These simple steps precipitated a big change in the culture from one characterized by confusion to one noted for clarity. That clarity, and the associated individual and organizational accountability, brought a dramatic improvement in progress toward meeting all four of the organization's most important objectives.

The third type of culture, a Culture of Intimidation, *forces* people to take accountability. Fearing that they will lose their job, their rank in the organization, or some future opportunity, they feel compelled to assume ownership. Unfortunately, they worry more about *whom* they are accountable to than about *what* they are accountable for. As a result, it is accountability by force of personality. Interestingly, the person holding people accountable may not actually use coercion to get people to listen and respond. For whatever reason, people may have simply gotten stuck Below the Line and can only muster enough courage to take accountability when their jobs are at stake. Even in this circumstance, the fact that they feel threatened legitimizes their sense of intimidation.

Feelings of intimidation, whether real and intended, imagined, or implied, can plummet people into a dangerous tell-me-what-to-do mode. We worked with a key executive, "Blair," who worked for an organization that permitted him to use intimidation as a management tool. A strong and charismatic personality, he knew what he wanted and when he wanted it. To make that clear, he would routinely yell at people to get their attention. He ruled by instilling fear in those around him. As a result, people worried more about the consequences of delivering bad news to Blair than about getting the job done. In one instance we attended a meeting Blair had convened with his extended senior team and watched as one of his directors offered a view about the company's direction that differed quite a bit from Blair's own view of the future. When he finished, you could have heard a pin drop. Blair's face turned red and, with the full force of his overbearing personality, he began shouting his disapproval. A chill settled over the whole room, as some fifty senior managers cast their eyes downward. Blair had made his point. He would not tolerate "that kind of thinking."

Stories about Blair's eruptions ran rampant through the company. People recounted episodes where he lost his temper, excoriated someone for a mistake or an honest opinion he didn't like, or fired someone without batting an eye. He had spun himself into a larger-than-life character with one overriding demand: be prepared, get results, or else! And he felt perfectly comfortable with that reputation. After all, it seemed to work for him. Just a year earlier he had received an award for leading the best performing business unit in the firm. In the end, however, all that intimidation, which had seemingly produced results in the short term and even led to a couple of performance awards, went sour when the fear he had instilled turned to resentment, resistance, and poor long-term results.

In a Culture of Abdication, people avoid taking accountability at all costs. We sometimes refer to it as "accountability by omission." The Metropolitan Transit Authority (MTA) of New York City suffered the ill effects of this sort of behavior when in the 1990s they invested close to $1 billion to install two hundred new escalators and elevators in the subway system. Despite that huge investment, problems plagued the project with one out of every six elevators and escalators going out of service for more than a month during the year following their installation. That year, 169 escalators incurred 68 breakdowns and two out of three elevators broke down at least once, trapping frightened passengers inside. Who could even begin to calculate the cost of these malfunctions? Certainly, they prompted swift attention? Nope. Not in a Culture of Abdication.

The issue did cause a lot of concern in some quarters. The *New York Times* spent months researching the problem, analyzing more than ten years of records. Their findings, eventually acknowledged by the Transit Authority itself, uncovered a myriad of problems that included several of the Inner Ring problems we've discussed: mechanics received as little as four weeks of training, when counterparts in other successful transit systems went through four-year apprenticeships involving thirteen hundred hours of classroom training; inefficiencies in organizational processes that allowed mechanics to spend only half of their shifts actually fixing mechanical issues; management decisions that rushed equipment back into service without solving the real problem; and design flaws that left equipment malfunctioning moments after installation. With all of these issues, no one seemed willing to take any accountability to make necessary fixes.

These elevators and escalators service five million subway riders every day. While the MTA has won recognition for its excellent work with subway car and bus maintenance, the department responsible for the auxiliary equipment, which included escalators and elevators, operates in a completely different culture. Mechanics would make minor adjustments, only to find the same elevator breaking down as many as five times over eight days. The Transit Authority knew their training procedures were woefully inadequate and that their mechanics were not equipped with the needed know-how to repair the machines, but they ignored this fact and dispatched the ill-prepared and consequently scarcely motivated mechanics anyway.

To his credit, Joseph Joyce, general superintendent of elevators and escalators, addressed the culture's problems when he said, "I'm trying to get these guys to think that, you know what, that could be your mom that's walking with a cane and needs that escalator. Nothing in this world is guaranteed. It could be one of us in a wheelchair next month. And if you want to enjoy the city, you want to be able to utilize our public transportation system. You need that elevator to work." The void left when people abdicate their accountability can be vast indeed. It results in a general sense of powerlessness that pervades everything that is done in the organization. And that's exactly how everyone on Joyce's team felt about the organization. In such an environment, people lose hope that anything will change for the better, succumb to the culture of abdication, and make no attempt to take accountability to make it better.

Finally, we arrive at the best possible culture, the one that all companies should desire and the one that most effectively produces results: a Culture of Accountability. This kind of culture maximizes the power of accountability and full ownership. In this culture, people choose to take personal accountability for both their successes and failures, always striving to operate Above the Line and apply the principles and practices of the Outer and Inner Rings of the Accountability Sequence Model. They make good things happen. When they encounter the inevitable unpleasant surprises and problems, they move swiftly to correct the situation.

When "Smithfields," a major publicly traded restaurant chain with over four hundred stores, experienced succeeding quarters of losses and a probable $40 million shortfall in projected profits, the new CEO, "Mario Rizzuto," announced that the plan for the new year was $42 million *in profit*. Because everyone in the organization had grown so accustomed to seeing loss after loss, that announcement struck most people as an absurd impossibility—from a $40 million loss to a $42 million profit? We assisted the new CEO in creating a Culture of Accountability where Below the Line behavior and attitudes would all but disappear throughout the Expectations Chain and Above the Line thought and behavior would become the rule of the day. Eighteen months later, the initiative turned all that initial astonishment into pride, when Smithfields reached $40 million in profit.

Their effort began by clearly defining results and eliminating all confusion around priorities. When Mario discovered at one point that the company had fallen $4 million behind plan, he broke that $4 million down in terms of the number of people visiting the restaurants and the number of shifts and the number of employees who served them. His analysis concluded that Smithfields only needed to generate 11 cents more in revenue per customer served. Achieving this would quickly put them back on plan. The management team went to work engaging everyone in the Expectations Chain to ask, "What else can I do to help achieve this result?"

The organization became energized as restaurant employees searched high and low for ways to make a difference. For their part, managers who had previously conducted table visits during their shifts made it a point to drop by each table to offer patrons a tiny card that highlighted a delectable appetizer that just happened to be the most profitable item on the menu. Servers never failed to present each table with a table-tree showcasing a tempting display of desserts. Everyone knew that in order to achieve the overall objective, all they really needed to do was sell one appetizer or dessert to every table. Within a month, they had made it happen and were securely back on track. A Culture of Accountability is the best kind of accountability culture; it produces results, motivates people, and creates excitement throughout the work environment.

Take a moment to review these Five Common Accountability Cultures and consider which one best describes the culture in which you presently work. Determine what is missing that could make a difference in your own ability to fulfill expectations.

THE FIVE COMMON ACCOUNTABILITY CULTURES

A CULTURE OF...	ACCOUNTABILITY IMPLEMENTED BY...	CHARACTERISTICS OF THIS ACCOUNTABILITY CULTURE...
ACCOUNTABILITY	Individual Choice	People willingly take personal accountability for both their successes and failures.
COMPLACENCY	Selective Compliance	People assume accountability only for their job, which they define as narrowly as possible.
CONFUSION	Surprise	People feel unsure about what they will be held accountable for, so they make their best guess and hope they are right.
INTIMIDATION	Force of Personality	People take accountability for the things they feel forced to own, worrying more about *who* they are accountable to, rather than *what* they are accountable to achieve.
ABDICATION	Omission	People go to great lengths to avoid taking accountability for anything, including their own jobs.

(BEST ↑ ... WORST ↓)

After determining the kind of accountability culture in which your Expectations Chain currently functions, use the Results Pyramid (see page 214)
to help you think through the experiences you will need to create in order
to drive the beliefs essential to a Culture of Accountability. Helping people
understand accountability (in the way we described it in the previous chapter), and then creating a supportive environment for it (as we discussed at
the beginning of this chapter), will put you well on your way to establishing
positive accountability as a defining characteristic of your culture. Such a
culture will include, among other attributes, three central values of Organizational Integrity.

THE THREE VALUES OF
ORGANIZATIONAL INTEGRITY

People working in a Culture of Accountability feel a strong sense of what
we call "Organizational Integrity." It is the collective version of individual
integrity where "*I* will do what *I* say *I* will do" becomes "*We* will do what *we*
say *we* will do." Karl G. Maeser, the founder of Brigham Young University,
once described what integrity meant to him. As he explained it, "Place me
behind prison walls—ever so high, ever so thick, reaching ever so far into
the ground—there is a possibility that in some way or another I will escape;
but stand me on a floor and draw a chalk line around me and have me give
my word of honor never to cross it. Can I get out of the Circle? No. Never!
I would die first." Integrity is all about doing what you say you will do and
keeping your word to the very best of your ability. Organizational Integrity,
then, is the idea that a group shares a commitment to operating with this
quality as a guiding principle. They do their utmost to keep their word to
one another and to do what they say they will do.

Every day, in almost any organization, you can hear people saying
things like:

"I'm sick of it. Almost every day someone tells me she'll have that report
on my desk by noon, and when three o'clock rolls around, my in-box is still
empty, without a word of explanation."

"I know our numbers are going to look lousy at the end of the third
quarter, but I'm *not* going to tell the executive team we'll miss the Wall
Street projections by 15 percent."

"Every time IT sets a deadline, they miss it. Nobody can plan on anything around here. Why doesn't anyone ever do what they say they'll do?"

In our practice we have learned that when complaints like these permeate an organization, they signal problems with Organizational Integrity and a potential accountability crisis. Organizations that do not address the issue can expect to pay a huge price for their inattention: unmet expectations throughout the Expectations Chain.

Unfortunately, the workforce coming into the job market over the past several years has been steeped in an environment that does not embrace integrity as a guiding value. One study by the Josephson Institute showed that 30 percent of almost thirty thousand students surveyed at one hundred American high schools acknowledged stealing from a store in the past year, 64 percent confessed to cheating on tests, 36 percent admitted that they had used the Internet to plagiarize an assignment, and 42 percent said they sometimes lie to save money. Astonishingly, 93 percent of those surveyed claimed a high level of personal ethics and character. Cheating in school is not something new, but when people see nothing wrong with bringing it into the workplace, that behavior will work counter to the values that form the foundation of a Culture of Accountability.

Why does Organizational Integrity matter so much? The answer's quite simple. When people do everything in their power to do what they say they will do, the work becomes predictable and commitments become a reality. When you can count on the people you work with to follow through, the process of holding people accountable becomes more positive. Bottom line, Organizational Integrity lies at the heart of keeping people in the Expectations Chain connected in a way that produces results and maintains relationships of trust and respect.

Three core values reside at the heart of any culture that maintains a climate of positive accountability, and those values comprise what we mean by Organizational Integrity. These values hold it all together and make a Culture of Accountability really work. Without them, Organizational Integrity erodes and eventually disappears. We have given these three values names that put them into action: Follow Through, Get Real, and Speak Up. Follow Through means "do what you say you will do"; Get Real means to "get to the truth"; and Speak Up means to "say what needs to be said." Each of them is an essential component of Organizational Integrity. No one can expect true accountability without these values and the actions they drive. A complete and constant focus on them allows people to hold others accountable for results in a positive, principled way. Incorporating and constantly stressing these three values will do more than anything else to make it possible for people to take accountability, fulfill expectations, and deliver results.

Follow Through

When you intend to follow through on what you say you will do, you think carefully about the commitments you make. You establish meaningful and achievable "By When's," and you take special pains not to overcommit and underdeliver. Other people never feel they need to chase you down for a status report because they know that they can count on you to do everything in your power to make it happen. When you commit to a deadline, people accept it because they know you have thought long and hard about it and feel confident you can deliver the expected result. When you express your commitment, people know you mean it and that you will follow through to make sure you honor it. They trust you.

Winston Churchill engendered so much trust among the British people that when he spoke to the House of Commons on June 4, 1940, an entire nation believed him when he said, "We shall go on to the end, we shall fight in France, we shall fight on the seas and oceans, we shall fight with growing confidence and growing strength in the air, we shall defend our island, whatever the cost may be, we shall fight on the beaches, we shall fight on the landing grounds, we shall fight in the fields and in the streets, we shall fight in the hills; we shall never surrender, and even if, which I do not for a moment believe, this island or a large part of it were subjugated and starving, then our Empire beyond the seas, armed and guarded by the British Fleet, would carry on the struggle, until, in God's good time, the new world, with all its power and might, steps forth to the rescue and the liberation of the old." As we all know, he followed through on that daunting commitment and got the job done.

When everyone in a culture adheres to a commitment to follow through, people believe all of the promises, commitments, and deadlines they make with each other and this trust establishes and reinforces the positive accountability connections needed to accelerate business processes.

Get Real

By "Get Real," we mean, "get to the truth." A commitment to get to the truth throughout the entire organization will also speed up business processes and improve your ability to get results. When people resist dealing with the truth, positive accountability grinds to a halt. We all find it hard at times to get to the "truth," particularly when we think it might make someone feel unhappy or look bad. However, "getting real" will do much more to move a project forward than any attempt to create a happy illusion, no matter how well intentioned. Creating an environment where people settle for nothing less than the truth will help them recognize the reality of their situation and enable them to clearly see the accountability they need to take in order to deliver results.

While working with one of our clients, a major Fortune 100 organization, "ADH," we heard a story that illustrates the value of getting to the truth. ADH manufactured and marketed a medication that addressed a medical condition afflicting a relatively small population of patients. While not a blockbuster profit-producer, the drug had been on the market for many years, but business conditions convinced ADH to stop manufacturing it. One father, whose daughter depended on the drug to stabilize her condition, went to refill the girl's prescription, only to find it back-ordered. He did not know that ADH was in the process of selling out its supply of the drug before announcing that it would cease production altogether. However, the fact that he could not obtain the drug right away prompted the worried father to write a letter to ADH's president explaining his distress. The president asked "Bill," a senior ADH executive, to look into it.

As Bill diligently delved into the situation, he discovered that not only did consumers not know that the drug would soon be discontinued, but neither did all but a few of ADH's own employees. Digging further, he learned that a widely available generic drug could effectively replace ADH's product, a fact he shared with the worried father. Grateful for this information, the father went to his local pharmacy only to learn that some of the inactive ingredients in the generic differed from ADH's formula and that the generic would not, according to a dietician and the pharmacy of a university medical center, provide an acceptable substitution.

That news did not deter Bill, who took the initiative to contact the manufacturer of the generic, who informed him that the generic alternative would, in fact, make a perfectly suitable alternative. Once again Bill called the father and explained the science to him. Then he called the university pharmacy to explain it to them as well. Bill then made sure ADH put together a letter for distribution to doctors throughout the nation that detailed the suitability of the generic drug as a replacement.

We like this story for several reasons. First, it underscores the importance of a rock-solid commitment to getting to the truth. It also shows how this value of truthfulness not only helped people solve a problem in the short run, but also benefited the organization in the long run. A less accountable person in a less accountable culture might have simply gone to the father and said, "We are discontinuing the product, so you will need to work with your doctor to find a suitable solution." Instead, he pursued the path of truthfulness and resourcefulness.

Speak Up

Finally, people operating in a Culture of Accountability say what needs to be said, when it needs to be said, and in a way that ensures others will hear it. To do that, they need an environment free from the fear of retaliation, because that fear can be overpowering to the point that anyone, even a normally assertive person, will clam up. A June 2001 survey at Clifton Springs Hospital & Clinic in Clifton Springs, New York, showed that more than 75 percent of the employees felt uncomfortable reporting medical errors, and a 2000 National Institute of Ethics survey of over one thousand law enforcement academy recruits indicated that almost half of them had personally witnessed misconduct by another employee but did not tell anyone about it. Almost 80 percent of those surveyed acknowledged an unwritten code of silence throughout law enforcement in this country. Those studies support our contention that speaking up is not always easy, even in those professions where lives can depend on doing so.

One of our clients frequently repeats a true story about the importance of speaking up. A doctor administered an injection to a patient in his office. Tragically, he mistakenly injected radiology cleaning fluid. Within twenty minutes, the patient lay dead, while family members, who had been assured that their loved one was undergoing a minor procedure, looked on in horror. The doctor almost immediately realized that two strikingly similar vials containing two radically different solutions had been sitting side by side on the counter and that he had used the wrong one. Despite the specter of a malpractice lawsuit, the doctor openly admitted to the family that he made a fatal error and took full accountability for what had happened. While the hospital's insurance provider made a financial settlement with the family, the patient's family, impressed with the doctor's openness and truthfulness, ended up not pressing a civil suit. As all of this took place, the family and doctor became friends. Because of the manner in which the family and the doctor approached this tragedy, the hospital has invited them, for the last few years, to present the hospital's safety award at its annual safety banquet.

But the story does not end there. It turned out that two years prior to this incident, exactly the same thing had happened at a sister hospital across town. Another doctor had made the same error using the deadly agent, and that patient had also died. But unlike the doctor who spoke up, this physician covered up his mistake, sweeping it under the carpet and under the radar of anyone else in the hospital. Had the doctor spoken up, the sister hospital surely would have taken steps to prevent the tragedy from occurring again. Creating an environment where people say what needs to be said, and when it needs to be said, helps establish an environment where accountability can flourish and sustain real results.

The values of Follow Through, Speak Up, and Get Real form the winning trifecta of Organizational Integrity. Establishing and promoting these values will help people within the Expectations Chain hold one another accountable the positive, principled way.

ACCOUNTABILITY REALITY CHECK

Take a few minutes now to consider where your organization (or your Expectations Chain) stands with respect to Organizational Integrity. Use the scorecard below to grade yourself, your team, department, division, or company (the people on whom you depend to get things done) by jotting down a letter grade (A-F, 1–5, or whatever your school grading systems may be). As you grade yourself and others, be sure to be completely open and honest.

ORGANIZATIONAL INTEGRITY VALUE	DESCRIPTION	SELF GRADE	ORGAN/ CHAIN GRADE
Follow Through	I do what I say I will do; I make every effort to meet deadlines and keep their commitments.		
Get Real	I am committed to getting to the truth; I strive to learn what people really think and to acknowledge the way things really are.		
Speak Up	I say what needs to be said, no matter what.		

If you awarded high grades, then congratulations! You more than likely enjoy the values associated with Organizational Integrity. If you assigned low grades, then you face some serious work using the Results Pyramid (see page 214) as your guide to establishing these values. Frank discussions with people about any attempt to shift toward these values will help put you on the right path to making that happen.

CONSIDER CULTURE WITH STYLE

As with all of the Inner Ring Solutions, your Accountability Style will influence your ability to solve the culture problems people face in your Expectations Chain. If you possess a Coerce & Compel style, you should bear in mind that you cannot create a Culture of Accountability by edict. It only happens by way of invitation. That is, you must openly campaign for it by working to persuade and convince the organization that the move Above the Line will benefit everyone. Creating new experiences to drive those new beliefs will help in the process of convincing others. Equally important, you will need to establish free-flowing feedback so that people Speak Up and Get Real about progress or the lack of it. Because people who tend to operate with this style often appear intimidating, it usually makes sense to create a network of informal communication that will help you grasp what is really going on in the organization and whether or not people are making genuine progress toward the results you expect.

If you tend toward the Wait & See style, you will most likely need to make an extra effort to emulate the three components of Organizational Integrity. Since someone with this style prefers a more informal and less vocal approach, you will want to make sure you create credible experiences for others by modeling your own ability to Follow Through, Get Real, and Speak Up. You will also want to make it clear that you wish them to do the same. If you do not make this a focused effort, you will find that it can take longer for people to believe that you really want to see these traits become a part of the culture and "the way we do things around here." Picking the right moments to demonstrate your seriousness will greatly enhance your ability to accelerate the culture change all along the Expectations Chain.

THE INNER RING

At some point in time, everyone will run into the culture as an obstacle for getting things done. Creating a Culture of Accountability will help the people whom you count on to move things through the Expectations Chain and deliver on what is expected. Creating a truly accountable culture requires establishing the three values of Organizational Integrity on which accountability depends. The real benefit of managing culture is that at some point it begins to manage you and those with whom you work. By creating a Culture of Accountability, success becomes more predictable as people take personal ownership for asking, "What else can I do?" to think and act in the manner necessary to achieve the result. It's the best kind of culture and fosters an environment where you can hold others accountable the positive, principled way.

Chapter Ten

THE POSITIVE, PRINCIPLED WAY

This recap summarizes the key concepts that will help you manage unmet expectations when culture offers the best solution. Building on the principles presented in our book *Journey to the Emerald City*, the tools in this chapter will help you make the shift to a Culture of Accountability.

A Culture of Accountability
In the best kind of culture, people take accountability to think and act on a daily basis in the manner necessary to develop successful solutions, find answers, and overcome obstacles.

The Results Pyramid
This description of "why people do what they do" includes four sequential steps: the Experiences we have drive our Beliefs, which determine our Actions and ultimately produce our Results.

Accountability Cultures
Five common types of cultures characterize the way an organization goes about understanding, creating, and sustaining accountability: a Culture of Complacency, a Culture of Confusion, a Culture of Intimidation, a Culture of Abdication, and a Culture of Accountability.

Organizational Integrity
Organizational Integrity is a defining characteristic of an accountable culture where people in the organization and in the Expectations Chain strive to do what they say they will do and adhere to three core values: Follow Through, Get Real, and Speak Up.

• Follow Through
People in a Culture of Accountability follow through to make sure they do what they say they will do.

• *Get Real*

People in a Culture of Accountability commit themselves to getting to the truth, no matter what.

• *Speak Up*

People in a Culture of Accountability feel free to say what needs to be said.

CONCLUSION

THE VOCABULARY OF ACCOUNTABILITY

With each client experience, we appreciate more and more how a shared vocabulary can enrich and clarify a conversation about getting results. In the case of fostering greater personal accountability, we have seen people speed up problem solving using the language we introduced in *The Oz Principle* by frequently asking themselves and each other, "Have we fallen Below the Line on this?" or "What do we need to do to get back Above the Line?" In this book, we have taken great care to craft a similar vocabulary to use when you hold others accountable for results the positive, principled way. When you get people in the Expectations Chain using the phrases "Outer Ring" and "Inner Ring" to establish and manage key expectations, then you will find them more quickly and effectively solving the problems that arise every day in your organization. This vocabulary not only provides a useful shorthand for describing what else people need to do in order to move forward and achieve results, but it also reinforces the positive, principled approach to accountability.

Imagine yourself in this scenario. You are the Southwest division manager for "Snow's," a major retail company headquartered in Chicago. While the executives in Chicago expect your team to hit certain ambitious numbers this year, you have set your sights on making your division number one in the company. Knowing it will take more than a written edict or a rousing pep talk to make that happen, you decide to use the Accountability Sequence to establish and manage this key expectation. First, you walk your team through the overall process. "I want us to get comfortable with the idea of establishing expectations and managing unmet expectations before we discuss our future as an important member of the Snow's family." You emphasize that this will require much more than a quick fix or a magic potion. "Our industry has suffered some hard times lately, and getting results will take more than the usual dedication and hard work."

Comfortable that your team understands the principles embodied in the full Accountability Sequence Model, you suggest that they begin their discussion on the Outer Ring.

THE OUTER RING:
ESTABLISHING EXPECTATIONS

Immediately, everyone recognizes that you are about to communicate an important expectation you need them to fulfill. Their antennae go up, and everyone listens intently to what you say next. "I've given this a lot of thought, discussed it with corporate as well as other partners in our Expectations Chain, and I've formed this key expectation: we will become the number one division in the company by the end of this fiscal year in all five performance categories on the scorecard. In order to achieve the number one ranking in each of these categories, each store will need to elevate its contribution." You emphasize the benefits people in the division will enjoy if they meet or surpass this key expectation: secure employment in an insecure economy, potential promotions, bonuses, and the satisfaction and pride that comes with a winning performance. You conclude by stressing that your expectation matches what corporate would like to see all of Snow's units achieve.

After communicating the expectation, you seek alignment by asking for candid feedback. Without hesitation, one manager speaks up. "It's a great goal. We all want to be the number one division, but, truthfully? Staffing issues in the stores will hold us back. Have you looked at the absenteeism rates lately? Off the chart!" You nod in agreement and comment, "Yes, I know that's a real issue, but I want to make sure we are all on the same page before we jump to the Inner Ring."

THE INNER RING:
MANAGING UNMET EXPECTATIONS

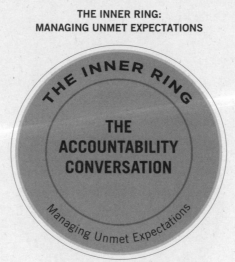

Before continuing with the Snow's scenario, let's pause for a moment to consider how you determine whether you should be working in the Outer or Inner Ring of the Accountability Sequence. Learning to spot certain triggers, shown in the chart on the next page, will help you and your team answer that fundamental question.

Once you learn to identify such triggers, you can expedite the right solution by better forming, communicating, aligning, and inspecting expectations or by working to improve motivation, training, personal accountability, or culture. Needless to say, you must first hold yourself accountable.

Returning to the Snow's scenario, one of your managers volunteers this: "I think it's clear that we are aligned behind this expectation. We all want to be the number one division in each category on the scorecard, and there's no question that we are each committed to doing what it takes to ensure that we move forward; but it's also clear that we have some Inner

Triggers That Move You to the Outer or Inner Ring

OUTER RING TRIGGERS	INNER RING TRIGGERS
People cannot accurately articulate what you expect.	People fail to deliver the result.
People signal that they find the expectations unrealistic or confusing.	People appear to lack the resourcefulness that only comes when they have invested their "hearts and minds" in the effort.
People do not seem to understand the "why" behind the expectations.	People clearly lack the skill to deliver on the expectation.
People show signs that they are not aligned with the direction you have set.	People fall Below the Line far too often; they make excuse after excuse for their lack of progress.
People do not proactively report the progress we expect.	People's beliefs about how things really work in the organization impede them from doing what needs to be done to achieve results.

Ring problems we need to tackle. I think we're ready to jump into the Inner Ring and identify the right solution."

THE INNER RING:
THE FOUR SOLUTIONS

As your team begins to engage in an Inner Ring discussion, yet another manager asks, "Isn't this a motivation problem? People get excellent training for their jobs, but they just don't see why it's so important to show up when they're scheduled to work, and they obviously don't appreciate the havoc they cause when they don't come in." That observation draws a few nods of agreement. Someone else, though, offers a different view. "I chalk it up to personal accountability. Our managers are afraid to follow through with the necessary performance coaching because they think replacing those who don't consistently show up is harder than coping with the absenteeism. Supervisors have come to believe that if you call people on the carpet for not showing up, they will just quit." Interesting point. You interrupt to ask, "How many of you would agree it's both?" The group expresses consensus. "So," a store manager ventures, "we need to enroll them in the 'cause,' and we need to follow through on performance plans when they don't show up." Beautiful. You move on, saying, "That's right, and when we're done with this discussion about our goal, we'll want to make sure we take accountability to do that."

With two options on the table, motivation and accountability, you suggest that the group pause for a moment to consider that perhaps the problem involves inadequate application of the steps in the Outer Ring. "Okay, folks, remember the three steps in the Accountability Conversation. Before we select an Inner Ring Solution and set about establishing it as a key expectation, we must ask ourselves whether we effectively applied the Outer Ring process to form, communicate, align, and inspect our previous performance expectations." That suggestion gets people thinking. "Good point!" says the person who raised the motivation issue. "If we want to make this new expectation work, we'd better figure out what else we could have done to prevent absenteeism from becoming a problem in the first place."

Another lively discussion results in the general agreement that while the team does a good job at forming and communicating expectations, it needs to pay more attention to alignment and inspection. "That," concludes another manager, "would help generate the buy-in, and the hearts-and-minds investment needed to motivate people to actually show up every single day."

You invite the team to raise other issues that might block the new initiative. A hand shoots up immediately, "What can we do about getting our salespeople properly trained to register new promotions at the point of sale?" Everyone recognizes that corporate is slow to provide training on any new cash register procedures needed for upcoming sales promotions. "Inner Ring!" someone shouts, sparking laughter around the room. You smile, too. "Good one. Now we can take the next step in the Accountability Conversation and select an Inner Ring Solution." Another team member volunteers an insight. "This is a culture issue. Corporate is always getting to our division after it works with each of the other divisions. It's been that way for the last ten years. They start their training sequentially by division number, and we happen to be division nine!" Someone suggests that, given division nine's solid past performance, you try to negotiate a change in the training sequence. You agree to take accountability for that.

Moving the group back to the Outer Ring, you lead a conversation about the group's feeling that you could all improve your skills in aligning and inspecting. Taking the third step in the Accountability Conversation, you take the team back to the Outer Ring to implement the plan. Eventually, everyone signs off on more frequent progress reports throughout the Expectations Chain. They also agree to address the motivation and accountability issues in their stores. "Good work," you say. "Now, can we also agree that each of us will apply the steps in the Outer Ring to do all we can to make sure we achieve this key expectation?" A chorus of "Yes, absolutely, you bet, definitely!" affirms the pledge. "And we'll keep our eyes out for any problems that demand an Inner Ring Solution?" Smiles and nods answer that question.

THE ACCOUNTABILITY SEQUENCE

You let the team know that you appreciate how they used the Outer and Inner Rings of the Accountability Sequence to guide a meaningful dialogue today, and that you look forward to many such meetings to stay on task and achieve the result you all expect: division nine at number one.

Throughout our careers, we have helped countless clients around the world create greater personal and organizational accountability for achieving results. We have watched people at every level of the organization, in every sector of the economy, and in every type of business imaginable struggle with the same fundamental question: "How do I effectively hold *other* people accountable for results?" Experience shows that it's not an easy question to answer. However, we can assure you that when you get accountability right, people respond. When you get it wrong, they rebel. And with that rebellion can go any hope for achieving key expectations and producing the results you want. The positive, principled way paves a simple, rational, and fair path to getting it right, a path you can take time and time again to hold people accountable in a way that builds morale and gets results. When that happens, people willingly invest their hearts and minds to meet and exceed expectations and deliver extraordinary results, the kinds of results that never leave you wondering, "How did that happen?"

Appendix

Models, Self-Assessments, Charts, and Lists

Index

University of Kansas Jayhawks, 130
University of Memphis Tigers, 130
Unmet expectations. *See* Expectations,
   unmet
USDA inspections, 116

Valassis, 168–69
van Rooijen, Wilco, 76–77
Vitality Curve, 126

Wait & See style: and alignment of
   expectations, 94; and
   communicating expectations,
   71–72; and culture of
   accountability, 230; and forming
   expectations, 51; and inspections,
   119; and motivation, 164–65; and
   personal accountability, 208–9;
   pros/cons of, 27–28; and training,
   187–88; traits of, 27–28, 94; and
   unmet expectations, 141–42
Walton, Sam, 114

Warren, J. Robin, 153
Warren, Rau'Shee, 125–26
WebEx conference, to inspect
   expectations, 101–2
Welch, Jack, 64–65; Vitality Curve, 126
What-When approach, 56–57
Whipping boys, 206
Why questions, about the cause, 159–62
Why-What-When approach, 59–70;
   Accountability Reality Check, 72;
   and Accountability Styles, 70–72;
   boundaries, discussing, 65–68;
   elements of, 59–60; seven times,
   seven ways, 64, 72–73; support
   discussion, 68–69; "what," clarity
   of, 64–65; versus What-When,
   56–57; "when" as concrete, 69–70;
   "why," crafting, 61–64; "why,"
   importance of, 60–61
Williams, Harland, 201
Wizard of Oz, The, 157–58, 195
Woods, Tiger, 80

ABOUT THE AUTHORS

Roger Connors and Tom Smith are co-CEOs and co-presidents of Partners In Leadership, Inc., a leadership training and management consulting company recognized as the premier provide of Accountability Training services around the world. They have co-authored three *New York Times* bestselling leadership books: *The Oz Principle: Getting Results Through Individual and Organizational Accountability, How Did That Happen? Holding People Accountable for Results the Positive, Principled Way,* and the recently released *Change the Culture, Change the Game: The Breakthrough Strategy for Energizing Your Organization and Creating Accountability for Results.* They are also the authors of the bestselling book *Journey to the Emerald City: Achieve a Competitive Edge by Creating a Culture of Accountability.* Their books have been translated into several languages and have appeared on numerous bestseller lists, including the *Wall Street Journal, USA Today,* Associated Press, *Publishers Weekly,* and Amazon.com lists. They offer the *Three Tracks to Creating Greater Accountability* as a comprehensive training program for helping organizations create greater accountability for individual, team, and organizational results.

Their company has thousands of clients in more than fifty countries and has trained hundreds of thousands of people—from the executive suite to the frontline worker—in understanding how greater accountability can increase efficiency, profits, and innovation at all levels of an organization. Their clients include many of the most admired companies in the world, almost half of the Dow Jones Industrial Average companies, all of the top twelve pharmaceutical companies in the world, and nearly half of the Fortune 50 largest companies in the United States.

Tom and Roger have appeared on numerous radio and television broadcasts, authored articles in major publications, and delivered keynote speeches at numerous major conferences. They have also led consulting engagements and major organizational interventions throughout the world, including most European countries, Japan, North America, South America, and the Middle East. Respected as trusted advisers to senior executives and recognized as the worldwide experts on the topic of workplace accountability, they bring extensive expertise to helping management team facilitate large-scale cultural transition through their Accountability Training. They both received MBA degrees from the Marriott School of Management at Brigham Young University.